Mastering Predictive Analytics with Python

Exploit the power of data in your business by building advanced predictive modeling applications with Python

Joseph Babcock

PUBLISHING

BIRMINGHAM - MUMBAI

Mastering Predictive Analytics with Python

First published: August 2016

Production reference: 1290816

Published by Packt Publishing Ltd.
Livery Place
35 Livery Street
Birmingham B3 2PB, UK.

ISBN 978-1-78588-271-5

www.packtpub.com

Credits

Author
Joseph Babcock

Reviewer
Dipanjan Deb

Commissioning Editor
Kartikey Pandey

Acquisition Editor
Aaron Lazar

Content Development Editor
Sumeet Sawant

Technical Editor
Utkarsha S. Kadam

Copy Editor
Vikrant Phadke

Project Coordinator
Shweta H Birwatkar

Proofreader
Safis Editing

Indexer
Monica Ajmera Mehta

Graphics
Kirk D'Pinha

Production Coordinator
Nilesh Mohite

Cover Work
Nilesh Mohite

About the Author

Joseph Babcock has spent almost a decade exploring complex datasets and combining predictive modeling with visualization to understand correlations and forecast anticipated outcomes. He received a PhD from the Solomon H. Snyder Department of Neuroscience at The Johns Hopkins University School of Medicine, where he used machine learning to predict adverse cardiac side effects of drugs. Outside the academy, he has tackled big data challenges in the healthcare and entertainment industries.

About the Reviewer

Dipanjan Deb is an experienced analytics professional with 16 years of cumulative experience in machine/statistical learning, data mining, and predictive analytics across the healthcare, maritime, automotive, energy, CPG, and human resource domains. He is highly proficient in developing cutting-edge analytic solutions using open source and commercial packages to integrate multiple systems in order to provide massively parallelized and large-scale optimization.

Dipanjan has extensive experience in building analytics teams of data scientists that deliver high-quality solutions. He strategizes and collaborates with industry experts, technical experts, and data scientists to build analytic solutions that shorten the transition from a POC to a commercial release.

He is well versed in overarching supervised, semi-supervised, and unsupervised learning algorithm implementations in R, Python, Vowpal Wabbit, Julia, and SAS. Distributed frameworks including Hadoop and Spark, both in-premise and in cloud environment. He is a part-time Kaggler and IOT/IIOT enthusiast (Raspberry Pi and Arduino prototyping).

www.PacktPub.com

eBooks, discount offers, and more

Did you know that Packt offers eBook versions of every book published, with PDF and ePub files available? You can upgrade to the eBook version at www.PacktPub.com and as a print book customer, you are entitled to a discount on the eBook copy. Get in touch with us at customercare@packtpub.com for more details.

At www.PacktPub.com, you can also read a collection of free technical articles, sign up for a range of free newsletters and receive exclusive discounts and offers on Packt books and eBooks.

https://www2.packtpub.com/books/subscription/packtlib

Do you need instant solutions to your IT questions? PacktLib is Packt's online digital book library. Here, you can search, access, and read Packt's entire library of books.

Why subscribe?

- Fully searchable across every book published by Packt
- Copy and paste, print, and bookmark content
- On demand and accessible via a web browser

Table of Contents

Preface

In *Mastering Predictive Analytics with Python*, you will work through a step-by-step process to turn raw data into powerful insights. Power-packed with case studies and code examples using popular open source Python libraries, this volume illustrates the complete development process for analytic applications. The detailed examples illustrate robust and scalable applications for common use cases. You will learn to quickly apply these methods to your own data.

What this book covers

Chapter 1, *From Data to Decisions – Getting Started with Analytic Applications*, teaches you to describe the core components of an analytic pipeline and the ways in which they interact. We also examine the differences between batch and streaming processes, and some use cases in which each type of application is well-suited. We walk through examples of both basic applications using both paradigms and the design decisions needed at each step.

Chapter 2, *Exploratory Data Analysis and Visualization in Python*, examines many of the tasks needed to start building analytical applications. Using the IPython notebook, we'll cover how to load data in a file into a data frame in pandas, rename columns in the dataset, filter unwanted rows, convert types, and create new columns. In addition, we'll join data from different sources and perform some basic statistical analyses using aggregations and pivots.

Chapter 3, Finding Patterns in the Noise – Clustering and Unsupervised Learning, shows you how to identify groups of similar items in a dataset. It's an exploratory analysis that we might frequently use as a first step in deciphering new datasets. We explore different ways of calculating the similarity between data points and describe what kinds of data these metrics might best apply to. We examine both divisive clustering algorithms, which split the data into smaller components starting from a single group, and agglomerative methods, where every data point starts as its own cluster. Using a number of datasets, we show examples where these algorithms will perform better or worse, and some ways to optimize them. We also see our first (small) data pipeline, a clustering application in PySpark using streaming data.

Chapter 4, Connecting the Dots with Models – Regression Methods, examines the fitting of several regression models, including transforming input variables to the correct scale and accounting for categorical features correctly. We fit and evaluate a linear regression, as well as regularized regression models. We also examine the use of tree-based regression models, and how to optimize parameter choices in fitting them. Finally, we will look at a sample of random forest modeling using PySpark, which can be applied to larger datasets.

Chapter 5, Putting Data in its Place – Classification Methods and Analysis, explains how to use classification models and some of the strategies for improving model performance. In addition to transforming categorical features, we look at the interpretation of logistic regression accuracy using the ROC curve. In an attempt to improve model performance, we demonstrate the use of SVMs. Finally, we will achieve good performance on the test set through Gradient-Boosted Decision Trees.

Chapter 6, Words and Pixels – Working with Unstructured Data, examines complex, unstructured data. Then we cover dimensionality reduction techniques such as the HashingVectorizer; matrix decompositions such as PCA, CUR, and NMR; and probabilistic models such as LDA. We also examine image data, including normalization and thresholding operations, and see how we can use dimensionality reduction techniques to find common patterns among images.

Chapter 7, Learning from the Bottom Up – Deep Networks and Unsupervised Features, introduces deep neural networks as a way to generate models for complex data types where features are difficult to engineer. We'll examine how neural networks are trained through back-propagation, and why additional layers make this optimization intractable.

Chapter 8, Sharing Models with Prediction Services, describes the three components of a basic prediction service, and discusses how this design will allow us to share the results of predictive modeling with other users or software systems.

Chapter 9, *Reporting and Testing – Iterating on Analytic Systems*, teaches several strategies for monitoring the performance of predictive models following initial design, and we look at a number of scenarios where the performance or components of the model change over time.

What you need for this book

You'll need latest Python version and PySpark version installed, along with the Jupyter notebook.

Who this book is for

This book is designed for business analysts, BI analysts, data scientists, or junior-level data analysts who are ready to move from a conceptual understanding of advanced analytics to an expertise in designing and building advanced analytics solutions using Python. You're expected to have basic development experience with Python.

Conventions

In this book, you will find a number of text styles that distinguish between different kinds of information. Here are some examples of these styles and an explanation of their meaning.

Code words in text, database table names, folder names, filenames, file extensions, pathnames, dummy URLs, user input, and Twitter handles are shown as follows: "Let's start by peeking at the beginning and end of the data using `head()` and `tail()`."

Any command-line input or output is written as follows:

```
rdd_data.coalesce(2).getNumPartitions()
```

New terms and **important words** are shown in bold. Words that you see on the screen, for example, in menus or dialog boxes, appear in the text like this: "Returning to the **Files** tab, you will notice two options in the top right-hand corner."

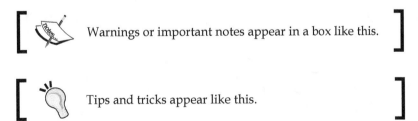

Warnings or important notes appear in a box like this.

Tips and tricks appear like this.

Reader feedback

Feedback from our readers is always welcome. Let us know what you think about this book—what you liked or disliked. Reader feedback is important for us as it helps us develop titles that you will really get the most out of.

To send us general feedback, simply e-mail feedback@packtpub.com, and mention the book's title in the subject of your message.

If there is a topic that you have expertise in and you are interested in either writing or contributing to a book, see our author guide at www.packtpub.com/authors.

Customer support

Now that you are the proud owner of a Packt book, we have a number of things to help you to get the most from your purchase.

Downloading the example code

You can download the example code files for this book from your account at http://www.packtpub.com. If you purchased this book elsewhere, you can visit http://www.packtpub.com/support and register to have the files e-mailed directly to you.

You can download the code files by following these steps:

1. Log in or register to our website using your e-mail address and password.
2. Hover the mouse pointer on the **SUPPORT** tab at the top.
3. Click on **Code Downloads & Errata**.
4. Enter the name of the book in the **Search** box.
5. Select the book for which you're looking to download the code files.
6. Choose from the drop-down menu where you purchased this book from.
7. Click on **Code Download**.

Once the file is downloaded, please make sure that you unzip or extract the folder using the latest version of:

- WinRAR / 7-Zip for Windows
- Zipeg / iZip / UnRarX for Mac
- 7-Zip / PeaZip for Linux

Downloading the color images of this book

We also provide you with a PDF file that has color images of the screenshots/diagrams used in this book. The color images will help you better understand the changes in the output. You can download this file from `https://www.packtpub.com/sites/default/files/downloads/MasteringPredictiveAnalyticswithPython_ColorImages.pdf`.

Errata

Although we have taken every care to ensure the accuracy of our content, mistakes do happen. If you find a mistake in one of our books—maybe a mistake in the text or the code—we would be grateful if you could report this to us. By doing so, you can save other readers from frustration and help us improve subsequent versions of this book. If you find any errata, please report them by visiting `http://www.packtpub.com/submit-errata`, selecting your book, clicking on the **Errata Submission Form** link, and entering the details of your errata. Once your errata are verified, your submission will be accepted and the errata will be uploaded to our website or added to any list of existing errata under the Errata section of that title.

To view the previously submitted errata, go to `https://www.packtpub.com/books/content/support` and enter the name of the book in the search field. The required information will appear under the **Errata** section.

Piracy

Piracy of copyrighted material on the Internet is an ongoing problem across all media. At Packt, we take the protection of our copyright and licenses very seriously. If you come across any illegal copies of our works in any form on the Internet, please provide us with the location address or website name immediately so that we can pursue a remedy.

Please contact us at `copyright@packtpub.com` with a link to the suspected pirated material.

We appreciate your help in protecting our authors and our ability to bring you valuable content.

Questions

If you have a problem with any aspect of this book, you can contact us at `questions@packtpub.com`, and we will do our best to address the problem.

1
From Data to Decisions – Getting Started with Analytic Applications

From quarterly financial projections to customer surveys, analytics help businesses to make decisions and plan for the future. While data visualizations such as pie charts and trend lines using spreadsheet programs have been used for decades, recent years have seen a growth in both the volume and diversity of data sources available to the business analyst and the sophistication of tools used to interpret this information.

The rapid growth of the Internet, through e-commerce and social media platforms, has generated a wealth of data, which is available faster than ever before for analysis. Photographs, search queries, and online forum posts are all examples of unstructured data that can't be easily examined in a traditional spreadsheet program. With the proper tools, these kinds of data offer new insights, in conjunction with or beyond traditional data sources.

Traditionally, data such as historical customer records appear in a structured, tabular form that is stored in an electronic data warehouse and easily imported into a spreadsheet program. Even in the case of such tabular data, the volume of records and the rate at which they are available are increasing in many industries. While the analyst might have historically transformed raw data through interactive manipulation, robust analytics increasingly requires automated processing that can scale with the volume and velocity of data being received by a business.

Along with the data itself, the methods used to examine it have become more powerful and complex. Beyond summarizing historical patterns or projecting future events using trend lines derived from a few key input variables, advanced analytics emphasizes the use of sophisticated predictive modeling (see the goals of predictive analytics, as follows) to understand the present and forecast near and long-term outcomes.

Diverse methods for generating such predictions typically require the following common elements:

- An outcome or target that we are trying to predict, such as a purchase or a **click-through-rate** (**CTR**) on a search result.

- A set of columns that comprise **features**, also known as **predictors** (for example, a customer's demographic information, past transactions on a sales account, or click behavior on a type of ad) describing individual properties of each record in our dataset (for example, an account or ad).

- A procedure that finds the model or set of models which best maps these features to the outcome of interest on a given sample of data.

- A way to evaluate the performance of the model on new data.

While predictive modeling techniques can be used in powerful analytic applications to discover complex relationships between seemingly unrelated inputs, they also present a new set of challenges to the business analyst:

- What method is the best suited for a particular problem?

- How does one correctly evaluate the performance of these techniques on historical and new data?

- What are the preferred strategies for tuning the performance of a given method?

- How does one robustly scale these techniques for both one-off analysis and ongoing insight?

In this book, we will show you how to address these challenges by developing analytic solutions that transform data into powerful insights for you and your business. The main tasks involved in building these applications are:

- Transforming raw data into a sanitized form that can be used for modeling. This may involve both cleaning anomalous data and converting unstructured data into a structured format.

- Feature engineering, by transforming these sanitized inputs into the format that is used to develop a predictive model.

- Calibrating a predictive model on a subset of this data and assessing its performance.

- Scoring new data while evaluating the ongoing performance of the model.

- Automating the transformation and modeling steps for regular updates.

- Exposing the output of the model to other systems and users, usually through a web application.

- Generating reports for the analyst and business user that distills the data and model into regular and robust insights.

Throughout this volume, we will use open-source tools written in the Python programming language to build these sorts of applications. Why Python? The Python language strikes an attractive balance between robust compiled languages such as Java, C++, and Scala, and pure statistical packages such as R, SAS, or MATLAB. We can work interactively with Python using the command line (or, as we will use in subsequent chapters, browser-based notebook environments), plotting data, and prototyping commands. Python also provides extensive libraries, allowing us to transform this exploratory work into web applications (such as Flask, CherryPy, and Celery, as we will see in *Chapter 8, Sharing Models with Prediction Services*), or scale them to large datasets (using PySpark, as we will explore in future chapters). Thus we can both analyze data and develop software applications within the same language.

Before diving into the technical details of these tools, let's take a high-level look at the concepts behind these applications and how they are structured. In this chapter, we will:

- Define the elements of an analytic pipeline: data transformation, sanity checking, preprocessing, model development, scoring, automation, deployment, and reporting.

- Explain the differences between batch-oriented and stream processing and their implications at each step of the pipeline.

- Examine how batch and stream processing can be jointly accommodated within the Lambda Architecture for data processing.

- Explore an example stream-processing pipeline to perform sentiment analysis of social media feeds.

- Explore an example of a batch-processing pipeline to generate targeted e-mail marketing campaigns.

The goals of predictive analytics

The term **predictive analytics**, along with others such as **data mining** and **machine learning**, are often used to describe the techniques used in this book to build analytic solutions. However, it is important to keep in mind that there are two distinct goals these methods can address. *Inference* involves building models in order to evaluate the significance of a parameter on an outcome and emphasizes interpretation and transparency over predictive performance. For example, the coefficients of a regression model (*Chapter 4, Connecting the Dots with Models – Regression Methods*) can be used to estimate the effect of variation in a particular model input (for example, customer age or income) on an output variable (for example, sales). The predictions from a model developed for inference may be less accurate than other techniques, but provide valuable conceptual insights that may guide business decisions. Conversely, *prediction* emphasizes the accuracy of the estimated outcome, even if the model itself is a black box where the connection between an input and the resulting output is not always clear. For example, Deep Learning (*Chapter 7, Learning from the Bottom Up – Deep Networks and Unsupervised Features*) can produce state-of-the-art models and extremely accurate predictions from complex sets of inputs, but the connection between the input parameters and the prediction may be hard to interpret.

Designing an advanced analytic solution

What are the essential components of an analytic solution? While the exact design can vary between applications, most consist of the following pieces (Figure 1):

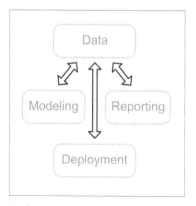

Figure 1: Reference architecture for an analytic pipeline

- **Data layer**: This stage deals with storage, processing, and persistence of the data, and how it is served to downstream applications such as the analytical applications we will build in this volume. As indicated in Figure 1, data serves as the **glue** the binds together the other pieces of our application, all of which rely on the data layer to store and update information about their state. This also reflects the **separation of concerns** that we will discuss in more detail in *Chapters 8, Sharing Models with Prediction Services* and *Chapter 9, Reporting and Testing – Iterating on Analytic Systems*, where the other three components of our application can be designed independently since they interact only through the data layer.

- **Modeling layer**: At this point, the data has been turned into a form that may be ingested by our modeling code in Python. Further feature engineering tasks may be involved to convert this sanitized data into model inputs, along with splitting data into subsets and performing iterative rounds of optimization and tuning. It will also be necessary to prepare the model in a way that can be persisted and deployed to downstream users. This stage is also involved with scoring new data as it is received or performing audits of model health over time.

- **Deployment layer**: The algorithm development and performance components in the modeling layer are usually exposed to either human users or other software systems through web services, which these consumers interact with through a server layer by means of network calls to both trigger new rounds of model development and query the results of previous analyses.

- **Reporting layer**: Predictions, model parameters, and insights can all be visualized and automated using reporting services.

With these broad components in mind, let's delve more deeply into the details of each of these pieces.

Data layer: warehouses, lakes, and streams

The beginning of any analytic pipeline is the data itself, which serves as the basis for predictive modeling. This input can vary both in the rate at which updates are available and the amount of transformation that needs to be applied to form the final set of features used in the predictive model. The data layer serves as the repository for this information.

Traditionally, data used for analytics might simply be stored on disk in flat files, such as a spreadsheet or document. As the diversity and scale of data have increased, so have the scale and complexity of resources needed to house and process them. Indeed, a modern view of the data layer encompasses both real-time (stream) data and batch data in the context of many potential downstream uses. This combined system, known as **Lambda Architecture** (Marz, Nathan, and James Warren. *Big Data: Principles and best practices of scalable realtime data systems.* Manning Publications Co., 2015.), is diagrammed in the following figure:

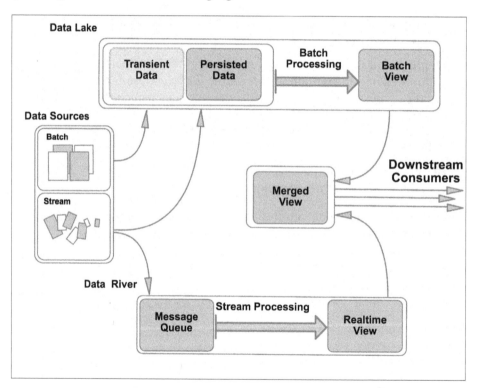

Figure 2: Data layer as a Lambda Architecture

The components of this data layer are:

- **Data sources**: These could be either real time data received in streams, or batch updates received on a periodic or discontinuous basis.

- **Data lake**: Both real-time and batch data is commonly saved in a data lake model, in which a distributed file system such as the **Hadoop File System (HDFS)** or **Amazon Web Services (AWS) Simple Storage Service (S3)** is used as a common storage medium for data received both in batch and in streams. This data can either be stored with a fixed lifetime (transient) or permanent (persisted) retention policy. This data may then be processed in ongoing batch transformations such as **Extract, Load, and Transform (ETL)** jobs running in frameworks such as MapReduce or Spark. ETL processes might involve cleaning the data, aggregating it into metrics of interest, or reshaping it into a tabular form from raw inputs. This processing forms the batch layer of the Lambda Architecture, where real-time availability is not expected and latency of minutes to days is acceptable in surfacing views of the data for downstream consumption.

- **Data river**: While the data lake accumulates all types of raw data in a central location, the data river forms an ongoing message queue where real-time data is dispatched to stream processing tasks. This is also termed the **speed layer** (Marz, Nathan, and James Warren. *Big Data: Principles and best practices of scalable realtime data systems*. Manning Publications Co., 2015.) of the architecture, as it operates on data as soon as it is available and real-time availability is expected.

- **Merged view**: Both real-time and batch views of the raw data may be merged into a common persistence layer, such as a data warehouse in structured tables, where they can be queried using **Structured Query Language (SQL)** and utilized in either transactional (for example, updating a bank balance in real time) or analytic (for example, running analyses or reports) applications. Examples of such warehouse systems include traditional relational systems such as MySQL and PostgreSQL (which usually store data with tabular schema in rows and columns), and NoSQL systems such as MongoDB or Redis (which arrange data more flexibly in key-value systems, where values can take on numerous formats outside the traditional rows and columns). This merged system is also referred to as the **serving layer** (Marz, Nathan, and James Warren. *Big Data: Principles and best practices of scalable realtime data systems*. Manning Publications Co., 2015.), and can either be directly queried using the database system, or surfaced to downstream applications.

- **Downstream applications**: Systems such as our advanced analytic pipelines can either directly consume the outputs of the batch and real-time processing layers, or interact with one or both of these sources through the merged view in the warehousing system.

How might streaming and batch data be processed differently in the data layer? In batch pipelines, the allowed delay between receiving and processing the data allows for potentially complex transformations of the source data: elements may be aggregated (such as calculating a user or product's average properties over a period of time), joined to other sources (for example, indexing additional website metadata on search logs), and filtered (for example, many web logging systems need to remove bot activity that would otherwise skew the results of predictive models). The source data could be obtained, for example, from simple text files posted to a server, a relational database system, or a mixture of different storage formats (see as follows).

Conversely, due to the speed at which incoming data must often be consumed, streaming processes typically involve less complex processing of inputs than batch jobs, and instead use simple filters or transformations. The sources for such applications are typically continuously updated streams from web services (such as social media or news feeds), events (such as geo-locations of vehicles and mobile phones), or customer activities (such as searches or clicks).

The choice between batch and stream processing at this stage is largely determined by the data source, which is either available as a continuously updated series of events (streaming) or larger, periodically available chunks (batch). In some cases, the nature of the data will also determine the form of the subsequent pipeline and an emphasis on real-time or higher latency processing. In others, the use of the application will take precedent in downstream choices. The normalized view surfaced in the data layer is used downstream in the next stage of the analytic pipeline, the modeling layer.

Modeling layer

The modeling layer involves a number of interconnected tasks, diagrammed in the following figure (**Figure 3**). As the data layer accommodates both real-time and batch data, we can imagine two main kinds of modeling systems:

- Streaming pipelines act upon a continuous source of data (such as instant messages or a news feed) as soon as it becomes available, potentially allowing real-time model updates or scoring. However, the ability to update the model in real time may vary by algorithm (for example it will work for models using stochastic updates, described in *Chapter 5, Putting Data in its Place – Classification Methods and Analysis*), and some can only be developed in an offline process. The potential volume of streaming data may also mean that it cannot be stored in its raw form, but only transformed into a more manageable format before the original record is discarded.

- **Batch processing**. Data sources that are updated on a periodic basis (often daily) are frequently processed using a batch-oriented framework. The input does not need to be used at the moment it is available, with a latency of hours or days between updates usually acceptable, meaning the data processing and model development are typically not occurring in real time.

 On the surface, the choice between the two classes of pipelines seems to involve the tradeoff between real-time (streaming) or offline (batch) analysis. In practice, the two classes can have real-time and non-real-time components intermingled within a single application.

If both types of pipeline are viable for a given problem (for example, if the streams are stock prices, a dataset whose volume and simple format – a set of numbers – should allow it to be readily stored offline and processed in its entirety at a later date), the choice between the two frameworks may be dictated by technical or business concerns. For example, sometimes the method used in a predictive model allows only for batch updates, meaning that continuously processing a stream as it is received does not add additional value. In other cases, the importance of the business decisions informed by the predictive model necessitates real-time updates and so would benefit from stream processing.

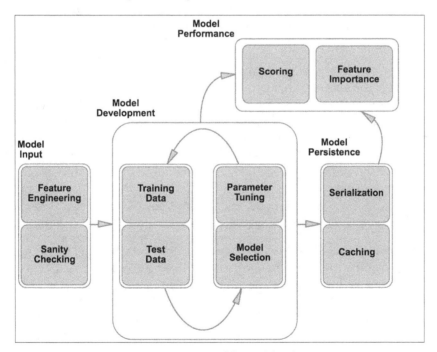

Figure 3: Overview of the modeling layer

The details of the generic components of each type of pipeline as shown in Figure 3 are as follows:

In the **Model Input** step the source data is loaded and potentially transformed by the pipeline into the inputs required for a predictive model. This can be as simple as exposing a subset of columns in a database table, or transforming an unstructured source such as text into a form that may be input to a predictive model. If we are fortunate, the kinds of features we wish to use in a model are already the form in which they are present in the raw data. In this case, the model fitting proceeds directly on the inputs. More often, the input data just contains the base information we might want to use as inputs to our model, but needs to be processed into a form that can be utilized in prediction.

In the case of numerical data, this might take the form of discretization or transformation. Discretization involves taking a continuous number (such as consumer tenure on a subscription service) and dividing it into bins (such as users with **<30** or **>=30** days of subscription) that either reduce the variation in the dataset (by thresholding an outlier on a continuous scale to a reasonable bin number) or turn a numerical range into a set of values that have more direct business implications. Another example of discretization is turning a continuous value into a rank, in cases where we don't care as much about the actual number as its relative value compared to others. Similarly, values that vary over exponential scales might be transformed using a natural logarithm to reduce the influence of large values on the modeling process.

In addition to these sorts of transformations, numerical features might be combined in ratios, sums, products, or other combinations, yielding a potential combinatorial explosion of features from even a few basic inputs. In some models, these sorts of interactions need to be explicitly represented by generating such combined features between inputs (such as the regression models we discuss in *Chapter 4, Connecting the Dots with Models – Regression Methods*). Other models have some ability to decipher these interactions in datasets without our direct creation of the feature (such as random forest algorithms in *Chapter 5, Putting Data in its Place – Classification Methods and Analysis* or gradient boosted decision trees in *Chapter 6, Words and Pixels – Working with Unstructured Data*).

In the case of categorical data, such as country codes or days of the week, we may need to transform the category into a numerical descriptor. This could be a number (if the data is ordinal, meaning for example that a value of 2 has an interpretation of being larger than another record with value 1 for that feature) or a vector with one or more non-zero entries indicating the class to which a categorical feature belongs (for example, a document could be represented by a vector the same length as the English vocabulary, with a number indicating how many times each word represented by a particular vector position appears in the document).

Finally, we might find cases where we wish to discover the hidden features represented by a particular set of inputs. For example, income, occupation, and age might all be correlated with the zip code in which a customer lives. If geographic variables aren't part of our dataset, we could still discover these common underlying patterns using dimensionality reduction, as we will discuss in *Chapter 6, Words and Pixels – Working with Unstructured Data*.

Sanity checking may also be performed at this stage, as it is crucial to spot data anomalies when they appear, such as outliers that might degrade the performance of the model. In the first phase of quality checks, the input data is evaluated to prevent outliers or incorrect data from impacting the quality of models in the following stages. These sanity checks could take many forms: for categorical data (for example, a state or country), there are only a fixed number of allowable values, making it easy to rule out incorrect inputs. In other cases, this quality check is based on an empirical distribution, such as variation from an average value, or a sensible minimum or maximum range. More complex scenarios usually arise from business rules (such as a product being unavailable in a given territory, or a particular combination of IP addresses in web sessions being illogical).

Such quality checks serve as more than safeguards for the modeling process: they can also serve as warnings of events such as bot traffic on websites that may indicate malicious activity. Consequently, these audit rules may also be incorporated as part of the visualization and reporting layer at the conclusion of the pipeline.

In the second round of quality checks following model development, we want to evaluate whether the parameters of the model make sense and whether the performance on the test data is in an acceptable range for deployment. The former might involve plotting the important parameters of a model if the technique permits, visualizations that can then also be utilized by the reporting step downstream. Similarly, the second class of checks can involve looking at accuracy statistics such as precision, recall, or squared error, or the similarity of the test set to data used in model generation in order to determine if the reported performance is reasonable.

As with the first round of sanity checks, not only can these quality control measures serve to monitor the health of the model development process, but also potentially highlight changes in the actual modeling code itself (especially if this code is expected to be regularly updated).

There isn't inherently much difference between streaming and batch-oriented processing in the sanity checking process, just the latency at which the application can uncover anomalies in the source data or modelling process and deliver them to the reporting layer. The complexity of the sanity checks may guide this decision: simple checks that can be done in real-time are well suited for stream processing, while evaluation of the properties of a predictive model could potentially take longer than the training of the algorithm itself, and is thus more suited for a batch process.

In the model development or update step, once the input data has undergone any necessary processing or transformation steps and passed the quality checks described above, it is ready to be used in developing a predictive model. This phase of the analytic pipeline can have several steps, with the exact form depending upon the application:

- **Data splitting**: At this stage we typically split data into disjoin sets, the training data (from which we will tune the parameters of the algorithm), and the test data (which is used for evaluation purposes). The important reason for making this split is so that the model generalizes to data beyond its initial inputs (the training data), which we can check by evaluating its performance on the test set.

- **Parameter tuning**: As we will examine in more detail in subsequent chapters, many predictive models have a number of hyperparameters— variables that need to be set before the parameters of the model can be optimized for a training set. Examples include the number of groups in a clustering application (*Chapter 3, Finding Patterns in the Noise – Clustering and Unsupervised Learning*), the number of trees used in a random forest *Chapter 4, Connecting the Dots with Models – Regression Methods*, or the learning rate and number of layers in a neural network (*Chapter 7, Learning from the Bottom Up – Deep Networks and Unsupervised Features*). These hyperparameters frequently need to be calibrated for optimal performance of a predictive model, through grid search (*Chapter 5, Putting Data in its Place – Classification Methods and Analysis*) or other methods. This tuning can occur only during the initial phase of model development, or as part of a regular retraining cycle. Following or jointly with hyperparameter tuning, the parameters, such as regression coefficients or decision splits in a tree model *Chapter 4, Connecting the Dots with Models – Regression Methods*, are optimized for a given set of training data. Depending upon the method, this step may also involve variable selection—the process of pruning uninformative features from the input data. Finally, we may perform the above tasks for multiple algorithms and choose the best performing technique.

Batch-oriented and streaming processes could differ at this stage depending upon the algorithm. For example, in models that allow for incremental updates through stochastic learning (*Chapter 5, Putting Data in its Place – Classification Methods and Analysis*), new data may be processed in a stream as each new training example can individually tune the model parameters. Conversely, data may arrive in a stream but be aggregated until a sufficient size is reached, at which point a batch process is launched to retrain the model. Some models allow for both kinds of training, and the choice depends more on the expected volatility of the input data. For example, rapidly trending signals in social media posts may suggest updating a model as soon as events are available, while models based on longer-term events such as household buying patterns may not justify such continuous updates.

- **Model performance**: Using either the test data split off during model development or an entirely new set of observations, the modeling layer is also responsible for scoring new data, surfacing important features in the model, and providing information about its ongoing performance. Once the model has been trained on a set of input data, it can be applied to new data in either in real-time computations, or through offline, batch processing to generate a predicted outcome or behavior.

  Depending upon the extent of initial data processing, new records may also need to be transformed to generate the appropriate features for evaluation by a model. The extent of such transformations may dictate whether scoring is best accomplished through a streaming or batch framework.

  Similarly, the use of the resulting prediction may guide the choice between streaming or batch-oriented processing. When such scores are used as inputs to other, responsive systems (such as in reordering search results or ads presented on a webpage), real-time updates from streaming pipelines, allow for immediate use of the new scores and so may be valuable. When the scores are primarily used for internal decision-making (such as prioritizing sales leads for follow-up), real-time updates may not be necessary and a batch-oriented framework can be used instead. This difference in latency may be correlated with whether the downstream consumer is another application (machine to machine interaction), or a human user relying upon the model for insight (machine to human).

- **Model persistence**: Once we have tuned the parameters of the predictive model, the result may also need to be packaged, or serialized into a format to allow deployment within a production environment. We will examine this in greater depth in *Chapter 8, Sharing Models with Prediction Services*, but in brief this process involves transforming the model output into a form for use by downstream systems and saving it back to the data layer for both disaster recovery and potential use by the reporting layer downstream described as follows.

Deployment layer

The output of our predictive modeling can be made broadly available to both individual users and other software services through a deployment layer, which encapsulates the modeling, scoring, and evaluation functions in the previous layer inside of web applications, as shown in the following Figure 4:

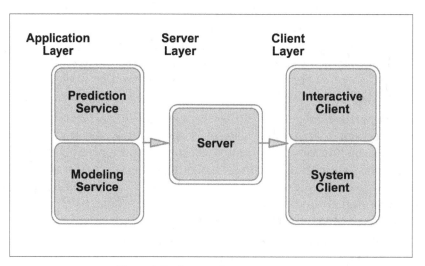

Figure 4: Deployment layer components

This **application layer** receives network calls over the web, transmitted either through a web browser or from a programmatic request generated by another software system. As we will describe in *Chapter 8, Sharing Models with Prediction Services*, these applications usually provide a standard set of commands to initiate an action, get a result, save new information, or delete unwanted information. They also typically interact with the data layer to both store results and, in the case of long-running tasks, to store information about the progress of modeling computations.

The network calls received by these applications are brokered by the Server Layer, which serves to route traffic between applications (usually based on `url` patterns). As we will cover in *Chapter 8, Sharing Models with Prediction Services*, this separation between the server and application allows us to scale our application by adding more machines, and independently add more servers to balance incoming requests.

The **client layer**, which initiates the requests received by the server, could be both interactive systems, such as a dashboard, or an independent system such as an e-mail server, that uses the output of a model to schedule outgoing messages.

Reporting layer

The output of the analytical pipeline may be surfaced by the reporting layer, which involves a number of distinct tasks, as shown in the following Figure 5:

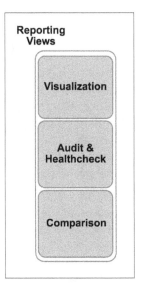

Figure 5: Reporting applications for prediction services

- **Visualizations**: This can allow interactive querying of the source data along with model data such as parameters and feature importance. It can also be used to visualize the output of a model, such as the set of recommendations that would be provided to a user on an e-commerce site, or the risk score assigned to a particular bank account. Because it is frequently used in interactive mode, we may also consider aggregating large model inputs into summarized datasets for lower latency during exploratory sessions. Additionally, visualizations can be either an ad hoc process (such as the interactive notebooks we will examine in future chapters), or a fixed series of graphics (such as the dashboards we will construct in *Chapter 9, Reporting and Testing – Iterating on Analytic Systems*).

- **Audit/Healthcheck**: The reporting service involves ongoing monitoring of the application. Indeed, an important factor in developing robust analytic pipelines is regular assessment to ensure that the model is performing as expected. Combining outputs from many previous steps, such as quality control checks and scores for new data, a reporting framework visualizes these statistics and compares them to previous values or a gold standard. This sort of reporting can be used both by the analyst, to monitor the application, and as a way to surface insights uncovered by the modeling process to the larger business organization.

- **Comparison reports**: This might be used as we iterate on model development through the process of experimentation, as we will discuss in *Chapter 9, Reporting and Testing – Iterating on Analytic Systems*. Because this analysis may involve statistical measurements, the visualizations might be combined with a service in the deployment layer to calculate significance metrics.

The choice of batch versus streaming processes will often determine whether such reports can be provided in real-time, but just because they are available immediately doesn't imply that such frequency is valuable to the user. For example, even if user response rates to an ad campaign can be collected in real-time, decisions about future advertising programs on these results may be constrained by quarterly business planning. In contrast, trending interest in particular search queries might also allow us to quickly tune the results of a recommendation algorithm, and thus this low-latency signal has value. Again, judgment based on the particular use-case is required.

To conclude this introduction, let's examine a pair of hypothetical applications that illustrates many of the components we've described above. Don't worry too much about the exact meaning of all the terminology, which will be expanded upon in following chapters.

Case study: sentiment analysis of social media feeds

Consider a marketing department that wants to evaluate the effectiveness of its campaigns by monitoring brand sentiment on social media sites. Because changes in sentiment could have negative effects on the larger company, this analysis is performed in real time. An overview of this example is shown in the Figure 6.

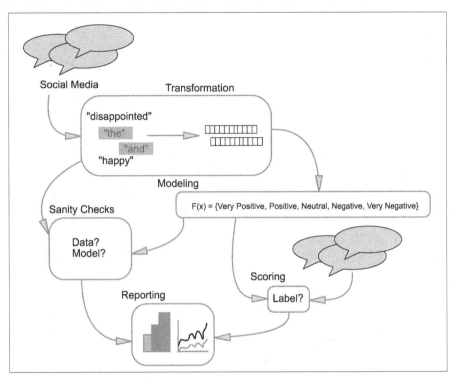

Figure 6: Diagram of social media sentiment analysis case study

Data input and transformation

The input data to this application are social media posts. This data is available in real time, but a number of steps need to be applied to make it usable by the sentiment-scoring model. Common words (such as **and** and **the**) need to be filtered, messages to be selected which actually refer to the company, and misspellings and word capitalization need to be normalized. Once this cleaning is done, further transformations may turn the message into a vector, with a count of each word in the model's allowed vocabulary, or hashed to populate a fixed-length vector.

Sanity checking

The outputs of the preceding transformations need to be sanity checked – are there any users who account for an unusually large number of messages (which might indicate bot spam)? Are there unexpected words in the input (which could be due to character encoding issues)? Are any of the input messages longer than the allowed message size for the service (which could indicate incorrect separation of messages in the input stream)?

Once the model is developed, sanity checking involves some human guidance. Do the sentiments predicted by the model correlate with the judgment of human readers? Do the words that correspond to high probability for a given sentiment in the model make intuitive sense?

These and other sanity checks can be visualized as a webpage or document summary that can be utilized by both the modeler, to evaluate model health, and the rest of the marketing staff to understand new topics that may correspond to positive or negative brand sentiment.

Model development

The model used in this pipeline is a multinomial logistic regression (*Chapter 5, Putting Data in its Place – Classification Methods and Analysis*) that takes as input counts of the words in each social media message and outputs a predicted probability that the message belongs to a given sentiment category: **VERY POSITIVE**, **POSITIVE**, **NEUTRAL**, **NEGATIVE**, and **VERY NEGATIVE**. While in theory (because the multinomial logistic regression can be trained using stochastic gradient updates), we could perform model training online, in practice this is not possible because the labels (sentiments) need to be assigned by a human expert. Therefore, our model is developed in an offline batch-process each week as a sufficient set of social media messages labelled by an expert becomes available. The hyperparameters of this model (the regularization weight and learning weight) have been estimated previously, so the batch retraining calculates the regression coefficient weights for a set of training messages and evaluates the performance on a separate batch of test messages.

Scoring

Incoming messages processed by this pipeline can be scored by the existing model and assigned to one of the five sentiment classes, and the volume of each category is updated in real time to allow monitoring of brand sentiment and immediate action if there is an extremely negative response to one of the marketing department's campaigns.

Visualization and reporting

As the model scores new social media messages, it updates a real-time dashboard with the volume of messages in each category compared to yesterday, the preceding week, and the preceding month, along with which words are given most weight in this week's model for the different classes. It also monitors the presence of new words, which may not have been present in the model's vocabulary, and which could indicate new features that the model cannot appropriately score, and suggest the need for inter-week retraining. In addition to this real-time dashboard, which the marketing department uses to monitor response to its campaigns, the analyst develops a more detailed report concerning model parameters and performance along with input dataset summary statistics, which they use to determine if the model training process each week is performing as expected, or if the quality of the model is degrading over time.

Case study: targeted e-mail campaigns

In our next example, our same marketing department wants to promote new items on their website to users who are mostly likely to be interested in purchasing them. Using a predictive model that includes features from both users and these new items, customers are sent e-mails containing a list of their most probable purchase. Unlike the real-time sentiment-monitoring example, e-mails are sent in batches and use data accumulated over a customer's whole transaction history as inputs to the model, which is a better fit for batch processing.

An overview of the processes used in this example is shown in Figure 7.

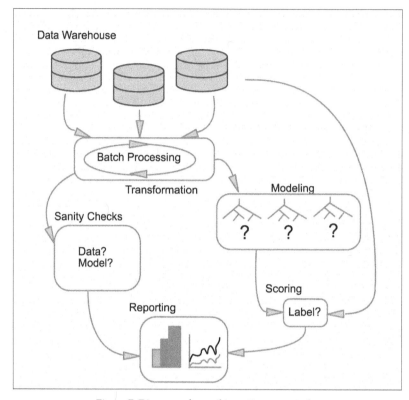

Figure 7: Diagram of e-mail targeting case study

Data input and transformation

During the initial data ingestion step, customer records stored in a company's data warehouse (a relational database system) are aggregated to generate features such as the average amount spent per week, frequency with which a customer visits the company's website, and the number of items purchased in a number of categories, such as furniture, electronics, clothing, and media. This is combined with a set of features for the set of items that are potentially promoted in the e-mail campaign, such as price, brand, and the average rating of similar items on the site. These features are constructed through a batch process that runs once per week, before e-mails are sent, on Mondays, to customers.

Sanity checking

The inputs to the model are checked for reasonable values: are the average purchase behaviors or transactions volume of a customer far outside the expected range? These could indicate errors in the data warehouse processing, or bot traffic on the website. Because the transformation logic involved in constructing features for the model is complex and may change over time as the model evolves, its outputs are also checked. For example, the purchase numbers and average prices should never be less than zero, and no category of merchandise should have zero records.

Following scoring of potential items prior to e-mail messaging, the top-scoring items per customer are sanity checked by comparing them to either the customer's historical transactions (to determine if they are sensible), or if no history is available, to the purchases of customers most similar in demographics.

Model development

In this example, the model is a random forest regression *Chapter 4, Connecting the Dots with Models – Regression Methods* that divides historical items – customer pairs into purchases (**labeled 1**) and non-purchases (**labeled 0**) and produces a scored probability that customer A purchases **item X**. One complexity in this model is that items which haven't been purchased might simply not have been seen by the customer yet, so a restriction is imposed in which the negative examples must be drawn from items already available for a month or more on the website. The hyperparameters of this model (the number and size of each tree) are calibrated during weekly retraining, along with the influence of individual variables on the resulting predictions.

Scoring

After the model is retrained each week using historical data, the set of new items on the website are scored using this model for each customer, and the top three are sent in the e-mail campaign.

Visualization and reporting

Either class of sanity checking (of either input data or model performance) can be part of a regular diagnostics report on the model. Because the random forest model is more complex than other approaches, it is particularly important to monitor changes in feature importance and model accuracy as problems may require more time to debug and resolve.

Because the predictions are used in a production system rather than delivering insights themselves, this reporting is primarily used by the analyst who developed the pipeline rather than the other members of the marketing department.

The success of these promotional e-mails will typically be monitored over the next month, and updates on the accuracy (for example, how many e-mails led to purchases above expected levels) can form the basis of a longer-term report that can help guide both the structure of the campaign itself (for example, varying the number of items in the messages) and the model (perhaps training should be performed more frequently if the predictions seem to become significantly worse between weeks).

Downloading the example code

You can download the example code files for this book from your account at http://www.packtpub.com. If you purchased this book elsewhere, you can visit http://www.packtpub.com/support and register to have the files e-mailed directly to you.

You can download the code files by following these steps:

- Log in or register to our website using your e-mail address and password.
- Hover the mouse pointer on the **SUPPORT** tab at the top.
- Click on **Code Downloads & Errata**.
- Enter the name of the book in the **Search** box.
- Select the book for which you're looking to download the code files.
- Choose from the drop-down menu where you purchased this book from.
- Click on **Code Download**.

Once the file is downloaded, please make sure that you unzip or extract the folder using the latest version of:

WinRAR / 7-Zip for Windows

- Zipeg / iZip / UnRarX for Mac
- 7-Zip / PeaZip for Linux

Summary

After finishing this chapter, you should now be able to describe the core components of an analytic pipeline and the ways in which they interact. We've also examined the differences between batch and streaming processes, and some of the use cases in which each type of application is well suited. We've also walked through examples using both paradigms and the design decisions needed at each step.

In the following sections we will develop the concepts previously described, and go into greater detail on some of the technical terms brought up in the case studies. In *Chapter 2, Exploratory Data Analysis and Visualization in Python,* we will introduce interactive data visualization and exploration using open source Python tools. *Chapter 3, Finding Patterns in the Noise – Clustering and Unsupervised Learning,* describes how to identify groups of related objects in a dataset using clustering methods, also known as unsupervised learning. In contrast, *Chapter 4, Connecting the Dots with Models – Regression Methods,* and *Chapter 5, Putting Data in its Place – Classification Methods and Analysis,* explore supervised learning, whether for continuous outcomes such as prices (using regression techniques in *Chapters 4, Connecting the Dots with Models – Regression Methods*), or categorical responses such as user sentiment (using classification models described in *Chapter 5, Putting Data in its Place – Classification Methods and Analysis*). Given a large number of features, or complex data such as text or image, we may benefit by performing dimensionality reduction, as described in *Chapter 6, Words and Pixels – Working with Unstructured Data.* Alternatively, we may fit textual or image data using more sophisticated models such as the deep neural networks covered in *Chapter 7, Learning from the Bottom Up – Deep Networks and Unsupervised Features,* which can capture complex interactions between input variables. In order to use these models in business applications, we will develop a web framework to deploy analytical solutions in *Chapter 8, Sharing Models with Prediction Services,* and describe ongoing monitoring and refinement of the system in *Chapter 9, Reporting and Testing – Iterating on Analytic Systems.*

Throughout, we will emphasize both how these methods work and practical tips for choosing between different approaches for various problems. Working through the code examples will illustrate the required components for building and maintaining an application for your own use case. With these preliminaries, let's dive next into some exploratory data analysis using notebooks: a powerful way to document and share analysis.

2
Exploratory Data Analysis and Visualization in Python

Analytic pipelines are not built from raw data in a single step. Rather, development is an iterative process that involves understanding the data in greater detail and systematically refining both model and inputs to solve a problem. A key part of this cycle is interactive data analysis and visualization, which can provide initial ideas for features in our predictive modeling or clues as to why an application is not behaving as expected.

Spreadsheet programs are one kind of interactive tool for this sort of exploration: they allow the user to import tabular information, pivot and summarize data, and generate charts. However, what if the data in question is too large for such a spreadsheet application? What if the data is not tabular, or is not displayed effectively as a line or bar chart? In the former case, we could simply obtain a more powerful computer, but the latter is more problematic. Simply put, many traditional data visualization tools are not well suited to complex data types such as text or images. Additionally, spreadsheet programs often assume data is in a finalized form, whereas in practice we will often need to clean up the raw data before analysis. We might also want to calculate more complex statistics than simple averages or sums. Finally, using the same programming tools to clean up and visualize our data as well as generate the model itself and test its performance allows a more streamlined development process.

In this chapter we introduce interactive Python (IPython) notebook applications (Pérez, Fernando, and Brian E. Granger. *IPython: a system for interactive scientific computing. Computing in Science & Engineering* 9.3 (2007): 21-29). The notebooks form a data preparation, exploration, and modeling environment that runs inside a web browser. The commands typed in the input cells of an IPython notebook are translated and executed as they are received: this kind of interactive programming is helpful for data exploration, where we may refine our efforts and successively develop more detailed analyses. Recording our work in these Notebooks will help to both backtrack during debugging and serve as a record of insights that can be easily shared with colleagues.

In this chapter we will discuss the following topics:

- Reading raw data into an IPython notebook, cleaning it, and manipulating it using the Pandas library.

- Using IPython to process numerical, categorical, geospatial, or time-series data, and perform basic statistical analyses.

- Basic exploratory analyses: summary statistics (mean, variance, median), distributions (histogram and kernel density), and auto-correlation (time-series).

- An introduction to distributed data processing with Spark RDDs and DataFrames.

Exploring categorical and numerical data in IPython

We will start our explorations in IPython by loading a text file into a DataFrame, calculating some summary statistics, and visualizing distributions. For this exercise we'll use a set of movie ratings and metadata from the Internet Movie Database (http://www.imdb.com/) to investigate what factors might correlate with high ratings for films on this website. Such information might be helpful, for example, in developing a recommendation system based on this kind of user feedback.

Installing IPython notebook

To follow along with the examples, you should have a Windows, Linux, or Mac OSX operating system installed on your computer and access to the Internet. There are a number of options available to install IPython: since each of these resources includes installation guides, we provide a summary of the available sources and direct the reader to the relevant documentation for more in-depth instructions.

- For most users, a pre-bundled Python environment such as Anaconda (Continuum Analytics) or Canopy (Enthought) provides an out-of-the-box distribution with IPython and all the libraries we will use in these exercises: these products are self-contained, and thus you should not have to worry about conflicting versions or dependency management.

- For more ambitious users, you can install a python distribution of your choice, followed by individual installation of the required libraries using package managers such as `pip` or `easy_install`.

The notebook interface

Let's get started with the following steps:

1. Once you've installed IPython, open the command prompt (terminal) on your computer and type:

   `jupyter notebook`

   Note that depending upon where you installed the program, the `jupyter` command may require the binary file that launches `jupyter` to be on your system path. You should see a series of commands like the following in your terminal:

```
[I 23:26:21.113 NotebookApp] Serving notebooks from local directory: /Users/jbabcock/Dropbox/Mastering_Predictive_Analy
[I 23:26:21.113 NotebookApp] 0 active kernels
[I 23:26:21.113 NotebookApp] The IPython Notebook is running at: http://localhost:8888/
[I 23:26:21.113 NotebookApp] Use Control-C to stop this server and shut down all kernels (twice to skip confirmation).
```

   This starts the **kernel**, the python interpreter that computes the result of commands entered into the notebook. If you want to stop the notebook, type *Ctrl + C*, and enter **yes**, and the kernel will shut down.

2. When the kernel starts, your default web browser should also open, giving you a homepage that looks like this:

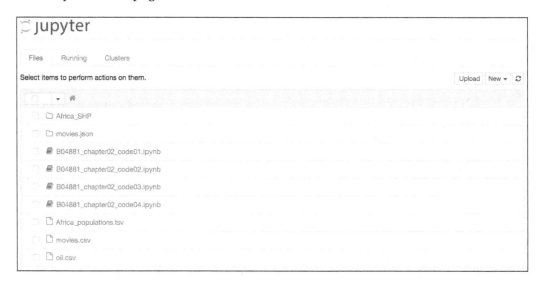

3. The **Files** tab (see above) will show you all of the files in the directory where you started the IPython process. Clicking **Running** will give you a list of all running notebooks – there are none when you start:

4. Finally, the Clusters panel gives a list of external clusters, should we decide to parallelize our calculations by submitting commands to be processed on more than one machine. We won't worry about this for now, but it will come in useful later when we begin to train predictive models, a task that may often be accelerated by distributing the work among many computers or processors.

5. Returning to the **Files** tab, you will notice two options in the top right-hand corner. One is to **Upload** a file: while we are running IPython locally, it could just as easily be running on a remote server, with the analyst accessing the notebook through a browser. In this case, to interact with files stored on our own machine, we can use this button to open a prompt and selected the desired files to upload to the server, where we could then analyze them in the notebook. The **New** tab lets you create a new folder, text file, a Python terminal running in the browser, or a notebook.

For now, let's open the sample notebook for this chapter by double clicking on **B04881_chapter02_code01.ipynb**. This opens the notebook:

The notebook consists of a series of cells, areas of text where we can type python code, execute it, and see the results of the commands. The python code in each cell can be executed by clicking the ⋈ button on the toolbar, and a new cell can be inserted below the current one by clicking ⋈ .

6. While the import statements in the first cell probably look familiar from your experience of using python in the command line or in a script, the `%matplotlib` inline command is not actually python: it is a markup instruction to the notebook that `matplotlib` images are to be displayed inline the browser. We enter this command at the beginning of the notebook so that all of our later plots use this setting. To run the import statements, click the ⋆ button or press *Ctrl + Enter*. The `ln[1]` on the cell may briefly change to `[*]` as the command executes. There will be no output in this case, as all we did was import library dependencies. Now that our environment is ready, we can start examining some data.

Loading and inspecting data

To start, we will import the data in `movies.csv` into a DataFrame object using the Pandas library (McKinney, Wes. *Python for data analysis: Data wrangling with Pandas*, NumPy, and IPython. O'Reilly Media, Inc., 2012). This DataFrame resembles traditional spreadsheet software and allows powerful extensions such as custom transformations and aggregations. These may be combined with numerical methods, such as those available in NumPy, for more advanced statistical analysis of the data. Let us continue our analysis:

1. If this were a new notebook, to add new cells we would go to the toolbar, click **Insert** and **Insert Cell Below**, or use the + . button. However, in this example all the cells are already generated, therefore we run the following command in the second cell:

   ```
   >>> imdb_ratings = pd.read_csv('movies.csv')
   ```

   We've now created a DataFrame object using the Pandas library, `imdb_ratings`, and can begin analyzing the data.

2. Let's start by peeking at the beginning and end of the data using `head()` and `tail()`. Notice that by default this command returns the first five rows of data, but we can supply an integer argument to the command to specify the number of lines to return. Also, by default the first line of the file is assumed to contain the column names, which in this case is correct. Typing:

   ```
   >>> imdb_ratings.head()
   ```

   Gives the following output:

	Unnamed: 0	title	year	length	budget	rating	votes	r1	r2	r3	...	r9	r10	mpaa	Action
0	1	$	1971	121	NaN	6.4	348	4.5	4.5	4.5	...	4.5	4.5	NaN	0
1	2	$1000 a Touchdown	1939	71	NaN	6.0	20	0.0	14.5	4.5	...	4.5	14.5	NaN	0
2	3	$21 a Day Once a Month	1941	7	NaN	8.2	5	0.0	0.0	0.0	...	24.5	24.5	NaN	0
3	4	$40,000	1996	70	NaN	8.2	6	14.5	0.0	0.0	...	34.5	45.5	NaN	0
4	5	$50,000 Climax Show, The	1975	71	NaN	3.4	17	24.5	4.5	0.0	...	0.0	24.5	NaN	0

We can similarly look at the last 15 lines of the data by typing:

```
>>> imdb_ratings.tail(15)
```

	Unnamed: 0	title	year	length	budget	rating	votes	r1	r2	r3
58773	58774	deadend.com	2002	120	NaN	6.9	53	64.5	4.5	0.0
58774	58775	e-Dreams	2001	94	NaN	6.8	86	4.5	0.0	0.0
58775	58776	eMale	2001	17	NaN	7.3	15	0.0	0.0	0.0
58776	58777	eRATicate	2003	9	NaN	6.0	5	0.0	0.0	0.0
58777	58778	eXXXorcismos	2002	78	NaN	4.2	11	34.5	0.0	0.0
58778	58779	eXistenZ	1999	97	NaN	6.7	14742	4.5	4.5	4.5
58779	58780	f2point8	2002	20	NaN	5.0	13	4.5	0.0	4.5
58780	58781	f8	2001	13	NaN	7.6	7	0.0	0.0	0.0
58781	58782	pURe kILLjoy	1998	87	NaN	5.2	6	0.0	14.5	14.5
58782	58783	sIDney	2002	15	NaN	7.0	8	14.5	0.0	0.0
58783	58784	tom thumb	1958	98	NaN	6.5	274	4.5	4.5	4.5
58784	58785	www.XXX.com	2003	105	NaN	1.1	12	45.5	0.0	0.0
58785	58786	www.hellssoapopera.com	1999	100	NaN	6.6	5	24.5	0.0	24.5

3. Looking at individual rows gives us a sense of what kind of data the file contains: we can also look at summaries for all rows in each column using the command describe(), which returns the number of records, mean value, and other aggregate statistics. Try typing:

```
>>> imdb_ratings.describe()
```

This gives the following output:

	Unnamed: 0	year	length	budget	rating	votes	r1
count	58788.00000	58788.000000	58788.000000	5.215000e+03	58788.000000	58788.000000	58788.000000
mean	29394.50000	1976.133582	82.337875	1.341251e+07	5.932850	632.130384	7.014382
std	16970.77815	23.735125	44.347717	2.335008e+07	1.553031	3829.621413	10.936759
min	1.00000	1893.000000	1.000000	0.000000e+00	1.000000	5.000000	0.000000
25%	14697.75000	1958.000000	74.000000	2.500000e+05	5.000000	11.000000	0.000000
50%	29394.50000	1983.000000	90.000000	3.000000e+06	6.100000	30.000000	4.500000
75%	44091.25000	1997.000000	100.000000	1.500000e+07	7.000000	112.000000	4.500000
max	58788.00000	2005.000000	5220.000000	2.000000e+08	10.000000	157608.000000	100.000000

4. Column names and their datatypes can be accessed using the properties
`columns` and `dtypes`. Typing:

```
>>> imdb_ratings.columns
```

Gives us the names of the columns:

```
Index(['Unnamed: 0', 'title', 'year', 'length', 'budget', 'rating', 'votes',
       'r1', 'r2', 'r3', 'r4', 'r5', 'r6', 'r7', 'r8', 'r9', 'r10', 'mpaa',
       'Action', 'Animation', 'Comedy', 'Drama', 'Documentary', 'Romance',
       'Short'],
      dtype='object')
```

If we issue the command:

```
>>> imdb_ratings.dtypes
```

5. As we can see, the datatypes of the columns have been automatically inferred
when we first loaded the file:

```
Unnamed: 0        int64
title             object
year              int64
length            int64
budget            float64
rating            float64
votes             int64
r1                float64
r2                float64
r3                float64
r4                float64
r5                float64
r6                float64
r7                float64
r8                float64
r9                float64
r10               float64
mpaa              object
Action            int64
Animation         int64
Comedy            int64
Drama             int64
Documentary       int64
Romance           int64
Short             int64
dtype: object
```

6. If we want to access the data in individual columns, we can do so using either `{DataFrame_name}.{column_name}` or `{DataFrame_name}['column_name']` (similar to a python dictionary). For example, typing:

```
>>> imdb_ratings.year.head()
```

or

```
>>> imdb_ratings['year'].head()
```

Gives the following output:

```
0      1971
1      1939
2      1941
3      1996
4      1975
Name: year, dtype: int64
```

Without much work, we can already use these simple commands to ask a number of diagnostic questions about the data. Do the summary statistics we generated using `describe()` make sense (for example, the max rating should be 10, while the minimum is 1)? Is the data correctly parsed into the columns we expect?

Looking back at the first five rows of data we visualized using the `head()` command, this initial inspection also reveals some formatting issues we might want to consider. In the **budget** column, several entries have the value NaN, representing missing values. If we were going to try to predict movie ratings based on features including **budget**, we might need to come up with a rule to fill in these missing values, or encode them in a way that is correctly represented to the algorithm.

Basic manipulations – grouping, filtering, mapping, and pivoting

Now that we have looked at the basic features of the Pandas DataFrame, let us start applying some transformations and calculations to this data beyond the simple statistics we obtained through `describe()`. For example, if we wanted to calculate how many films belong to each release year, we can use following command:

```
>>> imdb_ratings.value_counts()
```

Which gives the output:

2002	2168
2003	2158
2001	2121
2000	2048
2004	1945
1999	1927
1998	1705
1997	1568
1996	1390
1995	1248
1994	1199
1993	1016
1987	957
1992	948
1989	944
1988	944
1990	899
1991	888
1985	792
1986	792
1984	749

Notice that the result is by default sorted by the count of records in each year (with the most films in this dataset released in 2002). What if we wanted to sort by the release year? The sort_index() command orders the result by its index (the year to which the count belongs). The index is similar to the axis of a plot, with values representing the point at each axis tick. Using the command:

```
>>> imdb_ratings.year.value_counts().sort_index(ascending=False)
```

Gives the following output:

2005	349
2004	1945
2003	2158
2002	2168
2001	2121
2000	2048
1999	1927
1998	1705
1997	1568
1996	1390
1995	1248
1994	1199
1993	1016
1992	948
1991	888
1990	899
1989	944
1988	944
1987	957
1986	792
1985	792
1984	749
1983	698
1982	689

We can also use the DataFrame to begin asking analytical questions about the data, logically slicing and sub-selecting as we might in a database query. For example, let us select the subset of films released after 1999 with an R rating using the following command:

```
>>> imdb_ratings[(imdb_ratings.year > 1999) & (imdb_ratings.mpaa ==
'R')].head()
```

This gives the following output:

	Unnamed: 0	title	year	length	budget	rating	votes	r1	r2	r3	...	r9	r10	mpaa	Action	Animation
6	7	$windle	2002	93	NaN	5.3	200	4.5	0.0	4.5	...	4.5	14.5	R	1	0
42	43	'R Xmas	2001	83	NaN	4.9	288	14.5	4.5	4.5	...	4.5	4.5	R	0	0
122	123	100 Girls	2000	90	NaN	5.8	3349	4.5	4.5	4.5	...	4.5	4.5	R	0	0
123	124	100 Mile Rule	2002	98	1100000	5.6	181	4.5	4.5	4.5	...	4.5	14.5	R	0	0
152	153	11:11	2004	95	NaN	4.3	222	14.5	14.5	4.5	...	4.5	14.5	R	0	0

Similarly, we can group the data by any column(s) and calculate aggregated statistics using the `groupby` command and pass an array of calculations to perform as an argument to `aggregate`. Let us use the mean and standard deviation functions from NumPy to find the average and variation in ratings for films released in a given year:

```
>>> imdb_ratings.groupby('year').rating.aggregate([np.mean,np.std])
```

This gives:

year	mean	std
1893	7.000000	NaN
1894	4.888889	0.727056
1895	5.500000	0.624500
1896	5.269231	1.325635
1897	4.677778	0.732765
1898	5.040000	0.950263
1899	4.277778	0.713754
1900	4.731250	1.358783
1901	4.682143	1.081513
1902	4.900000	1.615549
1903	4.808108	1.334662
1904	4.223810	1.291588
1905	5.047059	1.196410
1906	5.676471	1.274034

However, sometimes the questions we want to ask require us to reshape or transform the raw data we are given. This will happen frequently in later chapters, when we develop features for predictive models. Pandas provide many tools for performing this kind of transformation. For example, while it would also be interesting to aggregate the data based on genre, we notice that in this dataset each genre is represented as a single column, with 1 or 0 indicating whether a film belongs to a given genre. It would be more useful for us to have a single column indicating which genre the film belongs to for use in aggregation operations. We can make such a column using the command idxmax() with the argument 1 to represent the maximum argument across columns (0 would represent the max index along rows), which returns the column with the greatest value out of those selected. Typing:

```
>>>imdb_ratings['genre']=imdb_
ratings[['Action','Animation','Comedy','Drama','Documentary','Romance']].
idxmax(1)
```

Gives the following result when we examine this new genre column using:

```
>>> imdb_ratings['genre'].head()
```

```
0         Comedy
1         Comedy
2      Animation
3         Comedy
4         Action
```

We may also perhaps like to plot the data with colors representing a particular genre. To generate a color code for each genre, we can use a custom mapping function with the following commands:

```
>>> genres_map = {"Action": 'red', "Animation": 'blue', "Comedy":
'yellow', "Drama": 'green', "Documentary": 'orange', "Romance": 'purple'}
>>> imdb_ratings['genre_color'] = imdb_ratings['genre'].apply(lambda x:
genres_map[x])
```

We can verify the output by typing:

```
>>> imdb_ratings['genre_color'].head()
```

Which gives:

```
0      yellow
1      yellow
2        blue
3      yellow
4         red
```

We can also transpose the table and perform statistical calculations using the `pivot_table` command, which can perform aggregate calculations on groupings of rows and columns as in a spreadsheet. For example, to calculate the average rating per genre per year we can use the following command:

```
>>>pd.pivot_table(imdb_
ratings,values='rating',index='year',columns=['genre'],aggfunc=np.mean)
```

Which gives the output:

genre	Action	Animation	Comedy	Documentary	Drama	Romance
year						
1893	7.000000	NaN	NaN	NaN	NaN	NaN
1894	5.100000	NaN	NaN	4.720000	NaN	NaN
1895	5.700000	NaN	NaN	5.400000	NaN	NaN
1896	5.875000	NaN	3.900000	5.571429	2.100000	NaN
1897	5.900000	NaN	5.200000	4.300000	NaN	NaN
1898	6.000000	NaN	5.050000	5.500000	3.600000	NaN
1899	4.533333	NaN	3.600000	3.866667	4.850000	NaN

Now that we have performed some exploratory calculations, let us look at some visualizations of this information.

Charting with Matplotlib

One of the practical features of IPython notebooks is the ability to plot data inline with our analyses. For example, if we wanted to visualize the distribution of film lengths we could use the command:

```
>>> imdb_ratings.length.plot()
```

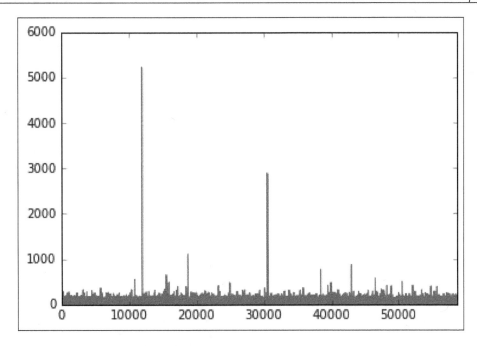

However, this is not really a very attractive image. To make a more aesthetically pleasing plot, we can change the default style using the style.use() command. Let us change the style to ggplot, which is used in the ggplot graphical library (Wickham, Hadley. *ggplot: An Implementation of the Grammar of Graphics*. R package version 0.4. 0 (2006)). Typing the following commands:

```
>>> matplotlib.style.use('ggplot')
>>> imdb_ratings.length.plot()
```

Gives a much more attractive graphic:

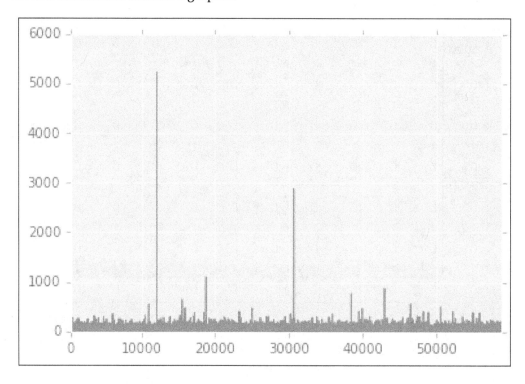

As you can see preceding, the default plot is a line chart. The line chart plots each datapoint (movie runtime) as a line, ordered from left to right by their row number in the DataFrame. To make a density plot of films by their genre, we can plot using the `groupby` command with the argument `type=kde`. **KDE** is an abbreviation for **Kernel Density Estimate** (Rosenblatt, Murray. Remarks on some nonparametric estimates of a density function. *The Annals of Mathematical Statistics 27.3 (1956): 832-837*; Parzen, Emanuel. On estimation of a probability density function and mode. The annals of mathematical statistics 33.3 (1962): 1065-1076), meaning that for each point (film runtime) we estimate the density (proportion of the population with that runtime) with the equation:

$$f(x) = \frac{1}{nh} \sum_{i=1}^{n} K\left(\frac{x - x_i}{h}\right)$$

Where `f(x)` is an estimate of the probability density, n is the number of records in our dataset, h is a bandwidth parameter, and `K` is a kernel function. As an example, if `K` were the Gaussian kernel given by:

$$K(x) = \frac{1}{\sigma\sqrt{2\pi}} e^{-\frac{(x-\mu)}{2\sigma^2}}$$

where σ is the standard deviation and μ is the mean of the normal distribution, then the KDE represents the average density of all other datapoints in a normally distributed 'window' around a given point x. The width of this window is given by *h*. Thus, the KDE allows us to plot a smoothed representation of a histogram by plotting not the absolute count at a given point, but a continuous probability estimate at the point. To this KDE plot, let us also add annotations for the axes, and limit the maximum runtime to 2 hrs using the following commands:

```
>>> plot1 = imdb_ratings.groupby('genre').length.
plot(kind='kde',xlim=(0,120),legend='genre')
>>>plot1[0].set_xlabel('Number of Minutes')
>>>plot1[0].set_title('Distribution of Films by Runtime Minutes')
```

Which gives the following plot:

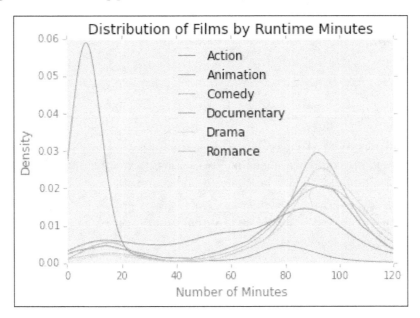

We see, unsurprisingly, that many animated films are short, while others categories average around 90 minutes in length. We can also plot similar density curves to examine the distribution of ratings between genres using the following commands:

```
>>> plot2 = imdb_ratings.groupby('genre').rating.
plot(kind='kde',xlim=(0,10),legend='genre')
>>> plot2[0].set_xlabel('Ratings')
>>> plot2[0].set_title('Distribution of Ratings')
```

Which gives the following plot:

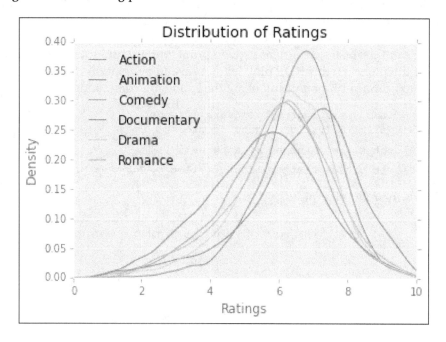

Interestingly, documentaries have on average the highest rating, while action films have the lowest. We could also visualize this same information using a boxplot using the following commands:

```
>>> pd.pivot_table(imdb_
ratings,values='rating',index='title',columns=['genre']).\
plot(kind='box',by='genre').\
set_ylabel('Rating')
```

This gives the boxplot as follows:

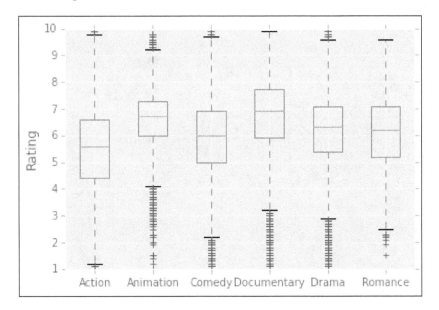

We can also use the notebook to start to make this sort of plotting automated for a dataset. For example, we often would like to look at the marginal plot of each variable (its single-dimensional distribution) compared to all others in order to find correlations between columns in our dataset. We can do this using the built-in `scatter_matrix` function:

```
>>> from pandas.tools.plotting import scatter_matrix
>>> scatter_matrix(imdb_
ratings[['year','length','budget','rating','votes']], alpha=0.2,
figsize=(6, 6), diagonal='kde')
```

This will allow us to plot the pairwise distribution of all the variables we have selected, giving us an overview of potential correlations between them:

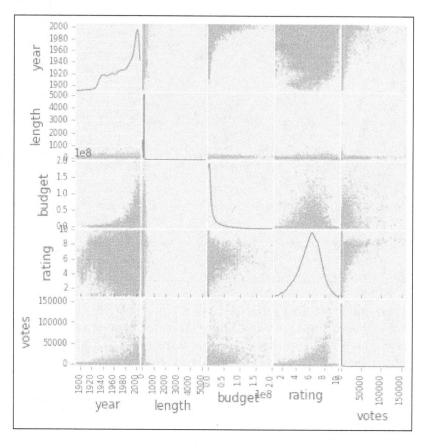

This single plot actually gives a lot of information. For example, it shows that in general higher budget films have higher ratings, and films made in the 1920s have higher average rating than those before. Using this sort of scatter matrix, we can look for correlations that might guide the development of a predictive model, such as a predictor of ratings given other movie features. All we need to do is give this function a subset of columns in the DataFrame to plot (since we want to exclude non-numerical data which cannot be visualized in this way), and we can replicate this analysis for any new dataset.

What if we want to visualize these distributions in more detail? As an example, lets break the correlation between length and rating by genre using the following commands:

```
>>> fig, axes = plt.subplots(nrows=3, ncols=2, figsize=(15,15))
>>> row = 0
>>> col = 0
>>> for index, genre in imdb_ratings.groupby('genre'):
...     if row > 2:
...         row = 0
...         col += 1
...     genre.groupby('genre').\
....plot(ax=axes[row,col],kind='scatter',x='length',y='rating',s=np.
sqrt(genre['votes']),c=genre['genre_
color'],xlim=(0,120),ylim=(0,10),alpha=0.5,label=index)
...     row += 1
```

In this command, we create a 3x2 grid to hold plots for our six genres. We then
iterate over the data groups by genre, and if we have reached the third row we reset
and move to the second column. We then plot the data, using the genre_color
column we generated previously, along with the index (the genre group) to label the
plot. We scale the size of each point (representing an individual film) by the number
of votes it received. The resulting scatterplots show the relationship between length
and genre, with the size of the point giving sense of how much confidence we should
place in the value of the point.

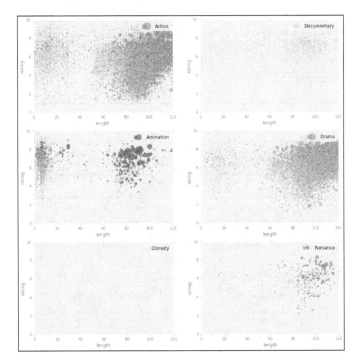

Now that we have looked at some basic analysis using categorical data and numerical data, let's continue with a special case of numerical data – time series.

Time series analysis

While the `imdb` data contained movie release years, fundamentally the objects of interest were the individual films and the ratings, not a linked series of events over time that might be correlated with one another. This latter type of data – a time series – raises a different set of questions. Are datapoints correlated with one another? If so, over what timeframe are they correlated? How noisy is the signal? Pandas DataFrames have many built-in tools for time series analysis, which we will examine in the next section.

Cleaning and converting

In our previous example, we were able to use the data more or less in the form in which it was supplied. However, there is not always a guarantee that this will be the case. In our second example, we'll look at a time series of oil prices in the US by year over the last century (Makridakis, Spyros, Steven C. Wheelwright, and Rob J. Hyndman. *Forecasting methods and applications*, John Wiley & Sons. Inc, New York(1998). We'll start again by loading this data into the notebook, and inspecting it visually using `tail()` by typing:

```
>>> oil_prices = pd.read_csv('oil.csv')
>>> oil_prices.tail()
```

Which gives the output:

	Year	Oil prices in constant 1997 dollars. 1870-1997
123	1993	17.15
124	1994	18.27
125	1995	19.40
126	1996	20.52
127	Oil prices in constant 1997 dollars. 1870-1997	NaN

The last row is unexpected, since it does not look like a year at all. In fact, it is a footer comment in the spreadsheet. As it is not actually part of the data, we will need to remove it from the dataset, which we can do with the following commands:

```
>>> oil_prices = oil_prices[~np.isnan(oil_prices[oil_prices.columns[1]])]
```

This will remove from the dataset and rows in which the second column is NaN (not a correctly formatted number). We can verify that we have cleaned up the dataset by using the tail command again

The second aspect of this data that we would like to clean up is the format. If we look at the format of the columns using:

```
>>> oil_prices.dtypes
```

we see that the year is not by default interpreted as a Python date type:

```
Year                                              object
Oil prices in constant 1997 dollars. 1870-1997    float64
dtype: object
```

We would like the **Year** column to be a Python date. type Pandas provides the built-in capability to perform this conversion using the `convert_object()` command:

```
>>> oil_prices = oil_prices.convert_objects(convert_dates='coerce')
```

At the same time, we can rename the column with prices something a little less verbose using the `rename` command:

```
>>> oil_prices.rename(columns = {oil_prices.columns[1]: 'Oil_Price_1997_
Dollars'},inplace=True)
```

We can then verify that the output from using the head() command shows these changes:

	Year	Oil_Price_1997_Dollars
0	1870-01-01	58.53
1	1871-01-01	49.09
2	1872-01-01	24.68
3	1873-01-01	16.71
4	1874-01-01	19.86

We now have the data in a format in which we can start running some diagnostics on this time series.

Time series diagnostics

We can plot this data using the `matplotlib` commands covered in the previous section using the following:

```
>>> oil_prices.plot(x='Year',y='Oil_Price_1997_Dollars')
```

This produces the time series plot as follows:

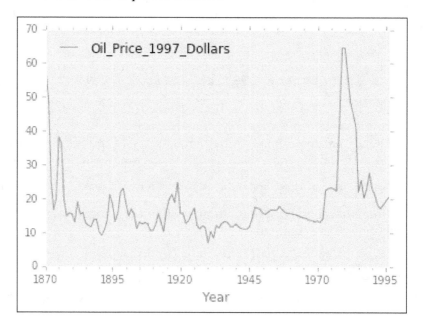

There are a number of natural questions we might ask of this data. Are the fluctuations in oil prices per year completely random, or do year-by-year measurements correlate with one another? There seem to be some cycles in the data, but it is difficult to quantify the degree of this correlation. A visual tool we can use to help diagnose this feature is a `lag_plot`, which is available in Pandas using the following commands:

```
>>> from pandas.tools.plotting import lag_plot
>>> lag_plot(oil_prices.Oil_Price_1997_Dollars)
```

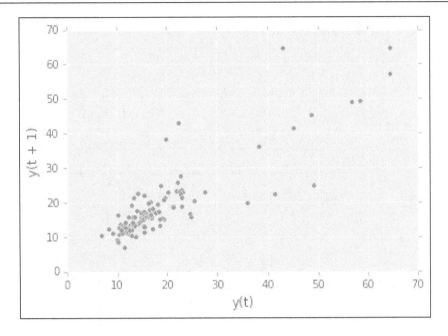

A lag plot simply plots a yearly oil price (x-axis) versus the oil price in the year immediately following it (y-axis). If there is no correlation, we would expect a circular cloud. The linear pattern here shows that there is some structure in the data, which fits with the fact that year-by-year prices go up or down. How strong is this correlation compared to expectation? We can use an autocorrelation plot to answer this question, using the following commands:

```
>>> from pandas.tools.plotting import autocorrelation_plot
>>> autocorrelation_plot(oil_prices['Oil_Price_1997_Dollars'])
```

Which gives the following autocorrelation plot:

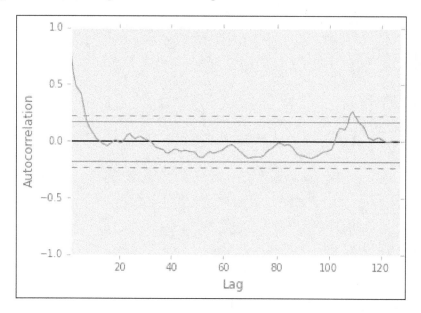

In this plot, the correlation between points at different lags (difference in years) is plotted along with a 95% confidence interval (solid) and 99% confidence interval (dashed) line for the expected range of correlation on random data. Based on this visualization, there appears to be exceptional correlation for lags of <10 years, which fits with the approximate duration of the peak price periods in the first plot of this data above.

Joining signals and correlation

Lastly, let us look at an example of comparing the oil price time series to another dataset, the number of car crash fatalities in the US for the given years (*List of Motor Vehicle Deaths in U.S. by Year*. Wikipedia. Wikimedia Foundation. Web. 02 May 2016. https://en.wikipedia.org/wiki/List_of_motor_vehicle_deaths_in_U.S._by_year).

We might hypothesize, for instance, that as the price of oil increases, on average consumers will drive less, leading to future car crashes. Again, we will need to convert the dataset time to date format, after first converting it from a number to a string, using the following commands:

```
>>> car_crashes=pd.read_csv("car_crashes.csv")
>>> car_crashes.Year=car_crashes.Year.astype(str)
>>> car_crashes=car_crashes.convert_objects(convert_dates='coerce')
```

Checking the first few lines with the `head()` command confirms that we have successfully formatted the data:

	Year	Car_Crash_Fatalities_US
0	1900-01-01	36
1	1901-01-01	54
2	1902-01-01	79
3	1903-01-01	117
4	1904-01-01	172

We can join this data to the oil prices statistics and compare the two trends over time. Notice that we need to rescale the crash data by dividing by 1000 so that it can be easily viewed on the same axis in the following command:

```
>>> car_crashes['Car_Crash_Fatalities_US']=car_crashes['Car_Crash_
Fatalities_US']/1000
```

We then use `merge()` to join the data, specifying the column to use to match rows in each dataset through the `on` variable, and plot the result using:

```
>>> oil_prices_car_crashes = pd.merge(oil_prices,car_crashes,on='Year')
>>> oil_prices_car_crashes.plot(x='Year')
```

The resulting plot is shown below:

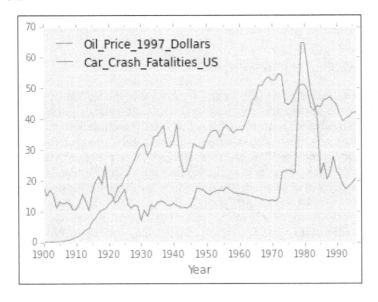

How correlated are these two signals? We can again use an `auto_correlation` plot to explore this question:

```
>>> autocorrelation_plot(oil_prices_car_crashes[['Car_Crash_Fatalities_
US','Oil_Price_1997_Dollars']])
```

Which gives:

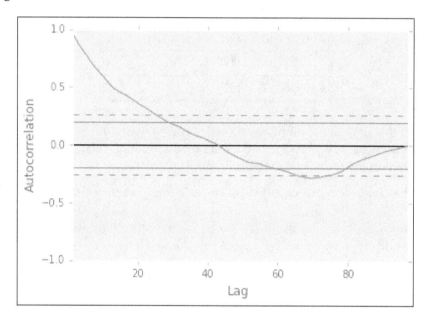

So it appears that the correlation is outside the expected fluctuation at 20 years or less, a longer range of correlation than appears in the oil prices alone.

Working with large datasets

The examples we give in this section are of modest size. In real-world applications, we may deal with datasets that will not fit on our computer, or require analyses that are so computationally intensive that they must be split across multiple machines to run in a reasonable timeframe. For these use cases, it may not be possible to use IPython Notebook in the form we have illustrated using Pandas DataFrames. A number of alternative applications are available for processing data at this scale, including PySpark, (http://spark.apache.org/docs/latest/api/python/), H20 (http://www.h2o.ai/), and XGBoost (https://github.com/dmlc/xgboost). We can also use many of these tools through a notebook, and thus achieve interactive manipulation and modeling for extremely large data volumes.

Working with geospatial data

For our last case study, let us explore the analysis of geospatial data using an extension to the Pandas library, GeoPandas. You will need to have GeoPandas installed in your IPython environment to follow this example. If it is not already installed, you can add it using `easy_install` or pip.

Loading geospatial data

In addition to our other dependencies, we will import the `GeoPandas` library using the command:

```
>>> import GeoPandas as geo.
```

We load dataset for this example, the coordinates of countries in Africa ("Africa." Maplibrary.org. Web. 02 May 2016. `http://www.mapmakerdata.co.uk.s3-website-eu-west-1.amazonaws.com/library/stacks/Africa/`) which are contained in a shape (`.shp`) file as before into a **GeoDataFrame**, an extension of the Pandas DataFrame, using:

```
>>> africa_map = geo.GeoDataFrame.from_file('Africa_SHP/Africa.shp')
```

Examining the first few lines using `head()`:

	CODE	COUNTRY	ID	geometry
0	ALG	Algeria	1	POLYGON ((-5.7636199999979 25.58624999999302, ...
1	ANG	Angola	2	POLYGON ((13.36632442474365 -8.32172966003418,...
2	ANG	Angola	3	POLYGON ((12.80576000000292 -4.806490000002668...
3	ANG	Angola	4	POLYGON ((11.76834011077881 -16.79932975769043...
4	ANG	Angola	5	POLYGON ((12.89840030670166 -5.988018989562988...

We can see that the data consists of identifier columns, along with a geometry object representing the shape of the country. The GeoDataFrame also has a `plot()` function, to which we can pass a `column` argument that gives the field to use for generating the color of each polygon using:

```
>>> africa_map.plot(column='CODE')
```

Which gives the following visualization:

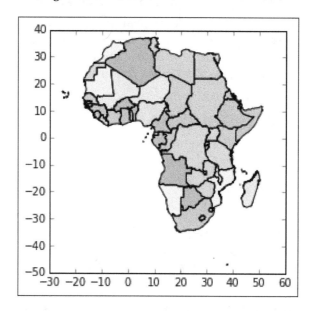

However, right now this color code is based on the country name, so does not offer much insight about the map. Instead, let us try to color each country based on its population using information about the population density of each country (*Population by Country – Thematic Map – World. Population by Country – Thematic Map-World*. Web. 02 May 2016, `http://www.indexmundi.com/map/?v=21`). First we read in the population using:

```
>>> africa_populations = pd.read_csv('Africa_populations.tsv',sep='\t')
```

Note that here we have applied the `sep='\t'` argument to `read_csv()`, as the columns in this file are not comma separated like the other examples thus far. Now we can join this data to the geographical coordinates using merge:

```
>>> africa_map = pd.merge(africa_map,africa_populations,left_
on='COUNTRY',right_on='Country_Name')
```

Unlike the example with oil prices and crash fatalities above, here the columns we wish to use to join the data has a different name in each dataset, so we must use the `left_on` and `right_on` arguments to specify the desired column in each table. We can then plot the map with colors derived from the population data using:

```
>>> africa_map.plot(column='Population',colormap='hot')
```

Which gives the new map as follows:

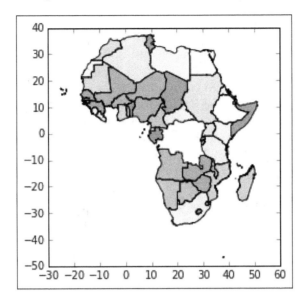

Now we can clearly see the most populous countries (Ethiopia, Democratic Republic of Congo, and Egypt) highlighted in white.

Working in the cloud

In the previous examples, we have assumed you are running the IPython notebook locally on your computer through your web browser. As mentioned, it is also possible for the application to run on an external server, with the user uploading files through the interface to interact with remotely. One convenient form of such external services are cloud platforms such as **Amazon Web Services** (**AWS**), Google Compute Cloud, and Microsoft Azure. Besides offering a hosting platform to run applications like the notebook, these services also offer storage for data sets much larger than what we would be able to store in our personal computers. By running our notebook in the cloud, we can more easily interact with these distributed storage systems using a shared infrastructure for data access and manipulation that also enforces desirable security and data governance. Lastly, cheap computing resources available via these cloud services may also allow us to scale the sorts of computation we describe in later chapters, adding extra servers to handle commands entered in the notebook on the backend.

Introduction to PySpark

So far we've mainly focused on datasets that can fit on a single machine. For larger datasets, we may need to access them through distributed file systems such as Amazon S3 or HDFS. For this purpose, we can utilize the open-source distributed computing framework PySpark (`http://spark.apache.org/docs/latest/api/python/`). PySpark is a distributed computing framework that uses the abstraction of **Resilient Distributed Datasets (RDDs)** for parallel collections of objects, which allows us to programmatically access a dataset as if it fits on a single machine. In later chapters we will demonstrate how to build predictive models in PySpark, but for this introduction we focus on data manipulation functions in PySpark.

Creating the SparkContext

The first step in any spark application is the generation of the SparkContext. The SparkContext contains any job-specific configurations (such as memory settings or the number of worker tasks), and allows us to connect to a Spark cluster by specifying the master. We start the SparkContext with the following command:

```
>>> sc = SparkContext('local','job_.{0}'.format(uuid.uuid4()))
```

The first argument gives the URL for our Spark master, the machine which coordinates execution of Spark jobs and distributes tasks to the worker machines in a cluster. All Spark jobs consist of two kinds of task: the **Driver** (which issues commands and collects information about the progress of the job), and **Executors** (which execute operations on the RDD). These could be created on the same machine (as is the case in our example), or on different machines, allowing a dataset that will not fit in memory on a single machine to be analyzed using parallel computation across several computers. In this case we will run locally, so give the argument for the master as `localhost`, but otherwise this could be the URL of a remote machine in our cluster. The second argument is just the name we give to our application, which we specify with a uniquely generated id using the `uuid` library. If this command is successful, you should see in your terminal where you are running the notebook a stack trace such as the following:

```
16/03/17 20:50:36 INFO SparkContext: Running Spark version 1.5.0
16/03/17 20:50:36 INFO SecurityManager: Changing view acls to: jbabcock
16/03/17 20:50:36 INFO SecurityManager: Changing modify acls to: jbabcock
16/03/17 20:50:36 INFO SecurityManager: SecurityManager: authentication disabled; ui acls disabled; users with view permission
s: Set(jbabcock); users with modify permissions: Set(jbabcock)
16/03/17 20:50:36 INFO Slf4jLogger: Slf4jLogger started
16/03/17 20:50:36 INFO Remoting: Starting remoting
16/03/17 20:50:36 INFO Remoting: Remoting started; listening on addresses :[akka.tcp://sparkDriver@localhost:50237]
16/03/17 20:50:36 INFO Utils: Successfully started service 'sparkDriver' on port 50237.
16/03/17 20:50:36 INFO SparkEnv: Registering MapOutputTracker
16/03/17 20:50:36 INFO SparkEnv: Registering BlockManagerMaster
16/03/17 20:50:36 INFO DiskBlockManager: Created local directory at /private/var/folders/nw/gf7_2mds3dd_01hq56rhbbqrqjxrx8/T/b
lockmgr-62785bc0-c764-4247-b9a0-8c2e1332c015
16/03/17 20:50:36 INFO MemoryStore: MemoryStore started with capacity 544.3 MB
16/03/17 20:50:36 INFO HttpFileServer: HTTP File server directory is /private/var/folders/nw/gf7_2mds3dd_01hq56rhbbqrqjxrx8/T/
spark-9a59fff7-5739-4691-aa5d-e38d324d4c36/httpd-6ec28393-7c40-42dd-956a-454026d11924
16/03/17 20:50:36 INFO HttpServer: Starting HTTP Server
16/03/17 20:50:36 INFO Server: jetty-8.y.z-SNAPSHOT
16/03/17 20:50:36 INFO AbstractConnector: Started SocketConnector@0.0.0.0:50238
16/03/17 20:50:36 INFO Utils: Successfully started service 'HTTP file server' on port 50238.
16/03/17 20:50:36 INFO SparkEnv: Registering OutputCommitCoordinator
16/03/17 20:50:36 INFO Server: jetty-8.y.z-SNAPSHOT
16/03/17 20:50:36 INFO AbstractConnector: Started SelectChannelConnector@0.0.0.0:4040
16/03/17 20:50:36 INFO Utils: Successfully started service 'SparkUI' on port 4040.
16/03/17 20:50:36 INFO SparkUI: Started SparkUI at http://localhost:4040
16/03/17 20:50:36 WARN MetricsSystem: Using default name DAGScheduler for source because spark.app.id is not set.
16/03/17 20:50:36 INFO Executor: Starting executor ID driver on host localhost
16/03/17 20:50:36 INFO Utils: Successfully started service 'org.apache.spark.network.netty.NettyBlockTransferService' on port
```

We can open the SparkUI using the address `http://localhost:4040`, which looks like this:

You can see our job name in the top-right hand corner, and we can use this page to track the progress of our jobs once we begin running them. The SparkContext is now ready to receive commands, and we can see the progress of any operations we execute in our notebook in the ui. If you want to stop the SparkContext, we can simply use the following command:

```
>>> sc.stop()
```

Note that if we are running locally we can only start one SparkContext on `localhost` at a time, so if we want to make changes to the context we will need to stop and restart it. Once we have created the base SparkContext, we can instantiate other contexts objects that contain parameters and functionality for particular kinds of datasets. For this example, we will use a SqlContext, which allows us to operate on DataFrames and use SQL logic to query a dataset. We generate the SqlContext using the SparkContext as an argument:

```
>>> sqlContext = SQLContext(sc)
```

Creating an RDD

To generate our first RDD, let us load the movies dataset again, and turn it into a list of tuples using all columns but the index and the row number:

```
>>> data = pd.read_csv("movies.csv")
>>> rdd_data = sc.parallelize([ list(r)[2:-1] for r in data.
itertuples()])
```

The `itertuples()` command returns each row of a pandas DataFrame as a tuple, which we then slice by turning it into a list and taking the indices 2 and greater (representing all columns but the index of the row, which is automatically inserted by Pandas, and the row number, which was one of the original columns in the file). To convert this local collection, we call `sc.parallelize`, which converts a collection into an RDD. We can examine how many partitions exist in this distributed collection using the function `getNumPartitions()`:

```
>>> rdd_data.getNumPartitions()
```

Since we just created this dataset locally, it only has one partition. We can change the number of partitions in an RDD, which can change the load of work done on each subset of data, using the `repartition()` (to increase the number of partitions) and `coalesce()` (to decrease) functions. You can verify that the following commands change the number of partitions in our example:

```
>>> rdd_data.repartition(10).getNumPartitions()
>>> rdd_data.coalesce(2).getNumPartitions()
```

If we want to examine a small sample of data from the RDD we can use the `take()` function. The following command will return five rows:

```
rdd_data.take(5)
```

You may notice that there is no activity on the Spark UI until you enter commands that require a result to be printed to the notebook, such as `getNumPartitions()` or `take()`. This is because Spark follows a model of lazy execution, only returning results when they are required for a downstream operation and otherwise waiting for such an operation. Besides those mentioned, other operations that will force execution are writes to disk and `collect()` (described below).

In order to load our data using the PySpark DataFrames API (similar to Pandas DataFrames) instead of an RDD (which does not have many of the utility functions for DataFrame manipulation we illustrated above), we will need a file in **JavaScript Object Notation** (**JSON**) format. We can generate this file using the following command, which maps the elements of each row into a dictionary and casts it to JSON:

```
>>> rdd_data.map( lambda x: json.JSONEncoder().encode({ str(k):str(v) for
(k,v) in zip(data.columns[2:-1],x)})).\
>>> saveAsTextFile('movies.json')
```

If you examine the output directory, you will notice that we have actually saved a directory with the name `movies.json` containing individual files (as many as there are partitions in our RDD). This is the same way in which data is stored in the **Hadoop distributed file system** (**HDFS**) in directories.

Note that we have just scratched the surface of everything we can do with an RDD. We can perform other actions such as filtering, grouping RDDs by a key, projecting subsets of each row, ordering data within groups, joining to other RDDs, and many other operations. The full range of available transformations and operations is documented at `http://spark.apache.org/docs/latest/api/python/pyspark.html`.

Creating a Spark DataFrame

Now that we have our file in the JSON format, we can load it as a Spark DataFrame using:

```
>>> df = sqlContext.read.json("movies.json")
```

If we intend to perform many operations on this data, we can cache it (persist it in temporary storage), allowing us to operate on the data Spark's own internal storage format, which is optimized for repeated access. We cache the dataset using the following command.

```
>>> df.cache()
```

`SqlContext` also allows us to declare a table alias for the dataset:

```
>>> df.registerTempTable('movies')
```

We can then query this data as if it were a table in a relational database system:

```
>>> sqlContext.sql(' select * from movies limit 5 ').show()
```

Like the Pandas DataFrames, we can aggregate them by particular columns:

```
>>> df.groupby('year').count().collect()
```

We can also access individual columns using similar syntax to Pandas:

```
>>> df.year
```

If we want to bring all data to a single machine rather than operating on dataset partitions which may be spread across several computers, we can call the `collect()` command. Use this command with caution: for large datasets it will cause all of the partitions of the data to be combined and sent to the Drive, which could potentially overload the memory of the Driver. The `collect()` command will return an array of row objects, for which we can use `get()` to access individual elements (columns):

```
>>> df.collect()[0].get(0)
```

Not all operations we are interested in performing on our data may be available in the DataFrame API, so if necessary we can convert the DataFrame into an RDD of rows using the following command:

```
>>> rdd_data = df.rdd
```

We can even convert a PySpark DataFrame into Pandas DataFrame using:

```
>>> df.toPandas()
```

In later chapters, we will cover setting up applications and building models in Spark, but you should now be able to perform many of the same basic data manipulations you used in Pandas.

Summary

We have now examined many of the tasks needed to start building analytical applications. Using the IPython notebook, we have covered how to load data in a file into a DataFrame in Pandas, rename columns in the dataset, filter unwanted rows, convert column data types, and create new columns. In addition, we have joined data from different sources and performed some basic statistical analyses using aggregations and pivots. We have visualized the data using histograms, scatter plots, and density plots as well as autocorrelation and log plots for time series. We also visualized geospatial data, using coordinate files to overlay data on maps. In addition, we processed the movies dataset using PySpark, creating both an RDD and a PySpark DataFrame, and performed some basic operations on these datatypes.

We will build on these tools in future sections, manipulating the raw input to develop features for building predictive analytics pipelines. We will later utilize similar tools to visualize and understand the features and performance of the predictive models we develop, as well as reporting the insights that they may deliver.

3
Finding Patterns in the Noise – Clustering and Unsupervised Learning

One of the natural questions to ask about a dataset is if it contains groups. For example, if we examine financial market data consisting of stock price fluctuations over time, are there groups of stocks that fall and rise with a similar pattern? Similarly, for a set of customer transactions from an e-commerce business we might ask if are there groups of user accounts distinguished by patterns of similar purchasing activity? By identifying groups of related items using the methods described in this chapter, we can understand data as a set of general patterns rather than just individual points. These patterns can help in making high-level summaries at the outset of a predictive modeling project, or as an ongoing way to report on the shape of the data we are modeling. The groupings produced can serve as insights themselves, or they can provide starting points for the models we will cover in later chapters. For example, the group to which a datapoint is assigned can become a feature of this observation, adding additional information beyond its individual values. Additionally, we can potentially calculate statistics (such as mean and standard deviation) item features within these groups, which may be more robust as model features than individual entries.

In contrast to the methods we will discuss in later chapters, grouping or *clustering* algorithms are known as **unsupervised learning**, meaning we have no response value, such as a sale price or click-through rate, which is used to determine the optimal parameters of the algorithm. Rather, we identify similar datapoints using only the features, and as a secondary analysis might ask whether the clusters we identify share a common pattern in their responses (and thus suggest the cluster is useful in finding groups associated with the outcome we are interested in).

The task of finding these groups, or *clusters*, has a few common ingredients that vary between algorithms. One is a notion of distance or similarity between items in the dataset, which will allow us to quantitatively compare them. A second is the number of groups we wish to identify; this can be specified initially using domain knowledge, or determined by running an algorithm with different numbers of clusters. We can then identify the best number of clusters that describes a dataset through statistics, such as examining numerical variance within the groups determined by the algorithm, or by visual inspection. In this chapter we will dive into:

- How to normalize data for use in a clustering algorithm and to compute similarity measurements for both categorical and numerical data
- How to use k-means clustering to identify an optimal number of clusters by examining the squared error function
- How to use agglomerative clustering to identify clusters at different scales
- Using affinity propagation to automatically identify the number of clusters in a dataset
- How to use spectral methods to cluster data with nonlinear relationships between points

Similarity and distance metrics

The first step in clustering any new dataset is to decide how to compare the similarity (or dissimilarity) between items. Sometimes the choice is dictated by what kinds of similarity we are most interested in trying to measure, in others it is restricted by the properties of the dataset. In the following sections we illustrate several kinds of distance for numerical, categorical, time series, and set-based data — while this list is not exhaustive, it should cover many of the common use cases you will encounter in business analysis. We will also cover normalizations that may be needed for different data types prior to running clustering algorithms.

Numerical distance metrics

Let us begin by exploring the data in the `wine.data` file. It contains a set of chemical measurements describing the properties of different kinds of wines, and the quality level (I-III) to which the wines are assigned (Forina, M., et al. *PARVUS An Extendible Package for Data Exploration*. Classification and Correla (1988)). Open the file in an iPython notebook and look at the first few rows with the following commands:

```
>>> df = pd.read_csv("wine.data",header=None)
>>> df.head()
```

	0	1	2	3	4	5	6	7	8	9	10	11	12	13
0	1	14.23	1.71	2.43	15.6	127	2.80	3.06	0.28	2.29	5.64	1.04	3.92	1065
1	1	13.20	1.78	2.14	11.2	100	2.65	2.76	0.26	1.28	4.38	1.05	3.40	1050
2	1	13.16	2.36	2.67	18.6	101	2.80	3.24	0.30	2.81	5.68	1.03	3.17	1185
3	1	14.37	1.95	2.50	16.8	113	3.85	3.49	0.24	2.18	7.80	0.86	3.45	1480
4	1	13.24	2.59	2.87	21.0	118	2.80	2.69	0.39	1.82	4.32	1.04	2.93	735

Notice that in this dataset we have no column descriptions, which makes the data hard to understand since we do not know what the features are. We need to parse the column names from the dataset description file wine.names, which in addition to the column names contains additional information about the dataset. With the following code, we generate a regular expression that will match a column name (using a pattern where a number followed by a parenthesis has a column name after it, as you can see in the list of column names in the file):

```
>>> import re
>>> expr = re.compile('.*[0-9]+\)\s?(\w+).*')
```

We then create an array where the first element is the class label of the wine (whether it belongs to quality category I-III).

```
>>> header_names = ['Class']
```

Iterating through the lines in the file, we extract those that match our regular expression:

```
>>> df_header = open("wine.names")
>>> for l in df_header.readlines():
        if len(expr.findall(l.strip()))!=0:
            header_names.append(expr.findall(l.strip())[0])
>>> df_header.close()
```

We then assign this list to the dataframe columns property, which contains the names of the columns:

```
>>> df.columns = header_names
```

Now that we have appended the column names, we can look at a summary of the dataset using the df.describe() method:

	Class	Alcohol	Malic	Ash	Alcalinity	Magnesium	Total	Flavanoids
count	178.000000	178.000000	178.000000	178.000000	178.000000	178.000000	178.000000	178.000000
mean	1.938202	13.000618	2.336348	2.366517	19.494944	99.741573	2.295112	2.029270
std	0.775035	0.811827	1.117146	0.274344	3.339564	14.282484	0.625851	0.998859
min	1.000000	11.030000	0.740000	1.360000	10.600000	70.000000	0.980000	0.340000
25%	1.000000	12.362500	1.602500	2.210000	17.200000	88.000000	1.742500	1.205000
50%	2.000000	13.050000	1.865000	2.360000	19.500000	98.000000	2.355000	2.135000
75%	3.000000	13.677500	3.082500	2.557500	21.500000	107.000000	2.800000	2.875000
max	3.000000	14.830000	5.800000	3.230000	30.000000	162.000000	3.880000	5.080000

Having performed some cleanup on the data, how can we calculate a similarity measurement between wines based on the information in each row? One option would be to consider each of the wines as a point in a thirteen-dimensional space specified by its dimensions (each of the columns other than Class). Since the resulting space has thirteen dimensions, we cannot directly visualize the datapoints using a scatterplot to see if they are nearby, but we can calculate distances just the same as with a more familiar 2- or 3-dimensional space using the Euclidean distance formula, which is simply the length of the straight line between two points. This formula for this length can be used whether the points are in a 2-dimensional plot or a more complex space such as this example, and is given by:

$$D(x, y) = \sqrt{\sum_{i=1}^{n}(x_i - y_i)^2}$$

Here x and y are rows of the dataset and n is the number of columns. One important aspect of the Euclidean distance formula is that columns whose scale is much different from others can dominate the overall result of the calculation. In our example, the values describing the magnesium content of each wine are ~100x greater than the magnitude of features describing the alcohol content or ash percentage.

If we were to calculate the distance between these datapoints, it would largely be determined by the magnesium concentration (as even small differences on this scale overwhelmingly determine the value of the distance calculation), rather than any of its other properties. While this might sometimes be desirable (for example, if the column with the largest numerical value is the one we most care about for judging similarity), in most applications we do not favor one feature over another and want to give equal weight to all columns. To get a fair distance comparison between these points, we need to normalize the columns so that they fall into the same numerical range (have similar maximal and minimal values). We can do so using the `scale()` function in scikit-learn and the following commands, which uses the array `header_names` we constructed previously to access all columns but the class label (the first element of the array):

```
>>> from sklearn import preprocessing
>>> df_normalized = pd.DataFrame(preprocessing.scale(df[header_
names[1:]]))
>>> df_normalized.columns = header_names[1:]
>>> df_normalized.describe()
```

	Alcohol	Malic	Ash	Alcalinity	Magnesium	Total	Flavanoids
count	1.780000e+02	1.780000e+02	1.780000e+02	1.780000e+02	1.780000e+02	178.000000	1.780000e+02
mean	-8.382808e-16	-1.197544e-16	-8.370333e-16	-3.991813e-17	-3.991813e-17	0.000000	-3.991813e-16
std	1.002821e+00	1.002821e+00	1.002821e+00	1.002821e+00	1.002821e+00	1.002821	1.002821e+00
min	-2.434235e+00	-1.432983e+00	-3.679162e+00	-2.671018e+00	-2.088255e+00	-2.107246	-1.695971e+00
25%	-7.882448e-01	-6.587486e-01	-5.721225e-01	-6.891372e-01	-8.244151e-01	-0.885468	-8.275393e-01
50%	6.099988e-02	-4.231120e-01	-2.382132e-02	1.518295e-03	-1.222817e-01	0.095960	1.061497e-01
75%	8.361286e-01	6.697929e-01	6.981085e-01	6.020883e-01	5.096384e-01	0.808997	8.490851e-01
max	2.259772e+00	3.109192e+00	3.156325e+00	3.154511e+00	4.371372e+00	2.539515	3.062832e+00

This function will subtract the mean value of a column from each element and then divide each point by the standard deviation of the column. This normalization centers the data in each column at mean 0 with variance 1, and in the case of normally distributed data this results in a standard normal distribution. Also, note that the `scale()` function returns a `numpy array`, which is why we must call `dataframe` on the output to use the pandas function `describe()`.

Now that we have scaled the data, we can calculate Euclidean distances between the rows using the following commands:

```
>>> import sklearn.metrics.pairwise as pairwise
>>> distances = pairwise.euclidean_distances(df_normalized)
```

You can verify that this command produces a square matrix of dimension 178 x 178 (the number of rows in the original dataset by the following command:

```
>>> distances.shape
```

We have now converted our dataset of 178 rows and 13 columns into a square matrix, giving the distance between each of these rows. In other words, row i, column j in this matrix represents the Euclidean distance between rows i and j in our dataset. This 'distance matrix' is the input we will use for clustering inputs in the following section.

If want to get a sense of how the points are distributed relative to one another using a given distance metric, we can use **multidimensional scaling (MDS)**—(Borg, Ingwer, and Patrick JF Groenen. Modern multidimensional scaling: Theory and applications. Springer Science & Business Media, 2005; Kruskal, Joseph B. *Nonmetric multidimensional scaling: a numerical method.* Psychometrika 29.2 (1964): 115-129; Kruskal, Joseph B. *Multidimensional scaling by optimizing goodness of fit to a nonmetric hypothesis.* Psychometrika 29.1 (1964): 1-27) to create a visualization. MDS attempts to find the set of lower dimensional coordinates (here, we will use two dimensions) that best represents the distances between points in the original, higher dimensions of a dataset (here, the pairwise Euclidean distances we calculated from the 13 dimensions). MDS finds the optimal 2-d coordinates according to the strain function:

$$Strain\left(x_1, x_2, \ldots, x_n\right) = \left(1 - \frac{\left(\sum_{i,j=1}^{n} D\left(x_i, x_j\right)\left\langle x_i, x_j\right\rangle\right)^2}{\left(\sum_{i,j=1}^{n} D\left(x_i, x_j\right)^2 \sum_{i,j=1}^{n}\left\langle x_i, x_j\right\rangle^2\right)}\right)^{1/2}$$

Where D are the distances we calculated between points. The 2-d coordinates that minimize this function are found using **Singular Value Decomposition (SVD)**, which we will discuss in more detail in *Chapter 6, Words and Pixels – Working with Unstructured Data*. After obtaining the coordinates from MDS, we can then plot the results using the `wine` class to color points in the diagram. Note that the coordinates themselves have no interpretation (in fact, they could change each time we run the algorithm due to numerical randomness in the algorithm). Rather, it is the relative position of points that we are interested in:

```
>>> from sklearn.manifold import MDS
>>> mds_coords = MDS().fit_transform(distances)
>>> pd.DataFrame(mds_coords).plot(kind='scatter',x=1,y=0,color=df.
Class[:],colormap='Reds')
```

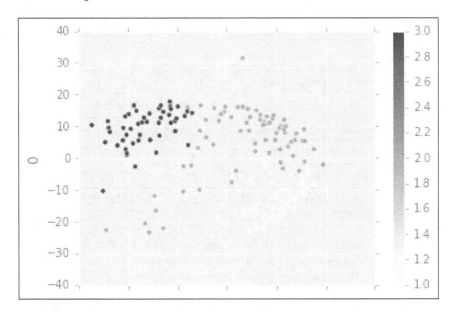

Given that there are many ways we could have calculated the distance between datapoints, is the Euclidean distance a good choice here? Visually, based on the multidimensional scaling plot, we can see there is separation between the classes based on the features we have used to calculate distance, so conceptually it appears that this is a reasonable choice in this case. However, the decision also depends on what we are trying to compare. If we are interested in detecting wines with similar attributes in absolute values, then it is a good metric. However, what if we're not interested so much in the absolute composition of the wine, but whether its variables follow similar trends among wines with different alcohol contents? In this case, we would not be interested in the absolute difference in values, but rather the *correlation* between the columns. This sort of comparison is common for time series, which we consider next.

Correlation similarity metrics and time series

For time series data, we are often concerned with whether the patterns between series exhibit the same variation over time, rather than their absolute differences in value. For example, if we were to compare stocks, we might want to identify groups of stocks whose prices move up and down in similar patterns over time. The absolute price is of less interest than this pattern of increase and decrease. Let us look at an example using the variation in prices of stocks in the **Dow Jones Industrial Average (DJIA)** over time (Brown, Michael Scott, Michael J. Pelosi, and Henry Dirska. *Dynamic-radius species-conserving genetic algorithm for the financial forecasting of Dow Jones index stocks.* Machine Learning and Data Mining in Pattern Recognition. Springer Berlin Heidelberg, 2013. 27-41.). Start by importing the data and examining the first rows:

```
>>> df = pd.read_csv("dow_jones_index/dow_jones_index.data")
>>> df.head()
```

	quarter	stock	date	open	high	low	close	volume	percent_change_price
0	1	AA	1/7/2011	$15.82	$16.72	$15.78	$16.42	239655616	3.79267
1	1	AA	1/14/2011	$16.71	$16.71	$15.64	$15.97	242963398	-4.42849
2	1	AA	1/21/2011	$16.19	$16.38	$15.60	$15.79	138428495	-2.47066
3	1	AA	1/28/2011	$15.87	$16.63	$15.82	$16.13	151379173	1.63831
4	1	AA	2/4/2011	$16.18	$17.39	$16.18	$17.14	154387761	5.93325

This data contains the daily stock price (for 6 months) for a set of 30 stocks. Because all of the numerical values (the prices) are on the same scale, we won't normalize this data as we did with the wine dimensions.

We notice two things about this data. First, the closing price per week (the variable we will use to calculate correlation) is presented as a string. Second, the date is not in the correct format for plotting. We will process both columns to fix this, converting these columns to a `float` and `datetime` object, respectively, using the following commands.

To convert the closing price to a number, we apply an anonymous function that takes all characters but the dollar sign and casts it as a float.

```
>>> df.close = df.close.apply( lambda x: float(x[1:]))
```

To convert the date, we also use an anonymous function on each row of the date column, splitting the string in to year, month, and day elements and casting them as integers to form a tuple input for a `datetime` object:

```
>>> import datetime
>>> df.date = df.date.apply( lambda x: datetime.\
    datetime(int(x.split('/')[2]),int(x.split('/')[0]),int(x.split('/')
[1]))))
```

With this transformation, we can now make a pivot table (as we covered in *Chapter 2, Exploratory Data Analysis and Visualization in Python*) to place the closing prices for each week as columns and individual stocks as rows using the following commands:

```
>>> df_pivot = df.pivot('stock','date','close').reset_index()
>>> df_pivot.head()
```

date	stock	2011-01-07 00:00:00	2011-01-14 00:00:00	2011-01-21 00:00:00	2011-01-28 00:00:00	2011-02-04 00:00:00	2011-02-11 00:00:00	2011-02-18 00:00:00	2011-02-25 00:00:00	2011-0 00:00:
0	AA	16.42	15.97	15.79	16.13	17.14	17.37	17.28	16.68	16.58
1	AXP	44.36	46.25	46.00	43.86	43.82	46.75	45.53	43.53	43.72
2	BA	69.38	70.07	71.68	69.23	71.38	72.14	73.04	72.30	71.80
3	BAC	14.25	15.25	14.25	13.60	14.29	14.77	14.75	14.20	14.12
4	CAT	93.73	94.01	92.75	95.68	99.59	103.54	105.86	102.00	103.04

As we can see, we only need columns after 2 to calculate correlations between rows, as the first two columns are the index and stock ticker symbol. Let us now calculate the correlation between these time series of stock prices by selecting the second column to end columns of the data frame for each row, calculating the pairwise correlations distance metric, and visualizing it using MDS, as before:

```
>>> import numpy as np
>>> correlations = np.corrcoef(np.float64(np.array(df_pivot)[:,2:]))
>>> mds_coords = MDS().fit_transform(correlations)
>>> pd.DataFrame(mds_coords).plot(kind='scatter',x=1,y=0)
```

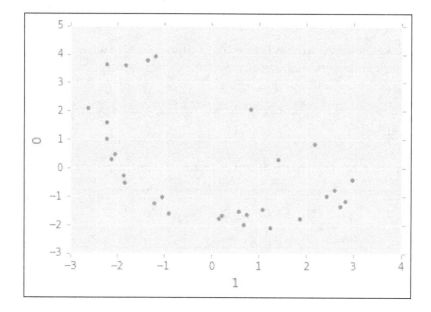

It is important to note that the Pearson coefficient, which we have calculated here, is a measure of linear correlation between these time series. In other words, it captures the linear increase (or decrease) of the trend in one price relative to another, but won't necessarily capture nonlinear trends (such as a parabola or sigmoidal pattern). We can see this by looking at the formula for the Pearson correlation, which is given by:

$$P(a,b) = \frac{Cov(a,b)}{\sigma(a)\sigma(b)} = \frac{\frac{1}{n}\sum_{i=1}^{n}(a_i - \mu(a))(b_i - \mu(b))}{\sqrt{\frac{1}{n}\sum_{i=1}^{n}(a_i - \mu(a))^2}\sqrt{\frac{1}{n}\sum_{i=1}^{n}(b_i - \mu(b))^2}}$$

Here μ and σ represent the mean and standard deviation of series *a* and *b*. This value varies from 1 (highly correlated) to -1 (inversely correlated), with 0 representing no correlation (such as a spherical cloud of points). You might recognize the numerator of this equation as the **covariance**, which is a measure of how much two datasets, *a* and *b*, vary in synch with one another. You can understand this by considering that the numerator is maximized when corresponding points in both datasets are above or below their mean value. However, whether this accurately captures the similarity in the data depends upon the scale. In data that is distributed in regular intervals between a maximum and minimum, with roughly the same difference between consecutive values it captures this pattern well. However, consider a case in which the data is exponentially distributed, with orders of magnitude differences between the minimum and maximum, and the difference between consecutive datapoints also varying widely. Here, the Pearson correlation would be numerically dominated by only the largest values in the series, which might or might not represent the overall similarity in the data. This numerical sensitivity also occurs in the denominator, which represents the product of the standard deviations of both datasets. The value of the correlation is maximized when the variation in the two datasets is roughly explained by the product of their individual variations; there is no left-over variation between the datasets that is not explained by their respective standard deviations. By extracting data for the first two stocks in this collection and plotting their pairwise values, we see that this assumption of linearity appears to be a valid one for comparing datapoints:

```
>>> df_pivot.iloc[0:2].transpose().iloc[2:].plot(kind='scatter',x=0,y=1)
```

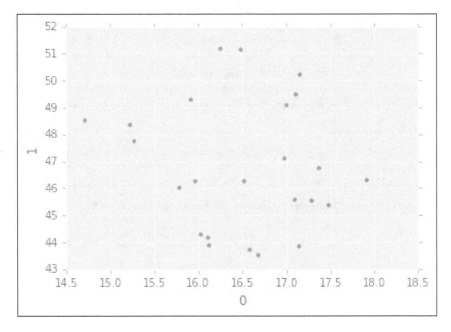

In addition to verifying that these stocks have a roughly linear correlation, this command introduces some new functions in pandas you may find useful. The first is iloc, which allows you to select indexed rows from a dataframe. The second is transpose, which inverts the rows and columns. Here, we select the first two rows, transpose, and then select all rows (prices) after the second (since the first is the index and the second is the *Ticker* symbol).

Despite the trend we see in this example, we could imagine there might a nonlinear trend between prices. In these cases, it might be better to measure not the linear correlation of the prices themselves, but whether the high prices for one stock coincide with another. In other words, the rank of market days by price should be the same, even if the prices are nonlinearly related. We can also calculate this rank correlation, also known as the Spearman's Rho, using SciPy, with the following formula:

$$\rho(a,b) = \frac{6 \sum_{i=1}^{n} d_i^2}{n(n^2 - 1)}$$

 Note that this formula assumes that the ranks are distinct (no ties); in the case of ties, we can instead calculate the Pearson correlation using the ranks of the datasets instead of their raw values.

Where n is the number of datapoints in each of two sets a and b, and d is the difference in ranks between each pair of datapoints ai and bi. Because we only compare the ranks of the data, not their actual values, this measure can capture variations between two datasets, even if their numerical value vary over wide ranges. Let us see if plotting the results using the Spearman correlation metric generates any differences in the pairwise distance of the stocks computed from MDS, using the following commands:

```
>>> import scipy.stats
>>> correlations2 = scipy.stats.spearmanr(np.float64(np.array(df_pivot)
[:,1:]))
>>> mds_coords = MDS().fit_transform(correlations2.correlation)
>>> pd.DataFrame(mds_coords).plot(kind='scatter',x=1,y=0)
```

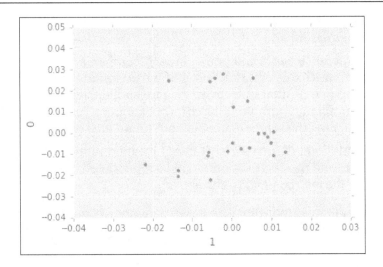

The Spearman correlation distances, based on the x and y axes, appear closer to each other than the Pearson distances, suggesting from the perspective of rank correlation that the time series are more similar.

Though they differ in their assumptions about how two datasets are distributed numerically, Pearson and Spearman correlations share the requirement that the two sets are of the same length. This is usually a reasonable assumption, and will be true of most of the examples we consider in this book. However, for cases where we wish to compare time series of unequal lengths, we can use **Dynamic Time Warping (DTW)**. Conceptually, the idea of DTW is to *warp* one time series to align with a second, by allowing us to open gaps in either dataset so that it becomes the same size as the second. What the algorithm needs to resolve is where the most similar points of the two series are, so that gaps can be places in the appropriate locations. In the simplest implementation, DTW consists of the following steps (see the following diagram):

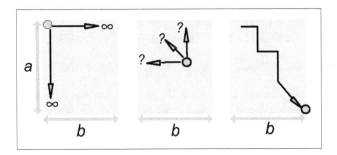

1. For dataset a of length n and a dataset b of length m, construct a matrix of size n by m.

2. Set the top row and the leftmost column of this matrix to both be infinity (left, in figure above).

3. For each point *i* in set *a*, and point *j* in set *b*, compare their similarity using a cost function. To this cost function, add the minimum of the element (*i-1, j-1*), (*i-1, j*), and (*j-1, i*) — that is, from moving up and left, left, or up in the matrix). These conceptually represent the costs of opening a gap in one of the series, versus aligning the same element in both (middle, above).

4. At the end of step 2, we will have traced the minimum cost path to align the two series, and the DTW distance will be represented by the bottommost corner of the matrix, (*n.m*) (right, above).

A negative aspect of this algorithm is that step 3 involves computing a value for every element of series *a* and *b*. For large time series or large datasets, this can be computationally prohibitive. While a full discussion of algorithmic improvements is beyond the scope of our present examples, we refer interested readers to FastDTW (which we will use in our example) and SparseDTW as examples of improvements that can be evaluated using many fewer calculations (Al-Naymat, Ghazi, Sanjay Chawla, and Javid Taheri. *Sparsedtw: A novel approach to speed up dynamic time warping*. Proceedings of the Eighth Australasian Data Mining Conference-Volume 101. Australian Computer Society, Inc., 2009. Salvador, Stan, and Philip Chan. *Toward accurate dynamic time warping in linear time and space*. Intelligent Data Analysis 11.5 (2007): 561-580.).

We can use the FastDTW algorithm to compare the stocks data and plot the results again using MDS. First we will compare pairwise each pair of stocks and record their DTW distance in a matrix:

```
>>> from fastdtw import fastdtw
>>> dtw_matrix = np.zeros(shape=(df_pivot.shape[0],df_pivot.shape[0]))
... for i in np.arange(0,df_pivot.shape[0]):
...     for j in np.arange(i+1,df_pivot.shape[0]):
...         dtw_matrix[i,j] = fastdtw(df_pivot.iloc[i,2:],df_pivot.iloc[j,2:])[0]
```

 This function is found in the fastdtw library, which you can install using pip or `easy_install`.

For computational efficiency (because the distance between i and j equals the distance between stocks j and i), we calculate only the upper triangle of this matrix. We then add the transpose (for example, the lower triangle) to this result to get the full distance matrix.

```
>>> dtw_matrix+=dtw_matrix.transpose()
```

Finally, we can use MDS again to plot the results:

```
>>> mds_coords = MDS().fit_transform(dtw_matrix)
>>> pd.DataFrame(mds_coords).plot(kind='scatter',x=1,y=0)
```

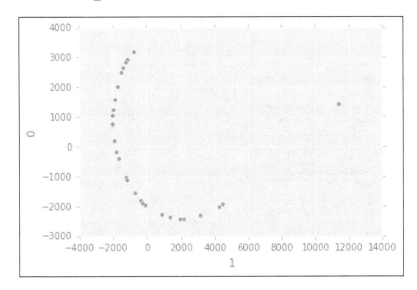

Compared to the distribution of coordinates along the *x* and *y* axis for Pearson correlation and rank correlation, the DTW distances appear to span a wider range, picking up more nuanced differences between the time series of stock prices.

Now that we have looked at numerical and time series data, as a last example let us examine calculating similarity measurements for categorical datasets.

Similarity metrics for categorical data

Text represents one class of categorical data: for instance, we might have use a vector to represent the presence or absence of a given keyword for a set of papers submitted to an academic conference, as in our example dataset (Moran, Kelly H., Byron C. Wallace, and Carla E. Brodley. *Discovering Better AAAI Keywords via Clustering with Community-sourced Constraints.* Twenty-Eighth AAAI Conference on Artificial Intelligence. 2014.). If we open the data, we see that the keywords are represented as a string in one column, which we will need to convert into a binary vector:

```
>>> df2 = pd.read_csv("Papers.csv",sep=",")
>>> df2.head()
```

	title	authors	groups	keywords	topics	abstract
0	Kernelized Bayesian Transfer Learning	Mehmet Gönen and Adam A. Margolin	Novel Machine Learning Algorithms (NMLA)	cross-domain learning\ndomain adaptation\nkern...	APP: Biomedical / Bioinformatics\nNMLA: Bayesi...	Transfer learning considers related but distin...
1	"Source Free" Transfer Learning for Text Class...	Zhongqi Lu, Yin Zhu, Sinno Pan, Evan Xiang, Yu...	AI and the Web (AIW)\nNovel Machine Learning A...	Transfer Learning\nAuxiliary Data Retrieval\nT...	AIW: Knowledge acquisition from the web\nAIW: ...	Transfer learning uses relevant auxiliary data...
2	A Generalization of Probabilistic Serial to Ra...	Haris Aziz and Paul Stursberg	Game Theory and Economic Paradigms (GTEP)	social choice theory\nvoting\nfair division\ns...	GTEP: Game Theory\nGTEP: Social Choice / Voting	The probabilistic serial (PS) rule is one of t...

While in *Chapter 6, Words and Pixels – Working with Unstructured Data*, we will examine special functions to do this conversion from text to vector, for illustrative purposes we will now code the solution ourselves. We need to gather all the unique keywords, and assign a unique index to each of them to generate a new column name 'keword_n' for each keyword:

```
>>> keywords_mapping = {}
>>> keyword_index = 0

>>> for k in df2.keywords:
...     k = k.split('\n')
...     for kw in k:
```

```
...        if keywords_mapping.get(kw,None) is None:
...            keywords_mapping[kw]='keyword_'+str(keyword_index)
...            keyword_index+=1
```

We then generate a new set of columns using this keyword to column name mapping, to set a 1 in each row where the keyword appears in that article's keywords:

```
>>>for (k,v) in keywords_mapping.items():
...        df2[v] = df2.keywords.map( lambda x: 1 if k in x.split('\n')
else 0 ) Image_B04881_03_18.png
```

These columns will be appended to the right of the existing columns and we can select out these binary indicators using the `iloc` command, as before:

```
>>> df2.head().iloc[:,6:]
```

	keyword_422	keyword_1174	keyword_640	keyword_1287	keyword_312	keyword_378	keyword_826	keyword_9
0 0	0	0	0	0	0	0	0
1 0	0	0	0	0	0	0	0
2 0	0	0	0	0	0	0	0
3 0	0	0	0	0	0	0	0
4 0	0	0	0	0	0	0	0

In this case, a Euclidean distance between articles could be computed, but because each coordinate is either 0 or 1, it does not provide the continuous distribution of distances we would like (we will get many ties, since there are only so many ways to add and subtract 1 and 0). Similarly, measurements of correlation between these binary vectors are less than ideal because the values can only be identical or non-identical, again leading to many duplicate correlation values.

What kinds of similarity metric could we use instead? One is the Jaccard coefficient:

$$J(a,b) = \frac{\|a \cap b\|}{\|a \cap b\|}$$

This is the number of intersecting items (positions where both *a* and *b* are set to *1* in our example) divided by the union (the total number of positions where either *a* or *b* are set to 1).This measure could be biased, however, if the articles have very different numbers of keywords, as a larger set of words will have a greater probability of being similar to another article. If we are concerned about such bias, we could use the cosine similarity, which measure the angle between vectors and is sensitive to the number of elements in each:

$$Cos(a,b) = \frac{a\sum b}{\|a\|\|b\|}$$

Where:

$$\|a\| = \sqrt{\sum_{i=1}^{n} a_i^2} \quad a\sum b = \sum_{i=1}^{n} a_i b_i$$

We could also use the Hamming distance (Hamming, Richard W. *Error detecting and error correcting codes*. Bell System technical journal 29.2 (1950): 147-160.), which simply sums whether the elements of two sets are identical or not:

$$H(a,b) = \sum_{i=1}^{n} 1 \, if \, a_i = b_i \, else \, 0$$

Clearly, this measure will be best if we are primarily looking for matches and mismatches. It is also, like the Jaccard coefficient, sensitive to the number of items in each set, as simply increasing the number of elements increases the possible upper bound of the distance. Similar to Hamming is the Manhattan distance, which does not require the data to be binary:

$$M(a,b) = \sum_{i=1}^{n} |a_i - b_i|$$

If we use the Manhattan distance as an example, we can use MDS again to plot the arrangement of the documents in keyword space using the following commands:

```
>>> distances = pairwise.pairwise_distances(np.float64(np.array(df2)
[:,6:]),metric='manhattan')
>>> mds_coords = MDS().fit_transform(distances)
pd.DataFrame(mds_coords).plot(kind='scatter',x=1,y=0)
```

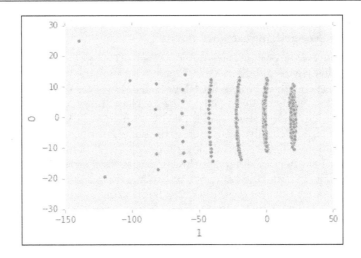

We see a number of groups of papers, suggesting that a simple comparison of common keywords provides a way to distinguish between articles.

The diagram below provides a summary of the different distance methods we have discussed and the decision process for choosing one over another for a particular problem. While it is not exhaustive, we hope it provides a starting point for your own clustering applications.

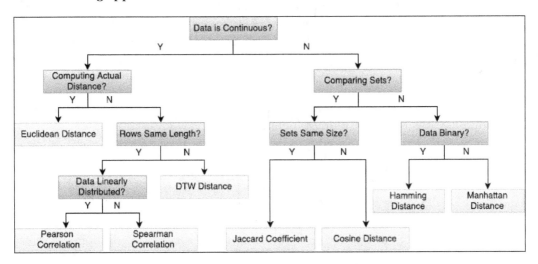

Aside: Normalizing categorical data

As you may have noted, we don't normalize categorical data in the same way that we used the `scale()` function for numerical data. The reason for this is twofold. First, with categorical data we are usually dealing with data in the range `[0,1]`, so the problem of one column of the dataset containing wildly larger values that overwhelm the distance metric is minimized. Secondly, the notion of the scale() function is that the data in the column is biased, and we are removing that bias by subtracting the mean. For categorical data, the 'mean' has a less clear interpretation, as the data can only take the value of 0 or 1, while the mean might be somewhere between the two (for example, 0.25). Subtracting this value doesn't make sense as it would make the data elements no longer binary indicators.

Aside: Blending distance metrics

In the examples considered so far in this chapter, we have dealt with data that may be described as either numerical, time series, or categorical. However, we might easily find examples where this is not true. For instance, we could have a dataset of stock values over time that also contains categorical information about which industry the stock belongs to and numerical information about the size and revenue of the company. In this case, it would be difficult to choose a single distance metric that adequately handles all of these features. Instead, we could calculate a different distance metric for each of the three sets of features (time-series, categorical, and numerical) and blend them (by taking their average, sum, or product, for instance). Since these distances might cover very different numerical scales, we might need to normalize them, for instance using the `scale()` function discussed above to convert each distance metric into a distribution with mean 0, standard deviation 1 before combining them.

Now that we have some ways to compare the similarity of items in a dataset, let us start implementing some clustering pipelines.

K-means clustering

K-means clustering is the classical divisive clustering algorithm. The idea is relatively simple: the **k** in the title comes from the number of clusters we wish to identify, which we need to decide before running the algorithm, while **means** denotes the fact that the algorithm attempts to assign datapoints to clusters where they are closest to the average value of the cluster. Thus a given datapoint chooses among k different means in order to be assigned to the most appropriate cluster. The basic steps of the simplest version of this algorithm are (MacKay, David. *An example inference task: clustering.* Information theory, inference and learning algorithms (2003): 284-292):

1. Choose a desired number of groups *k*.

    Assign k cluster centers; these could simply be k random points from the dataset, which is known as the Forgy method (Hamerly, Greg, and Charles Elkan. *Alternatives to the k-means algorithm that find better clusterings.* Proceedings of the eleventh international conference on Information and knowledge management. ACM, 2002.). Alternatively, we could assign a random cluster to each datapoint, and compute the average of the datapoints assigned to the same cluster as the k centers, a method called Random Partitioning (Hamerly, Greg, and Charles Elkan. *Alternatives to the k-means algorithm that find better clusterings.* Proceedings of the eleventh international conference on Information and knowledge management. ACM, 2002). More sophisticated methods are also possible, as we will see shortly.

2. Assign any remaining datapoints to the nearest cluster, based on some similarity measure (such as the squared Euclidean distance).

3. Recalculate the center of each of the *k* groups by averaging the points assigned to them. Note that at this point the center may no longer represent the location of a single datapoint, but is the weighted center of mass of all points in the group.

4. Repeat 3 and 4 until no points change cluster assignment or the maximum number of iterations is reached.

K-means ++

In the initialization of the algorithm in step 2 above, there are two potential problems. If we simple choose random points as cluster centers, they may not be optimally distributed within the data (particularly if the size of the clusters is unequal). The k points may not actually end up in the k clusters in the data (for example, multiple random points may reside within the largest cluster in the dataset, as in the figure below, top middle panel), which means the algorithm may not converge to the 'correct' solution or may take a long time to do so. Similarly, the Random Partitioning method will tend to place all the centers near the greatest mass of datapoints (see figure below, top right panel), as any random set of points will be dominated by the largest cluster. To improve the initial choice of parameters, we can use instead the k++ initialization proposed in 2007 (Arthur, David, and Sergei Vassilvitskii. "k-means++: The advantages of careful seeding." Proceedings of the eighteenth annual ACM-SIAM symposium on Discrete algorithms. Society for Industrial and Applied Mathematics, 2007.). In this algorithm, we choose an initial datapoint at random to be the center of the first cluster. We then calculate the squared distance from every other datapoint to the chosen datapoint, and choose the next cluster center with probability proportional to this distance. Subsequently, we choose the remaining clusters by calculating this squared distance to the previously selected centers for a given datapoint. Thus, this initialization will choose points with higher probability that are far from any previously chosen point, and spread the initial centers more evenly in the space. This algorithm is the default used in scikit-learn.

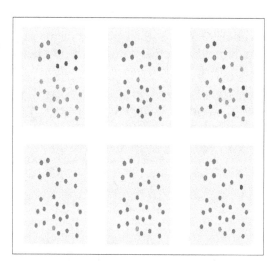

Kmeans++ clustering. (Top, left): Example data with three clusters of unequal size. (Top, middle). Random choice of cluster centers is biased towards points in the largest underlying cluster. (Top, right): Random partitioning results in center of mass for all three random clusters near the bottom of the plot. (Bottom panels). Kmeans++ results in sequential selection of three cluster centers that are evenly spaced across the dataset.

Let's think for a moment about why this works; even if we start with random group centers, once we assign points to these groups the centers are pulled towards the average position of observations in our dataset. The updated center is nearer to this average value. After many iterations, the center of each group will be dominated by the average position of datapoints near the randomly chosen starting point. If the center was poorly chosen to begin with, it will be dragged towards this average, while datapoints that were perhaps incorrectly assigned to this group will gradually be reassigned. During this process, the overall value that is minimized is typically the sum of squared errors (when we are using the Euclidean distance metric), given by:

$$SSE = \sum_{i=1}^{n} D\left(x_i, c_i\right)^2$$

Where D is the Euclidean distance and c is the cluster center for the cluster to which a point is assigned. This value is also sometimes referred to as the inertia. If we think about this for a moment, we can see that this has the effect that the algorithm works best for data that is composed of circles (or spheres in higher dimensions); the overall SSE for a cluster is minimized when points are uniformly distant from it in a spherical cloud. In contrast, a non-uniform shape (such as an ellipse) will tend to have higher SSE values, and the algorithm will be optimized by splitting the data into two clusters, even if visually we can see that they appear to be represented well by one. This fact reinforces why normalization is often beneficial (as the 0 mean, 1 standard deviation normalization attempts to approximate the shape of a normal distribution for all dimensions, thus forming circles of spheres of data), and the important role of data visualization in addition to numerical statistics in judging the quality of clusters.

It is also important to consider the implications of this minimization criteria for step 3. The SSE is equivalent to the summed squared Euclidean distance between cluster points and their centroid. Thus, using the squared Euclidean distance as the metric for comparison, we guarantee that the cluster assignment is also optimizing the minimization criteria. We could use other distance metrics, but then this will not be guaranteed. If we are using Manhattan or Hamming distance, we could instead make our minimization criteria the sum of distances to the cluster center, which we term the k-median, since the value that optimizes this statistic is the cluster median (Jain, Anil K., and Richard C. Dubes. Algorithms for clustering data. Prentice-Hall, Inc., 1988.). Alternatively, we could use an arbitrary distance metric with an algorithm such as k-medoids (see below).

Clearly, this method will be sensitive to our initial choice of group centers, so we will usually run the algorithm many times and use the best result.

Let's look at an example: type the following commands in the notebook to read in a sample dataset.

```
>>> df = pd.read_csv('kmeans.txt',sep='\t')
>>> df.plot(kind='scatter',x='x_coord',y='y_coord')
```

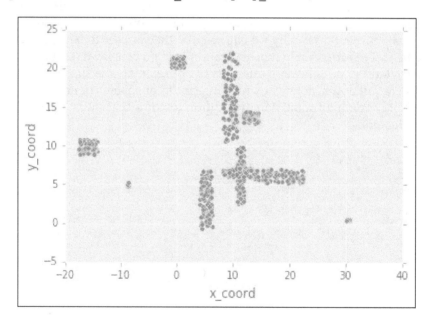

By visual inspection, this dataset clearly has a number of clusters in it. Let's try clustering with *k=5*.

```
>>> from sklearn.cluster import KMeans
>>> kmeans_clusters = KMeans(5).fit_predict(X=np.array(df)[:,1:])
>>> df.plot(kind='scatter', x='x_coord', y='y_coord', c=kmeans_clusters)
```

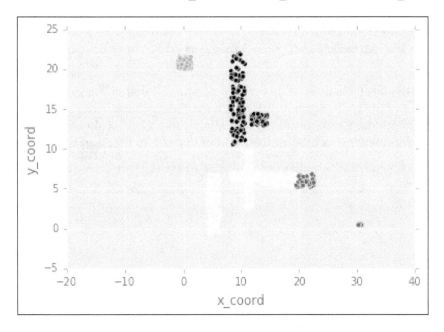

You will notice that we use the slice operators '[]' to index a numpy array that we create from the input dataframe, and select all rows and the columns after the first (the first contains the label, so we don't need it as it isn't part of the data being used for clustering). We call the KMeans model using a pattern that will become familiar for many algorithms in scikit-learn and PySpark: we create model object (KMeans) with parameters (here, 5, which is the number of clusters), and call 'fit_predict' to both calibrate the model parameters and apply the model to the input data. Here, applying the model generates cluster centers, while in regression or classification models that we will discuss in *Chapters 4, Connecting the Dots with Models – Regression Methods* and *Chapter 5, Putting Data in its Place – Classification Methods and Analysis*, 'predict' will yield an estimated continuous response or class label, respectively, for each data point. We could also simply call the `fit` method for KMeans, which would simply return an object describing the cluster centers and the statistics resulting from fitting the model, such as the inertia measure we describe above.

Is this a good number of clusters to fit to the data or not? We can explore this question if we cluster using several values of k and plot the inertia at each. In Python we can use the following commands.

```
>>> inertias = []
>>> ks = np.arange(1,20)
>>> for k in ks:
...         inertias.append(KMeans(k).fit(X=np.array(df)[:,1:]).inertia_)
>>> results = pd.DataFrame({"num_clusters": ks, "sum_distance": inertias})
```

Recall that the inertia is defined as the sum of squared distance points in a cluster to the center of the cluster to which they are assigned, which is the objective we are trying to optimize in k-means. By visualizing this inertia value at each cluster number *k*, we can get a feeling for the number of clusters that best fits the data:

```
>>> results.plot(kind='scatter', x='num_clusters', y='sum_distance')
```

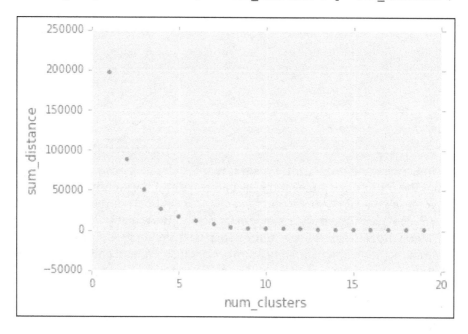

We notice there is an *elbow* around the five-cluster mark, which fortunately was the value we initially selected. This elbow indicates that after five clusters we do not significantly decrease the inertia as we add more clusters, suggesting that at k=5 we have captured the important group structure in the data.

This exercise also illustrates some problems: as you can see from the plot, some of our clusters might be formed from what appear to be overlapping segments, forming a cross shape. Is this a single cluster or two mixed clusters? Unfortunately, without a specification in our cluster model of what shape the clusters should conform to, the results are driven entirely by distance metrics, not pattern which you might notice yourself visually. This underscores the importance of visualizing the results and examining them with domain experts to judge whether the obtained clusters makes sense. In the absence of a domain expert, we could also see whether the obtained clusters contain all points labeled with a known assignment – if a high percentage of the clusters are enriched for a single label, this indicates the clusters are of good conceptual quality as well as minimizing our distance metric.

We could also try using a method that will automatically calculate the best number of clusters for a dataset.

Affinity propagation – automatically choosing cluster numbers

One of the weaknesses of the k-means algorithm is that we need to define upfront the number of clusters we expect to find in the data. When we are not sure what an appropriate choice is, we may need to run many iterations to find a reasonable value. In contrast, the Affinity Propagation algorithm (Frey, Brendan J., and Delbert Dueck. *Clustering by passing messages between data points*. science 315.5814 (2007): 972-976.) finds the number of clusters automatically from a dataset. The algorithm takes a similarity matrix as input (S) (which might be the inverse Euclidean distance, for example – thus, closer points have larger values in S), and performs the following steps after initializing a matrix of *responsibility* and *availability* values with all zeroes. It calculates the *responsibility* for one datapoint k to be the cluster center for another datapoint i. This is represented numerically by the similarity between the two datapoints. Since all availabilities begin at zero, in the first round we simply subtract the highest similarity to any other point (k') for i. Thus, a high responsibility score occurs when point k is much more similar to i than any other point.

$$r(i,k) = s(i,k) - \max_{k' \neq k}\left\{a(i,k') + s(i,k')\right\}$$

Where i is the point for which we are trying to find the cluster center, k is a potential cluster center to which point i might be assigned, s is their similarity, and a is the 'availability' described below. In the next step, the algorithm calculates the availability of the datapoint k as a cluster center for point i, which represents how appropriate k is as a cluster center for i by judging if it is the center for other points as well. Points which are chosen with high responsibility by many other points have high availability, as per the formula:

$$a(i,k) = \min\left(0, r(k,k) + \sum_{i' \notin \{i,k\}} \max\left(0, r(i',k)\right)\right)$$

Where r is the responsibility given above. If $i=k$, then this formula is:

$$a(k,k) = \sum_{i' \notin \{i,k\}} \max\left(0, r(i',k)\right)$$

These steps are sometimes described as **message passing,** as they represent information being *exchanged* by the two datapoints about the relative probability of one being a cluster center for another. Looking at steps 1 and 2, you can see that as the algorithm proceeds the responsibility will drop for many of the datapoints to a negative number (as we subtract not only the highest similarity of other datapoints, but also the availability score of these points, leaving only a few positives that will determine the cluster centers. At the end of the algorithm (once the responsibilities and availabilities are no longer changing by an appreciable numerical amount), each datapoint points at another as a cluster center, meaning the number of clusters is automatically determined from the data. This method has the advantage that we don't need to know the number of clusters in advance, but does not scale as well as other methods, since in the simplest implantation we need an n-by-n similarity matrix as the input. If we fit this algorithm on our dataset from before, we see that it detects far more clusters than our elbow plot suggests, since running the following commands gives a cluster number of 309.

```
>>> affinity_p_clusters = sklearn.cluster.AffinityPropagation().fit_
predict(X=np.array(df)[:,1:])
>>> len(np.unique(affinity_p_clusters))
```

However, if we look at a histogram of the number of datapoints in each cluster, using the command:

```
>>> pd.DataFrame(affinity_p_clusters).plot(kind='hist',bins=np.
unique(affinity_p_clusters))
```

We can see that only a few clusters are large, while many points are identified as belonging to their own group:

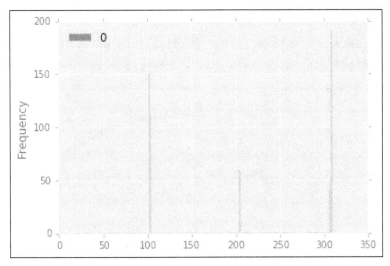

Where K-Means Fails: Clustering Concentric Circles

So far, our data has been well clustered using k-means or variants such as affinity propagation. What examples might this algorithm perform poorly on? Let's take one example by loading our second example dataset and plotting it using the commands:

```
>>> df = pd.read_csv("kmeans2.txt",sep="\t")
>>> df.plot(x='x_coord',y='y_coord',kind='scatter')
```

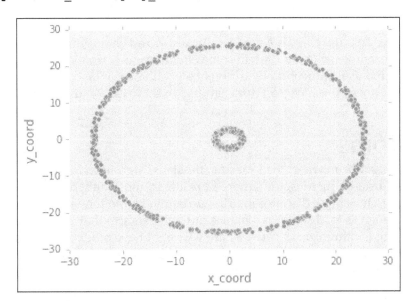

By eye alone, you can clearly see that there are two groups: two circles nested one within the other. However, if we try to run k-means clustering on this data, we get an unsatisfactory result, as you can see from running the following commands and plotting the result:

```
>>> kmeans_clusters = KMeans(2).fit_predict(X=np.array(df)[:,1:])
>>> df.plot(kind='scatter', x='x_coord', y='y_coord', c=kmeans_clusters)
```

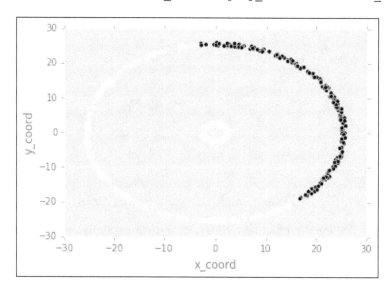

In this case, the algorithm was unable to identify the two natural clusters in the data—because the center ring of data is the same distance to the outer ring at many points, the randomly assigned cluster center (which is more likely to land somewhere in the outer ring) is a mathematically sound choice for the nearest cluster. This example suggests that, in some circumstances, we may need to change our strategy and use a conceptually different algorithm. Maybe our objective of squared error (inertia) is incorrect, for example. In this case, we might try k-medoids.

k-medoids

As we have described earlier, the k-means (medians) algorithm is best suited to particular distance metrics, the squared Euclidean and Manhattan distance (respectively), since these distance metrics are equivalent to the optimal value for the statistic (such as total squared distance or total distance) that these algorithms are attempting to minimize. In cases where we might have other distance metrics (such as correlations), we might also use the k-medoid method (Theodoridis, Sergios, and Konstantinos Koutroumbas. *Pattern recognition*. (2003).), which consists of the following steps:

1. Select k initial points as the initial cluster centers.

2. Calculate the nearest cluster center for each datapoint by any distance metric and assign it to that cluster.

3. For each point and each cluster center, swap the cluster center with the point and calculate the reduction in overall distances to the cluster center across all cluster members using this swap. If it doesn't improve, undo it. Iterate step 3 for all points.

This is obviously not an exhaustive search (since we don't repeat step 1), but has the advantage that the optimality criterion is not a specific optimization function but rather improving the compactness of the clusters by a flexible distance metric. Can k-medoids improve our clustering of concentric circles? Let's try running using the following commands and plotting the result:

```
>>> from pyclust import KMedoids
>>> kmedoids_clusters = KMedoids(2).fit_predict(np.array(df)[:,1:])
>>> df.plot(kind='scatter', x='x_coord', y='y_coord', c=kmedoids_
clusters)
```

 Note that k-medoids is not included in sci-kit learn, so you will need to install the pyclust library using `easy_install` or `pip`.

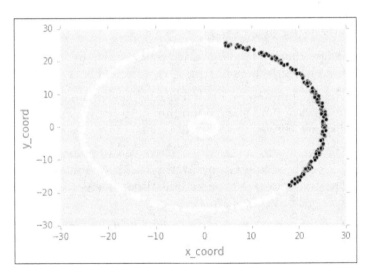

There isn't much improvement over k-means, so perhaps we need to change our clustering algorithm entirely. Perhaps instead of generating a similarity between datapoints in a single stage, we could examine hierarchical measures of similarity and clustering, which is the goal of the agglomerative clustering algorithms we will examine next.

Agglomerative clustering

In contrast to algorithms, such as k-means, where the dataset is partitioned into individual groups, **agglomerative** or **hierarchical** clustering techniques start by considering each datapoint as its own cluster and merging them together into larger groups from the bottom up (Maimon, Oded, and Lior Rokach, eds. *Data mining and knowledge discovery handbook*. Vol. 2. New York: Springer, 2005). The classical application of this idea is in phylogenetic trees in evolution, where common ancestors connect individual organisms. Indeed, these methods organize the data into tree diagrams, known as **dendrograms**, which visualize how the data is sequentially merged into larger groups.

The basic steps of an agglomerative algorithm are (diagrammed visually in the figure below):

1. Start with each point in its own cluster.
2. Compare each pair of datapoints using a distance metric. This could be any of the methods discussed above.
3. Use a linkage criterion to merge datapoints (at the first stage) or clusters (in subsequent phases), where linkage is represented by a function such as:
    - The maximum (also known as complete linkage) distance between two sets of points.The minimum (also known as single linkage) distance between two sets of points.
    - The average distance between two sets of points, also known as **Unweighted Pair Group Method with Arithmetic Mean (UPGMA)**. The points in each group could also be weighted to give a weighted average, or WUPGMA.
    - The difference between centroids (centers of mass), or UPGMC.
    - The squared Euclidean distance between two sets of points, or Ward's Method (Ward Jr, Joe H. *Hierarchical grouping to optimize an objective function. Journal of the American statistical association* 58.301 (1963): 236-244).

    °   Repeat steps 2-3 until there is only a single cluster containing all data points. Note that following the first round, the first stage of clusters become a new point to compare with all other clusters, and at each stage the clusters formed become larger as the algorithm proceeds. Along the way, we will construct a tree diagram as we sequentially merge clusters from the prior steps together.

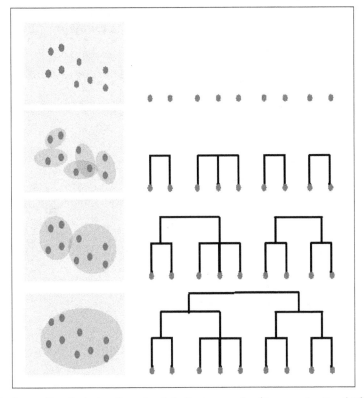

Agglomerative clustering: From top to bottom, example of tree construction (right) from a dataset (left) by sequentially merging closest points

Note that we could also run this process in reverse, taking an initial dataset and splitting it into individual points, which would also construct a tree diagram. In either case, we could then find clusters at several levels of resolution by choosing a cutoff depth of the tree and assigning points to the largest cluster they have been assigned to below that cutoff. This depth is often calculated using the linkage score given in step 3, allowing us conceptually to choose an appropriate distance between groups to consider a cluster (either relatively close or far away as we move up the tree).

Where agglomerative clustering fails

Agglomerative algorithms have many of the same ingredients as k-means; we choose a number of clusters (which will determine where we cut the tree generated by clustering—in the most extreme case, all points become members of a single cluster) and a similarity metric. We also need to choose a **linkage metric** for step 3, which determines the rules for merging individual branches of our tree. Can agglomerative clustering succeed where k-means failed? Trying this approach on the circular data suggests otherwise, as shown by plotting results of the following commands:

```
>>> from sklearn.cluster import AgglomerativeClustering
>>> agglomerative_clusters = AgglomerativeClustering(2,linkage='ward').
fit_predict(X=np.array(df)[:,1:])
>>> df.plot(kind='scatter', x='x_coord', y='y_coord', c=agglomerative_
clusters)
```

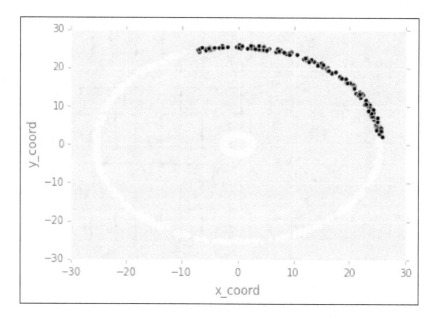

In order to correctly group the inner and outer circle, we can attempt to modify our notion of similarity using connectivity, a concept taken from graph analysis in which a set of nodes are connected by edges, and connectivity refers to whether two nodes share an edge between them. Here, we essentially construct a graph between pairs of points by thresholding the number of points that can be considered similar to one another, rather than measuring a continuous distance metric between each pair of points. This potentially reduces our difficulties with the concentric circles data, since if we set a very small value (say 10 nearby points), the uniform distance from the middle to the outer ring is no longer problematic because the central points will always be closer to each other than to the periphery. To construct this connectivity-based similarity, we could take a distance matrix such as those we've already calculated, and threshold it for some value of similarity by which we think points are connected, giving us a binary matrix of 0 and 1. This kind of matrix, representing the presence or absence of an edge between nodes in a graph, is also known as an **adjacency matrix**. We could choose this value through inspecting the distribution of pairwise similarity scores, or based on prior knowledge. We can then supply this matrix as an argument to our agglomerative clustering routine, providing a neighborhood of points to be considered when comparing datapoints, which gives an initial structure to the clusters. We can see that this makes a huge difference to the algorithms results after running the following commands. Note that when we generate the adjacency matrix L, we may end up with an asymmetric matrix since we threshold the ten most similar points for each member of the data. This could lead to situations where two points are not mutually closest to each other, leading to an edge represented in only the top or bottom triangle of the adjacency matrix. To generate a symmetric input for our clustering algorithm, we take the average of the matrix L added to its transpose, which effectively adds edges in both directions between two points.

```
>>> from sklearn.cluster import AgglomerativeClustering
>>> from sklearn.neighbors import kneighbors_graph
>>> L = kneighbors_graph(np.array(df)[:,1:], n_neighbors=10, include_self=False)
>>> L = 0.5 * (L + L.T)
>>> agglomerative_clusters = AgglomerativeClustering(n_clusters=2,connectivity=L,linkage='average').fit_predict(X=np.array(df)[:,1:])
>>> df.plot(kind='scatter', x='x_coord', y='y_coord', c=agglomerative_clusters)
```

Now, as you can see, this algorithm can correctly identify and separate two clusters:

Interestingly, constructing this neighborhood graph and partitioning it into sub graphs (splitting the whole graph into a set of nodes and edges that are primarily connected to each other, rather than to other elements of the network) is equivalent to performing k-means clustering on a transformed distance matrix, an approach known as Spectral Clustering (Von Luxburg, Ulrike. *A tutorial on spectral clustering.* Statistics and computing 17.4 (2007): 395-416). The transformation here is from taking the Euclidean distance D we calculated earlier and calculating the kernel score – the Gaussian kernel given by:

$$e^{-\gamma D\left(x_i,x_j\right)^2}$$

between each pair of points i and j, with a bandwidth γ instead of making a hard threshold as when we constructed the neighborhood before. Using the pairwise kernel matrix K calculated from all points i and j, we can then construct the Laplacian matrix of a graph, which is given by:

$$L = I - D^{1/2} K D^{1/2}$$

Here, I is the identity matrix (with a one along the diagonal and zero elsewhere), and D is the diagonal matrix whose elements are :

$$D_{ii} = \sum_{j=1}^{n} K_{ij}$$

Giving the number of neighbors for each point i. In essence by calculating L we now represent the dataset as a series of nodes (points) connected by edges (the elements of this matrix), which have been normalized so that the total value of all edges for each node sums to 1. Since the Gaussian kernel score is continuous, in this normalization divides pairwise distances between a given point and all others into a probability distribution where the distances (edges) sum to 1.

You may recall from linear algebra that Eigenvectors of a matrix A are vectors v for which, if we multiply the matrix by the eigenvector v, we get the same result as if we had multiplied the vector by a constant amount λ: $Av = \lambda v$. Thus, the matrix here represents a kind of operation on the vector. For example, the identity matrix gives an eigenvalue of 1, since multiplying v by the identity gives v itself. We could also have a matrix such as:

$$\begin{bmatrix} 2 & 0 & 0 \\ 0 & 2 & 0 \\ 0 & 0 & 2 \end{bmatrix}$$

which doubles the value of the vector with which it is multiplied, suggesting the matrix acts as a 'stretching' operation on the vector. From this perspective, larger eigenvalues correspond to greater stretching of the vector, while the eigenvector gives the direction in which the stretching occurs. This is useful because it gives us the primary axes along which the matrix operation acts. In our example, if we take the two eigenvectors with the largest eigenvalues (in essence, the directions in which the matrix represents the greatest transformation of a vector), we are extracting the two greatest axes of variation in the matrix. We will return to this concept in more detail when we discuss *Principal components* in *Chapter 6, Words and Pixels – Working with Unstructured Data*, but suffice to say that if we run `run-kmeans` on these eigenvectors (an approach known as **spectral clustering**, since the eigenvalues of a matrix that we cluster are known as the spectrum of a matrix), we get a result very similar to the previous agglomerative clustering approach using neighborhoods, as we can see from executing the following commands:

```
>>> spectral_clusters = sklearn.cluster.SpectralClustering(2).fit_
predict(np.array(df)[:,1:])
```

```
>>> df.plot(kind='scatter', x='x_coord', y='y_coord', c=spectral_
clusters)
```

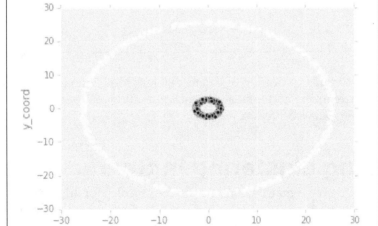

We can successfully capture this nonlinear separation boundary because we've represented the points in the space of the greatest variation in pairwise distance, which is the difference between the inner and outermost circle in the data:

The preceding examples should have given you a number of approaches you can use to tackle clustering problems, and as a rule of thumb guide, the following diagram illustrates the decision process for choosing between them:

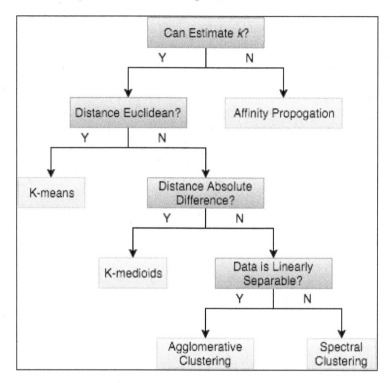

For the last part of our exploration of clustering, let's look at an example application utilizing Spark Streaming and k-means, which will allow us to incrementally update our clusters as they are received.

Streaming clustering in Spark

Up to this point, we have mainly demonstrated examples for ad hoc exploratory analysis. In building up analytical applications, we need to begin putting these into a more robust framework. As an example, we will demonstrate the use of a streaming clustering pipeline using PySpark. This application will potentially scale to very large datasets, and we will compose the pieces of the analysis in such a way that it is robust to failure in the case of malformed data.

As we will be using similar examples with PySpark in the following chapters, let's review the key ingredients we need in such application, some of which we already saw in *Chapter 2, Exploratory Data Analysis and Visualization in Python*. Most PySpark jobs we will create in this book consist of the following steps:

1. Construct a Spark context. The context contains information about the name of the application, and parameters such as memory and number of tasks.

2. The Spark context may be used to construct secondary context objects, such as the streaming context we will use in this example. This context object contains parameters specifically about a particular kind of task, such as a streaming dataset, and inherits all the information we have previously initialized in the base Spark context.

3. Construct a dataset, which is represented in Spark as a **Resilient Distributed Dataset (RDD)**. While from a programmatic standpoint we can operate on this RDD just as we do with, for example, a pandas dataframe, under the hood it is potentially parallelized across many machines during analysis. We may parallelize the data after reading it from a source file, or reading from parallel file systems such as Hadoop. Ideally we don't want to fail our whole job if one line of data is erroneous, so we would like to place an error handling mechanism here that will alert us to a failure to parse a row without blocking the whole job.

4. We frequently need to transform our input dataset into a subclass of RDD known as a **Labeled RDD**. Labeled RDDs contain a label (such as the cluster label for the clustering algorithms we have been studying in this chapter) and a set of features. For our clustering problems, we will only perform this transformation when we predict (as we usually don't know the cluster ahead of time), but for the regression and classification models we will look at in *Chapter 4, Connecting the Dots with Models – Regression Methods*, and *Chapter 5, Putting Data in its Place – Classification Methods and Analysis*, the label is used as a part of fitting the model.

5. We'll frequently want a way to save the output of our modeling to be used by downstream applications, either on disk or in a database, where we can later query models indexed by history.

Let's look at some of these components using the Python notebook. Assuming we have Spark installed on our system, we'll start by importing the required dependencies:

```
>>> from pyspark import SparkContext
>>> from pyspark.streaming import StreamingContext
```

We can then test starting the `SparkContext`:

```
>>> sc = SparkContext( 'local', 'streaming-kmeans')
```

Recall that the first argument gives the URL for our Spark master, the machine that coordinates execution of Spark jobs and distributes tasks to the worker machines in a cluster. In this case, we will run it locally, so give this argument as `localhost`, but otherwise this could be the URL of a remote machine in our cluster. The second argument is just the name we give to our application. With a context running, we can also generate the streaming context, which contains information about our streaming application, using the following:

```
>>> ssc = StreamingContext(sc, 10)
```

The first argument is simply the `SparkContext` used as a parent of the `StreamingContext`: the second is the frequency in seconds at which we will check our streaming data source for new data. If we expect regularly arriving data we could make this lower, or make it higher if we expect new data to be available less frequently.

Now that we have a `StreamingContext`, we can add data sources. Let's assume for now we'll have two sources for training data (which could be historical). We want the job not to die if we give one line of bad data, and so we use a `Parser` class that gives this flexibility:

```
>>> class Parser():
    def __init__(self,type='train',delimiter=',',num_elements=5, job_
uuid=''):
        self.type=type
        self.delimiter=delimiter
        self.num_elements=num_elements
        self.job_uuid=job_uuid

    def parse(self,l):
        try:
            line = l.split(self.delimiter)
            if self.type=='train':
                category = float(line[0])
                feature_vector = Vectors.dense(line[1:])
                return LabeledPoint(category, feature_vector)
            elif self.type=='test':
                category = -1
                feature_vector = Vectors.dense(line)
```

```
                    return LabeledPoint(category, feature_vector)
            else:
                # log exceptions
                f = open('/errors_events/{0}.txt'.format(self.job_
uuid),'a')
                f.write('Unknown type: {0}'.format(self.type))
                f.close()
        except:
            # log errors
            f = open('/error_events/{0}.txt'.format(self.job_uuid),'a')
            f.write('Error parsing line: {0}'.format)
            f.close()
```

We log error lines to a file with the name of our job ID, which will allow us to locate them later if we need to. We can then use this parser to train and evaluate the model. To train the model, we move files with three columns (a label and the data to be clustered) into the training directory. We can also add to the test data directory files with two columns only the coordinate features:

```
>>> num_features = 2
num_clusters = 3

training_parser = Parser('train',',',num_features+1,job_uuid)
test_parser = Parser('test',',',num_features,job_uuid)

trainingData = ssc.textFileStream("/training_data").\
    map(lambda x: training_parser.parse(x)).map(lambda x: x.features)
testData = ssc.textFileStream("/test_data").\
    map(lambda x: test_parser.parse(x)).map(lambda x: x.features)
streaming_clustering = StreamingKMeans(k=num_clusters, decayFactor=1.0).\
    setRandomCenters(num_features,0,0)
streaming_clustering.trainOn(trainingData)
streaming_clustering.predictOn(testData).\
    pprint()
ssc.start()
```

The decay factor in the parameters gives the recipe for combining current cluster centers and old ones. For parameter 1.0, we use an equal weight between old and new, while for the other extreme, at 0, we only use the new data. If we stop the model at any point we, can inspect it using the `lastestModel()` function:

```
>>>   streaming_clustering.latestModel().clusterCenters
```

We could also predict using the `predict()` function on an appropriately sized vector:

```
>> streaming_clustering.latestModel().predict([ … ])
```

Summary

In this section, we learned how to identify groups of similar items in a dataset, an exploratory analysis that we might frequently use as a first step in deciphering new datasets. We explored different ways of calculating the similarity between datapoints and described what kinds of data these metrics might best apply to. We examined both divisive clustering algorithms, which split the data into smaller components starting from a single group, and agglomerative methods, where every datapoint starts as its own cluster. Using a number of datasets, we showed examples where these algorithms will perform better or worse, and some ways to optimize them. We also saw our first (small) data pipeline, a clustering application in PySpark using streaming data.

4
Connecting the Dots with Models – Regression Methods

The trend line is a common feature of many business analyses. How much do purchases increase when ads are shown more often on a homepage? What is the average rating of videos on social media based on user age? What is the likelihood that a customer will buy a second product from your website if they bought their first more than 6 months ago? These sorts of questions can be answered by drawing a line representing the average change in our response (for example, purchases or ratings) as we vary the input (for example, user age or amount of past purchases) based on historical data, and using it to extrapolate the response for future data (where we only know the input, but not output yet). Calculating this line is termed *regression*, based on the hypothesis that our observations are scattered around the true relationship between the two variables, and on average future observations will regress (approach) the trend line between input and output.

Several complexities complicate this analysis in practice. First, the relationships we fit usually involve not one, but several inputs. We can no longer draw a two dimensional line to represent this multi-variate relationship, and so must increasingly rely on more advanced computational methods to calculate this trend in a high-dimensional space. Secondly, the trend we are trying to calculate may not even be a straight line – it could be a curve, a wave, or even more complex patterns. We may also have more variables than we need, and need to decide which, if any, are relevant for the problem at hand. Finally, we need to determine not just the trend that best fits the data we have, but also generalizes best to new data.

In this chapter we will learn:

- How to prepare data for a regression problem
- How to choose between linear and nonlinear methods for a given problem
- How to perform variable selection and assess over-fitting

Linear regression

Ordinary Least Squares (OLS).

We will start with the simplest model of linear regression, where we will simply try to fit the best straight line through the data points we have available. Recall that the formula for linear regression is:

$$y = X\beta$$

Where y is a vector of n responses we are trying to predict, X is a vector of our input variable also of length n, and β is the slope response (how much the response y increases for each 1-unit increase in the value of X). However, we rarely have only a single input; rather, X will represent a set of input variables, and the response y is a linear combination of these inputs. In this case, known as multiple linear regression, X is a matrix of n rows (observations) and m columns (features), and β is a vector set of slopes or coefficients which, when multiplied by the features, gives the output. In essence, it is just the trend line incorporating many inputs, but will also allow us to compare the magnitude effect of different inputs on the outcome. When we are trying to fit a model using multiple linear regression, we also assume that the response incorporates a white noise error term ε, which is a normal distribution with mean 0 and a constant variance for all data points.

To solve for the coefficients β in this model, we can perform the following calculations:

$$y = X\beta$$
$$X^T y = X^T X \beta$$
$$\beta = \frac{X^T y}{\left(X^T X\right)^{-1}}$$

The value of β is known the ordinary least squares estimate of the coefficients. The result will be a vector of coefficients β for the input variables. We make the following assumptions about the data:

- We assume the input variables (X) are accurately measured (there is no error in the values we are given). If they were not, and incorporated error, then they represent random variables, and we would need to incorporate this error in our estimate of the response in order to be accurate.

- The response is a linear combination of the input variables – in other words, we need to be able to fit a straight line through the response. As we will see later in this chapter, we can frequently perform transformations to change nonlinear data into a linear form to satisfy this assumption.

- The residual (the difference between the fitted and actual response) of the response y is assumed to have constant variance over the range of its values. If this is not the case (for example, if smaller values of y have smaller errors than larger values), then it suggests we are not appropriately incorporating a source of error in our model, because the only variation left after we account for the predictors X should be the error term ε. As previously mentioned, this error term ε should have constant variance, meaning the fit should have constant residual variance.

- The residuals are assumed to be un-correlated based on the value of the predictors X. This is important because we assume we are trying to fit a line that goes through the average of the response data points at each predictor value, which would be accurate if we assume that the residual error is randomly distributed about 0. If the residuals are correlated with the value of a predictor, then the line that accurately fits the data may not go through the average, but rather be determined by the underlying correlation in the data. For example, if we are looking at time-series data, days of the week may have more correlated error at a 7-day pattern, meaning that our model should fit this periodicity rather than trying to simply draw a line through the data points for all days together.

- The predictors are assumed not to be collinear (correlated with one another). If two predictors are identical, then they cancel each other out when we make a linear combination of the input matrix X. As we can see in the derivation of β above, to calculate the coefficients we need to take an inverse. If columns in the matrix exactly cancel each other out, then this matrix $(X^TX)^{-1}$ is rank deficient and has no inverse. Recall that if a matrix is full rank, its columns (rows) cannot be represented by a linear combination of the other columns (rows). A rank-deficient does not have an inverse because if we attempt to solve the linear system represented by:

$$I = \left(X^T X\right) A$$

Where A is the inverse we are trying to solve and I is the identity matrix, we will end up with columns in the solution the exactly cancel each-other, meaning any set of coefficients will solve the equation and we cannot have a unique solution.

Why does the OLS formula for β represent the best estimate of the coefficients? The reason is that this value minimizes the squared error:

$$L(\beta) = \sum_{i=1}^{n}(y - \hat{y})^2 = \sum_{i=1}^{n}(y - X\beta)^2$$

While a derivation of this fact is outside the scope of this text, this result is known as the Gauss Markov Theorem, and states that the OLS estimate is the Best Linear Unbiased Estimator (BLUE) of the coefficients β. Recall that when we are estimating these coefficients, we are doing so under the assumption that our calculations have some error, and deviate from the real (unseen) values. The BLUE is then the set of coefficients β that have the smallest mean error from these real values. For more details, we refer the reader to more comprehensive texts (Greene, William H. Econometric analysis. Pearson Education India, 2003; Plackett, Ronald L. "Some theorems in least squares." Biometrika 37.1/2 (1950): 149-157).

Depending upon the problem and dataset, we can relax many of the assumptions described above using alternative methods that are extensions of the basic linear model. Before we explore these alternatives, however, let us start with a practical example. The data we will be using for this exercise is a set of news articles from the website `http://mashable.com/`. (Fernandes, Kelwin, Pedro Vinagre, and Paulo Cortez. "A Proactive Intelligent Decision Support System for Predicting the Popularity of Online News." Progress in Artificial Intelligence. Springer International Publishing, 2015. 535-546.). Each article has been annotated using a number of features such as its number of words and what day it was posted - a complete list appears in the data file associated with this exercise. The task is to predict the popularity (the share column in the dataset) using these other features. In the process of fitting this first model, we will examine some of the common feature preparation tasks that arise in such analyses.

Data preparation

Let us start by taking a look at the data by typing the following commands:

```
>>> news = pd.read_csv('OnlineNewsPopularity.csv',sep=',')
>>> news.columns
```

Which gives the output:

```
Index(['url', ' timedelta', ' n_tokens_title', ' n_tokens_content',
' n_unique_tokens', ' n_non_stop_words', ' n_non_stop_unique_tokens',
' num_hrefs', ' num_self_hrefs', ' num_imgs', ' num_videos',          '
average_token_length', ' num_keywords', ' data_channel_is_lifestyle',
' data_channel_is_entertainment', ' data_channel_is_bus',          ' data_
channel_is_socmed', ' data_channel_is_tech',          ' data_channel_is_
world', ' kw_min_min', ' kw_max_min', ' kw_avg_min',          ' kw_min_
max', ' kw_max_max', ' kw_avg_max', ' kw_min_avg',          ' kw_max_avg',
' kw_avg_avg', ' self_reference_min_shares',          ' self_reference_
max_shares', ' self_reference_avg_sharess',          ' weekday_is_monday',
' weekday_is_tuesday', ' weekday_is_wednesday',          ' weekday_is_
thursday', ' weekday_is_friday', ' weekday_is_saturday',          '
weekday_is_sunday', ' is_weekend', ' LDA_00', ' LDA_01', ' LDA_02',
' LDA_03', ' LDA_04', ' global_subjectivity',          ' global_sentiment_
polarity', ' global_rate_positive_words',          ' global_rate_negative_
words', ' rate_positive_words',          ' rate_negative_words', ' avg_
positive_polarity',          ' min_positive_polarity', ' max_positive_
polarity',          ' avg_negative_polarity', ' min_negative_polarity',
' max_negative_polarity', ' title_subjectivity',          ' title_
sentiment_polarity', ' abs_title_subjectivity',          ' abs_title_
sentiment_polarity', ' shares'],          dtype='object')
```

If you look carefully, you will realize that all the column names have a leading whitespace; you probably would have found out anyway the first time you try to extract one of the columns by using the name as an index. The first step of our data preparation is to fix this formatting using the following code to strip whitespace from every column name:

```
>>> news.columns = [ x.strip() for x in news.columns]
```

Now that we have correctly formatted the column headers, let us examine the distribution of the data using the describe() command as we have seen in previous chapters:

	timedelta	n_tokens_title	n_tokens_content	n_unique_tokens	n_non_stop_words	n_non_stop_unique_tok
count	39644.000000	39644.000000	39644.000000	39644.000000	39644.000000	39644.000000
mean	354.530471	10.398749	546.514731	0.548216	0.996469	0.689175
std	214.163767	2.114037	471.107508	3.520708	5.231231	3.264816
min	8.000000	2.000000	0.000000	0.000000	0.000000	0.000000
25%	164.000000	9.000000	246.000000	0.470870	1.000000	0.625739
50%	339.000000	10.000000	409.000000	0.539226	1.000000	0.690476
75%	542.000000	12.000000	716.000000	0.608696	1.000000	0.754630
max	731.000000	23.000000	8474.000000	701.000000	1042.000000	650.000000

As you scroll from left to right along the columns, you will notice that the range of the values in each column is very different. Some columns have maximum values in the hundreds or thousands, while others are strictly between 0 and 1. In particular, the value that we are trying to predict, shares, has a very wide distribution, as we can see if we plot the distribution using the following command:

```
>>> news['shares'].plot(kind='hist',bins=100)
```

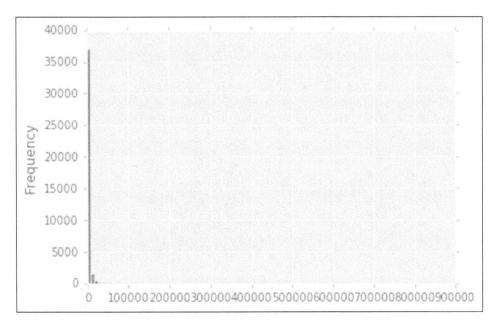

Why is this distribution a problem? Recall that conceptually, when we fit a line through a dataset, we are finding the solution to the equation:

$$y = X\beta$$

Where y is a response variable (such as shares), and β is the vector slopes by which we increase/decrease the value of the response for a 1-unit change in a column of X. If our response is logarithmically distributed, then the coefficients will be biased to accommodate extremely large points in order to minimize the total error of the fit given by:

$$\sum_{i=1}^{n}(y - X\beta)^2$$

To reduce this effect, we can logarithmically transform the response variable, which as you can see through the following code makes a distribution that looks much more like a normal curve:

```
>>> news['shares'].map( lambda x: np.log10(x)
).plot(kind='hist',bins=100)
```

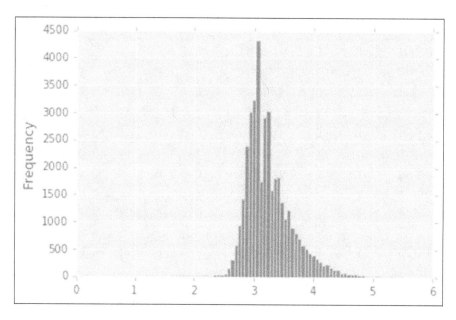

This same rule of thumb holds true for our predictor variables, X. If some predictors are much larger than others, the solution of our equation will mainly emphasize those with the largest range, as they will contribute most to the overall error. In this example, we can systemically scale all of our variables using a logarithmic transformation. First, we remove all uninformative columns, such as the URL, which simply gives website location for the article.

```
>>> news_trimmed_features = news.ix[:,'timedelta':'shares']
```

 Note that in *Chapter 6, Words and Pixels – Working with Unstructured Data* we will explore potential ways to utilize information in textual data such as the url, but for now we will simply discard it.

Then, we identify the variables we wish to transform (here an easy rule of thumb is that their max, given by the 8th row (index 7) of the describe() data frame is > 1, indicating that they are not in the range 0 to 1) and use the following code to apply the logarithmic transform. Note that we add the number 1 to each logarithmically transformed variable so that we avoid errors for taking the logarithm of 0.

```
>>> log_values = list(news_trimmed_features.columns[news_trimmed_
features.describe().reset_index().loc[7][1:]>1])
>>> for l in log_values:
...     news_trimmed_features[l] = np.log10(news_trimmed_features[l]+1)
```

Using the describe() command again confirms that the columns now have comparable distributions:

	timedelta	n_tokens_title	n_tokens_content	n_unique_tokens	n_non_stop_words	n_non_stop_unique_tokens	num_hrefs
count	39644.000000	39644.000000	39644.000000	39644.000000	39644.000000	39644.000000	39644.000000
mean	0.531735	0.311212	0.542389	0.072653	0.110895	0.086453	0.279180
std	0.053246	0.017761	0.102107	0.016611	0.019587	0.017908	0.085195
min	0.290978	0.169416	0.000000	0.000000	0.000000	0.000000	0.000000
25%	0.507516	0.301030	0.530545	0.067285	0.114287	0.083162	0.230186
50%	0.547957	0.309927	0.557842	0.074561	0.114287	0.089202	0.290978
75%	0.572267	0.325093	0.586083	0.081518	0.114287	0.094885	0.337677
max	0.587095	0.376616	0.692683	0.585047	0.604041	0.581333	0.542116

We also need to remove infinite or nonexistent values from the dataset. We first convert infinite values to the placeholder 'not a number', or NaN, using the following:

```
>>> news_trimmed_features = news_trimmed_features.replace([np.inf, -np.
inf], np.nan)
```

We then use the `fill` function to substitute the *NaN* placeholder with the proceeding value in the column (we could also have specified a fixed value, or used the preceding value in the column) using the following:

```
>>> news_trimmed_features = news_trimmed_features.fillna(method='pad')
```

Now we can split the data into the response variable ('shares') and the features (all columns from 'timedelta' to 'abs_title_sentiment_polarity'), which we will use as inputs in the regression models described later using the commands:

```
>>> news_response = news_trimmed_features['shares']
>>> news_trimmed_features = news_trimmed_features.ix[:,'timedelta':'abs_
title_sentiment_polarity']
```

Let us now also take another look at variables that we did not transform logarithmically. If you try to fit a linear model using the dataset at this point, you will find that the slopes for many of these are extremely large or small. This can be explained by looking at what the remaining variables represent. For example, one set of columns which we did not logarithmically transform encodes a 0/1 value for whether a news article was published on a given day of the week. Another (annotated LDA) gives a 0/1 indicator for whether an article was tagged with a particular algorithmically-defined topic (we will cover this algorithm, known as Latent Dirichlet Allocation, in more detail in *Chapter 6, Words and Pixels – Working with Unstructured Data*). In both cases, any row in the dataset must have the value 1 in one of the columns of these features (for example, the day of week has to take one of the seven potential values). Why is this a problem?

Recall that in most linear fits, we have both a slope and an intercept, which is the offset of the line vertically from the origin *(0, 0)* of the *x-y* plane. In a linear model with many variables, we represent this multi-dimensional intercept by a column of all 1 in the feature matrix X, which will be added by default in many model-fitting libraries. This means that a set of columns (for example, the days of the week), since they are independent, could form a linear combination that exactly equals the intercept column, making it impossible to find a unique solution for the slopes β. This is the same issue as the last assumption of linear regression we discussed previously, in which the matrix (XTX) is not invertible, and thus we cannot obtain a numerically stable solution for the coefficients. This instability results in the unreasonably large coefficient values you will observe if you were to fit a regression model on this dataset. It is for this reason that we either need to leave out the intercept column (an option you usually need to specify in a modeling library), or leave out one of the columns for these binary variables. Here we will do the second, dropping one column from each set of binary features using the following code:

```
>>> news_trimmed_features = news_trimmed_features.drop('weekday_is_
sunday',1)

>>> news_trimmed_features = news_trimmed_features.drop('LDA_00',1)
```

Now that we have taken care of these feature engineering concerns, we are ready to fit a regression model to our data.

Model fitting and evaluation

Now that we are ready to fit a regression model to our data, it is important to clarify the goal of our analysis. As we discussed briefly in *Chapter 1, From Data to Decisions – Getting Started with Analytic Applications*, the goals of modeling can be either a) to predict a future response given historical data, or b) infer the statistical significance and effect of a given variable on an outcome.

In the first scenario, we will choose a subset of data to train our model, and then evaluate the goodness of fit of the linear model on an independent data set not used to derive the model parameters. In this case, we want to validate that the trends represented by the model generalize beyond a particular set of data points. While the coefficient outputs of the linear model are interpretable, we are still more concerned in this scenario about whether we can accurately predict future responses rather than the meaning of the coefficients.

In the second scenario, we may not use a test data set at all for validation, and instead fit a linear model using all of our data. In this case, we are more interested in the coefficients of the model and whether they are statistically significant. In this scenario, we are also frequently interested in comparing models with more or fewer coefficients to determine the most important parameters that predict an outcome.

We will return to this second case, but for now let us continue under the assumption that we are trying to predict future data. To obtain test and validation data, we use the following commands to split the response and predictor data into 60% training and 40% test splits:

```
>>> from sklearn import cross_validation
>>> news_features_train, news_features_test, news_shares_train, news_
shares_test = \
>>> cross_validation.train_test_split(news_trimmed_features, news_
response, test_size=0.4, random_state=0)
```

We use the 'random state' argument to set a fixed outcome for this randomization, so that we can reproduce the same train/test split if we want to rerun the analysis at later date. With these training and test sets we can then fit the model and compare the predicted and observed values visually using the following code:

```
>>> from sklearn import linear_model
>>> lmodel = linear_model.LinearRegression().fit(news_features_train,
news_shares_train)
>>> plt.scatter(news_shares_train,lmodel.predict(news_features_
train),color='black')
>>> plt.xlabel('Observed')
>>> plt.ylabel('Predicted')
```

Which gives the following plot:

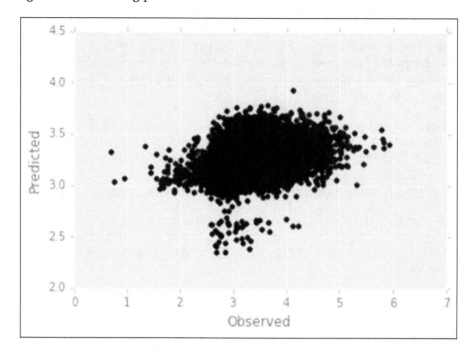

Similarly, we can look at the performance of the model on the test data set using the commands:

```
>>> plt.scatter(news_shares_test,lmodel.predict(news_features_
test),color='red')
>>> plt.xlabel('Observed')
>>> plt.ylabel('Predicted')
```

Which gives the plot:

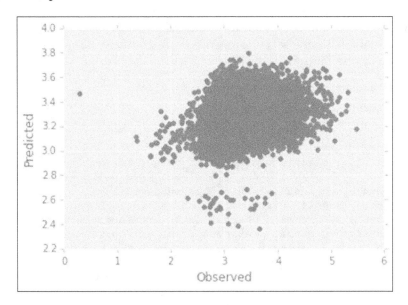

The visual similarities are confirmed by looking at the coefficient of variation, or 'R-squared' value. This is a metric often used in regression problems, which defines how much of the variation in the response is explained by the variation in the predictors according to the model. It is computed as:

$$R^2 = \left(\frac{Cov\left(predicted, observed\right)}{Var\left(predicted\right)Var\left(observed\right)} \right)^2$$

Where `Cov` and `Var` are the **Covariance** and **Variance** (respectively) of the two variables (the observed response y, and the predicted response given by yβ). A perfect score is 1 (a straight line), while 0 represents no correlation between a predicted and observed value (an example would be a spherical cloud of points). Using scikit learn, we can obtain the R^2 value using the `score()` method of the linear model, with arguments the features and response variable. Running the following for our data:

```
>>> lmodel.score(news_features_train, news_shares_train)
>>> lmodel.score(news_features_test, news_shares_test)
```

We get a value of `0.129` for the training data and `0.109` for the test set. Thus, we see that while there is some relationship between the predicted and observed response captured in the news article data, though we have room for improvement.

In addition to looking for overall performance, we may also be interested in which variables from our inputs are most important in the model. We can sort the coefficients of the model by their absolute magnitude to analyse this using the following code to obtain the sorted positions of the coefficients, and reorder the column names using this new index:

```
>>> ix = np.argsort(abs(lmodel.coef_))[::-1][:]
>>> news_trimmed_features.columns[ix]
```

This gives the following output:

```
Index([u'n_unique_tokens', u'n_non_stop_unique_tokens', u'n_non_
stop_words',        u'kw_avg_avg', u'global_rate_positive_words',
u'self_reference_avg_sharess', u'global_subjectivity', u'LDA_02',
u'num_keywords', u'self_reference_max_shares', u'n_tokens_content',
u'LDA_03', u'LDA_01', u'data_channel_is_entertainment', u'num_hrefs',
u'num_self_hrefs', u'global_sentiment_polarity', u'kw_max_max',
u'is_weekend', u'rate_positive_words', u'LDA_04',        u'average_
token_length', u'min_positive_polarity',      u'data_channel_is_bus',
u'data_channel_is_world', u'num_videos',      u'global_rate_negative_
words', u'data_channel_is_lifestyle',      u'num_imgs', u'avg_positive_
polarity', u'abs_title_subjectivity',      u'data_channel_is_socmed',
u'n_tokens_title', u'kw_max_avg',      u'self_reference_min_shares',
u'rate_negative_words',      u'title_sentiment_polarity', u'weekday_
is_tuesday',       u'min_negative_polarity', u'weekday_is_wednesday',
u'max_positive_polarity', u'title_subjectivity', u'weekday_is_thursday',
u'data_channel_is_tech', u'kw_min_avg', u'kw_min_max', u'kw_avg_max',
u'timedelta', u'kw_avg_min', u'kw_max_min', u'max_negative_polarity',
u'kw_min_min', u'avg_negative_polarity', u'weekday_is_saturday',
u'weekday_is_friday', u'weekday_is_monday',      u'abs_title_sentiment_
polarity'],        dtype='object')
```

You will notice that there is no information on the variance of the parameter values. In other words, we do not know the confidence interval for a given coefficient value, nor whether it is statistically significant. In fact, the scikit-learn regression method does not calculate statistical significance measurements, and for this sort of inference analysis—the second kind of regression analysis discussed previously and in *Chapter 1, From Data to Decisions - Getting Started with Analytic Applications*—we will turn to a second Python library, statsmodels (http://statsmodels.sourceforge.net/).

Statistical significance of regression outputs

After installing the `statsmodels` library, we can perform the same linear model analysis as previously, using all of the data rather than a train/test split. With `statsmodels`, we can use two different methods to fit the linear model, `api` and `formula.api`, which we import using the following commands:

```
>>> import statsmodels
>>> import statsmodels.api as sm
>>> import statsmodels.formula.api as smf
```

The `api` methods first resembles the scikit-learn function call, except we get a lot more detailed output about the statistical significance of the model after running the following:

```
>>> results = sm.OLS(news_response, news_trimmed_features).fit()
>>> results.summary()
```

Which gives the following output:

OLS Regression Results

Dep. Variable:	shares	R-squared:	0.123
Model:	OLS	Adj. R-squared:	0.121
Method:	Least Squares	F-statistic:	98.80
Date:	Mon, 21 Mar 2016	Prob (F-statistic):	0.00
Time:	00:03:53	Log-Likelihood:	-17704.
No. Observations:	39644	AIC:	3.552e+04
Df Residuals:	39587	BIC:	3.601e+04
Df Model:	56		
Covariance Type:	nonrobust		

What do all these parameters mean? The number of observations and number of dependent variables are probably obvious, but the others we have not seen before. Briefly, their names and interpretation are:

- **Df model**: This is the number of independent elements in the model parameters. We have 57 columns; once we know the value of 56 of them, the last is fixed by the need to minimize the remaining error, so there are only 56 degrees of freedom overall.

- **Df residuals**: This is the number of independent pieces of information in the error estimates of the model. Recall that we obtain the errors by y-x.We only have up to m independent columns in x, where m is the number of predictors. So our estimate of the error has n-1 independent elements from the data itself, from which we subtract another m which is determined by the inputs, giving us n-m-1.

- **Covariance type**: This is the kind of covariance used in the model; here we just use white noise (a mean 0, normally distributed error), but we could just as easily have specified a particular structure that would accommodate, for example, a case where the error is correlated with the magnitude of the response.

- **Adj. R-squared**: If we include more variables in a model, we can start to increase the R2 by simply having more degrees of freedom with which to fit the data. If we wish to fairly compare the R2 for models with different numbers of parameters, then we can adjust the R2 calculation with the following formula:

$$R_{adj}^2 = R^2 - \left(\frac{p}{n-p-1} \right)\left(1 - R^2\right)$$

Using this formula, for models with larger numbers of parameters, we penalize the R2 by the amount of error in the fit.

- **F-statistics**: This measure is used to compare (through a Chi-squared distribution) that any of the regression coefficients are statistically different than 0.

- **Prob (F-statistic)**: This is the p-value (from the F-statistic) that the null hypothesis (that the coefficients are 0 and the fit is no better than the intercept-only model) is true.

- **Log-likelihood**: Recall that we assume the error of the residuals in the linear model is normally distributed. Therefore, to determine how well our result fits this assumption, we can compute the likelihood function:

$$L(\beta) = \prod_{i=1}^{n} \frac{1}{\sigma\sqrt{2\pi}} e^{\frac{((y_i - x_i\beta) - \mu)^2}{2\sigma^2}}$$

Where σ is the standard deviation of the residuals and μ is the mean of the residuals (which we expect be very near 0 based on the linear regression assumptions above). Because the log of a product is a sum, which is easier to work with numerically, we usually take the logarithm of this value, expressed as:

$$Log(L(\beta)) = \frac{1}{\sigma\sqrt{2\pi}} \sum_{i=1}^{n} \frac{((y_i - x_i\beta) - \mu)^2}{2\sigma^2}$$

While this value is not very useful on its own, it can help us compare two models (for example with different numbers of coefficients). Better goodness of fit is represented by a larger log likelihood, or a lower negative log likelihood.

In practice, we usually minimize the negative log likelihood instead of maximizing the log likelihood, as most optimization algorithms that we might use to obtain the optimal parameters assume minimization as the default objective.

- **AIC/BIC**: AIC and BIC are abbreviations for the Akaike Information Criterion and Bayes Information Criterion. These are two statistics that help to compare models with different numbers of coefficients, thus giving a sense of the benefit of greater model complexity from adding more features. AIC is given by:

$$2m - 2\ln(L(\beta))$$

Where *m* is the number of coefficients in the model and *L* is the likelihood, as described previously. Better goodness of fit is represented by lower AIC. Thus, increasing the number of parameters penalizes the model, while improving the likelihood that it decreases the AIC. BIC is similar, but uses the formula:

$$-2L(\beta) + m\ln(n)$$

Where n is the number of data points in the model. For a fuller comparison of AIC and BIC, please see (Burnham, Kenneth P., and David R. Anderson. *Model selection and multimodel inference: a practical information-theoretic approach.* Springer Science & Business Media, 2003).

Along with these, we also receive an output of the statistical significance of each coefficient, as judged by a *t-test* of its standard error:

	coef	std err	t	P>|t|	[95.0% Conf. Int.]
timedelta	0.0142	0.006	2.322	0.020	0.002 0.026
n_tokens_title	0.0640	0.024	2.626	0.009	0.016 0.112
n_tokens_content	-0.0897	0.020	-4.451	0.000	-0.129 -0.050
n_unique_tokens	-1.3315	0.320	-4.164	0.000	-1.958 -0.705
n_non_stop_words	0.8054	0.215	3.740	0.000	0.383 1.228
n_non_stop_unique_tokens	0.5612	0.233	2.411	0.016	0.105 1.017
num_hrefs	0.0973	0.008	11.474	0.000	0.081 0.114
num_self_hrefs	-0.1083	0.011	-9.649	0.000	-0.130 -0.086
num_imgs	0.0487	0.006	7.981	0.000	0.037 0.061
num_videos	0.0667	0.008	8.620	0.000	0.052 0.082
average_token_length	-0.2459	0.103	-2.390	0.017	-0.448 -0.044
num_keywords	0.1209	0.024	5.130	0.000	0.075 0.167
data_channel_is_lifestyle	-0.0592	0.013	-4.545	0.000	-0.085 -0.034
data_channel_is_entertainment	-0.1166	0.008	-14.059	0.000	-0.133 -0.100

We also receive a final block of statistics:

Omnibus:	7432.190	Durbin-Watson:	1.940
Prob(Omnibus):	0.000	Jarque-Bera (JB):	19103.164
Skew:	1.030	Prob(JB):	0.00
Kurtosis:	5.705	Cond. No.	3.16e+03

Most of these are outside the scope of this volume, but the Durbin-Watson (DW) statistic will be important later, when we discuss dealing with time series data. The DW statistic is given by:

$$\frac{\sum_{t=2}^{T}\left(e_t - e_{t-1}\right)^2}{\sum_{t=1}^{T} e_t^2}$$

Where e are the residuals (here y-$X\beta$ for the linear model). In essence, this statistic asks whether the residuals are positively or negatively correlated. If its value is >2, this suggests a positive correlation. Values between 1 and 2 indicate little to correlation, with 2 indicating no correlation. Values less than 1 represent negative correlation between successive residuals. For more detail please see (Chatterjee, Samprit, and Jeffrey S. Simonoff. *Handbook of regression analysis*. Vol. 5. John Wiley & Sons, 2013).

We could also have fit the model using the `formula.api` commands, by constructing a string from the input data representing the formula for the linear model. We generate the formula using the following code:

```
>>> model_formula = news_response.name+" ~ "+ " + ".join(news_trimmed_
features.columns)
```

You can print this formula to the console to verify it gives the correct output:

```
shares ~ timedelta + n_tokens_title + n_tokens_content + n_unique_tokens
+ n_non_stop_words + n_non_stop_unique_tokens + num_hrefs + num_self_
hrefs + num_imgs + num_videos + average_token_length + num_keywords +
data_channel_is_lifestyle + data_channel_is_entertainment + data_channel_
is_bus + data_channel_is_socmed + data_channel_is_tech + data_channel_is_
world + kw_min_min + kw_max_min + kw_avg_min + kw_min_max + kw_max_max
+ kw_avg_max + kw_min_avg + kw_max_avg + kw_avg_avg + self_reference_
min_shares + self_reference_max_shares + self_reference_avg_sharess +
weekday_is_monday + weekday_is_tuesday + weekday_is_wednesday + weekday_
is_thursday + weekday_is_friday + weekday_is_saturday + is_weekend
+ LDA_01 + LDA_02 + LDA_03 + LDA_04 + global_subjectivity + global_
sentiment_polarity + global_rate_positive_words + global_rate_negative_
words + rate_positive_words + rate_negative_words + avg_positive_polarity
+ min_positive_polarity + max_positive_polarity + avg_negative_polarity
+ min_negative_polarity + max_negative_polarity + title_subjectivity +
title_sentiment_polarity + abs_title_subjectivity + abs_title_sentiment_
polarity
```

We can then use this formula to fit the full pandas dataframe containing both the response and the input variables, by concatenating the response and feature variables along their columns (axis 1) and calling the `ols` method of the formula API we imported previously:

```
>>> news_all_data = pd.concat([news_trimmed_features,news_
response],axis=1)
>>> results = smf.ols(formula=model_formula,data=news_all_data).fit()
```

In this example, it seems reasonable to assume that the residuals in the model we fit for popularity as a function of new article features are independent. For other cases, we might make multiple observations on the same set of inputs (such as when a given customer appears more than once in a dataset), and this data may be correlated with time (as when records of a single customer are more likely to be correlated when they appear closer together in time). Both scenarios violate our assumptions of independence among the residuals in a model. In the following sections we will introduce three methods to deal with these cases.

Generalize estimating equations

In our next set of exercises we will use an example of student grades in a math course in several schools recorded over three terms, expressed by the symbols (G1-3) (Cortez, Paulo, and Alice Maria Gonçalves Silva. "Using data mining to predict secondary school student performance." (2008)). It might be expected that there is a correlation between the school in which the student is enrolled and their math grades each term, and we do see some evidence of this when we plot the data using the following commands:

```
>>> students = pd.read_csv('student-mat.csv',sep=';')
>>> students.boxplot(by='school',column=['G1','G2','G3'])
```

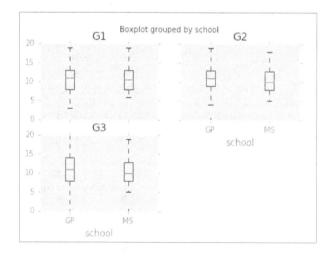

We can see that there is some correlation between a decline in math grades in terms 2 and 3, and the school. If we want to estimate the effect of other variables on student grades, then we want to account for this correlation. How we do so depends upon what our objective is. If we want to simply have an accurate estimate of the coefficients β of the model at the population level, without being able to predict individual students' responses with our model, we can use the **Generalize Estimating Equations** (GEE) (Liang, Kung-Yee, and Scott L. Zeger. "Longitudinal data analysis using generalized linear models." *Biometrika* 73.1 (1986): 13-22). The motivating idea of the GEE is that we treat this correlation between school and grade as an additional parameter (which we estimate by performing a linear regression on the data and calculating the residuals) in the model. By doing so, we account for the effect of this correlation on the coefficient estimate, and thus obtain a better estimate of their value. However, we still usually assume that the responses within a group are exchangeable (in other words, the order does not matter), which is not the case with clustered data that might have a time-dependent component.

Unlike the linear model, GEE parameter estimates are obtained through nonlinear optimization of the objective function U(β), using the following formula:

$$U\left(\beta\right)=\sum_{k=1}^{K}\frac{\partial\mu_k}{\partial\beta}V_k^{-1}\left(Y_k-\mu_k\left(\beta\right)\right)$$

Where μ_k is the mean response of a group k (such as a school, in our example), V_k is the variance matrix giving the correlation between residuals for members of the group k and Y_k - μ_k is the vector of residuals within this group. This is usually solved using the Newton-Raphson equation, which we will look at in more detail in *Chapter 5, Putting Data in its Place – Classification Methods and Analysis*. Conceptually, we can estimate the variance matrix V using the residuals from a regression, and optimize the formula above until convergence. Thus, by optimizing both the correlation structure between grouped data samples given by V along with the coefficients β, we have effectively obtained an estimate β independent of V.

To apply this method to our data, we can again create the model string using the following command:

```
>>> model_formula = "G3 ~ "+" + ".join(students.columns[1:len(students.columns)-3])
```

We can then run the GEE using the school as the grouping variable:

```
>>> results = smf.gee(model_formula,"school",data=students).fit()
>>> results.summary()
```

However, in some cases we would instead like to obtain an estimate of individual, not population-level, responses, even with the kind of group correlations we discussed previously. In this scenario, we could instead use mixed effects models.

Mixed effects models

Recall that in the linear models we have fitted in this chapter, we assume the response is modeled as:

$$y = X\beta + \varepsilon$$

Where ε is an error term. However, when we have correlation between data points belonging to a group, we can also use a model of the form:

$$y = X\beta + Zu + \varepsilon$$

Where z and u are group-level variables and coefficients, respectively. The coefficient u has a mean 0 and a variance structure that needs to be specified. It could be uncorrelated between groups, for example, or have a more complex covariance relationship where certain groups are correlated with one another more strongly than others. Unlike the GEE model, we are not attempting to simply estimate the group level effect of the coefficients (after factoring out the effect of group membership), but within-group coefficients that control for the effect of belonging to a particular group. The name of mixed effects models comes from the fact that the variables ⊠ are fixed effects whose value is exactly known, while u are random effects, where the value u represents an observation of a group level coefficient which is a random variable. The coefficients u could either be a set of group-level intercepts (random intercepts model), or combined with group-level slopes (random slopes model). Groups may even be nested within one another (hierarchical mixed effects models), such as if town-level groups capture one kind of correlated variation, while state-level groups capture another. A full discussion of the many variations of mixed effects models is outside the scope of this book, but we refer the interested reader to references such as (West, Brady T., Kathleen B. Welch, and Andrzej T. Galecki. *Linear mixed models: a practical guide using statistical software.* CRC Press, 2014; Stroup, Walter W. *Generalized linear mixed models: modern concepts, methods and applications.* CRC press, 2012). As with GEE, we can fit this model similar to the linear model by including a group-level variable using the following commands:

```
>>> results = smf.mixedlm(model_formula,groups="school",data=students).
fit()

>>> results.summary()
```

Time series data

The last category of model assumptions that we will consider are where clustered data is temporally correlated, for example if a given customer has periodic buying activity based on the day of the week. While GEE and mixed effects models generally deal with data in which the inter-group correlations are exchangeable (the order does not matter), in time series data, the order is important for the interpretation of the data. If we assume exchangeability, then we may incorrectly estimate the error in our model, since we will assume the best fit goes through the middle of the data in a given group, rather than following the correlation structure of repeated measurements in a time series.

A particularly flexible model for time series data uses a formula known as the Kalman filter. Superficially, the Kalman filter resembles the equation for mixed effects models; consider an observation that at a given point in time has an unobserved state which we want to infer in the model (such as whether a given stock is increasing or decreasing in price), which is obscured by noise (such as market variation in stock price). The state of the data point is given by:

$$x_t = F_t x_{t-1} + \beta_t u_t + w_t$$

Where F represents the matrix of transition probabilities between states, xt-1 is the state at the last time step, w_t is noise, and B_t and u_t represent regression variables that could incorporate, for example, seasonal effects. In this case, u would be a binary indicator of a season or time of day, and β the amount we should add or subtract from x based on this indicator. The state x is used to predict the observed response using:

$$y_t = H_t x_t + v_t$$

Where xt is the state from the previous equation, H is a set of coefficients for each underlying state, and vt is noise. The Kalman filter uses the observations at time t-1 to update our estimates of both the underlying state x and the response y at time t.

The family of equations given previously is also known by the more general term "Structural Time Series Equations". For the derivations of the update equations and further details on "Structural Time Series Models", we refer the reader to more advanced references (Simon, Dan. *Optimal state estimation: Kalman, H infinity, and nonlinear approaches.* John Wiley & Sons, 2006; Harvey, Andrew C. *Forecasting, structural time series models and the Kalman filter.* Cambridge University Press, 1990).

In the `statsmodels` package, the Kalman filter is used in **auto-regressive moving average (ARMA)** models, which are fit with the following command:

```
>>> statsmodels.tsa.arima_model.ARMA()
```

Generalized linear models

In most of the preceding examples, we assume that the response variable may be modeled as a linear combination of the responses. However, we can often relax this assumption by fitting a generalized linear model. Instead of the formula:

$$y = X\beta + \varepsilon$$

We substitute a `link` function (G) that transforms the nonlinear output into a linear response:

$$G(Y) = X\beta + \varepsilon$$

Examples of `link` functions include:

- **Logit**: This `link` function maps the responses in the range 0 to 1 to a linear scale using the function $X\beta=ln(y/1-y)$, where y is usually a probability between 0 and 1. This `link` function is used in logistic and multinomial regression, covered in *Chapter 5, Putting Data in its Place – Classification Methods and Analysis*.

- **Poisson**: This `link` function maps count data to a linear scale using the relationship $X\beta=ln(y)$, where y is count data.

- **Exponential**: This `link` function maps data from an exponential scale to a linear one with the formula $X\beta=y-1$.

While these sorts of transformations make it possible to transform many nonlinear problems into linear ones, they also make it more difficult to estimate parameters of the model. Indeed, the matrix algebra used to derive the coefficients for simple linear regression do not apply, and the equations do not have any closed solution we could represent by a single step or calculation. Instead, we need iterative update equations such as those used for GEE and mixed effects models. We will cover these sorts of methods in more detail in *Chapter 5, Putting Data in its Place – Classification Methods and Analysis*.

Now we have now covered some of the diverse cases of fitting models to data that violate the linear regression assumptions in order to correctly interpret coefficients. Let us return now to the task of trying to improve the predictive performance of our linear model by selecting a subset of variables in the hope of removing correlated inputs and reducing over-fitting, an approach known as *regularization*.

Applying regularization to linear models

After observing that the performance of our linear model is not optimal, one relevant question is whether all of the features in this model are necessary, or whether the coefficients we have estimated are suboptimal. For instance, two columns may be highly correlated with one another, meaning that the matrix XTX can be rank-deficient and thus not invertible, leading to numerical instability in calculating the coefficients. Alternatively, we may have included enough input variables to make an excellent fit on the training data, but this fit may not generalize to the test data as it precisely captures nuanced patterns present only in the training data. The high number of variables gives us great flexibility to make the predicted responses exactly match the observed responses in the training set, leading to overfitting. In both cases, it may be helpful to apply regularization to the model. Using regularization, we try to apply a penalty to the magnitude and/or number of coefficients, in order to control for over-fitting and multicollinearity. For regression models, two of the most popular forms of regularization are Ridge and Lasso Regression.

In Ridge Regression, we want to constrain the coefficient magnitude to a reasonable level, which is accomplished by applying a squared penalty to the size of the coefficients in the loss function equation:

$$L(\beta) = \sum_{i=1}^{n}(y_i - x_i\beta)^2 + \alpha\sum_{j=1}^{m}\beta_j^2$$

 Please note this L(β), though using the same symbols, is not the same as the likelihood equations discussed earlier.

In other words, by applying the penalty a to the sum of squares of the coefficients, we constrain the model not only to approximate y as well as possible, using the slopes β multiplied by the features, but also constrain the size of the coefficients β. The effect of this penalty is controlled by the weighting factor a. When alpha is 0, the model is just normal linear regression. Models with $a > 0$ increasingly penalizes large β values. How can we choose the right value for a? The scikit-learn library offers a helpful cross-validation function that can find the optimal value for a on the training set using the following commands:

```
>>> lmodel_ridge = linear_model.RidgeCV().fit(news_features_train, news_shares_train)
>>> lmodel_ridge.alpha_
```

Which gives the optimal α value as 0.100.

However, making this change does not seem to influence predictive accuracy on the test set when we evaluate the new *R2* value using the following commands:

```
>>> lmodel_ridge.score(news_features_test, news_shares_test)
```

In fact, we obtain the same result as the original linear model, which gave a test set *R2* of `0.109`.

Another method of regularization is referred to as Lasso, where we minimize the following equation. It is similar to the Ridge Regression formula above, except that the squared penalty on the values of β have been replaced with an absolute value term.

$$L(\beta) = \sum_{i=1}^{n}(y_i - x_i\beta)^2 + \alpha\sum_{j=1}^{m}|\beta_j|$$

This absolute value penalty has the practical effect that many of the slopes are optimized to be zero. This could be useful if we have many inputs and wish to select only the most important to try and derive insights. It may also help in cases where two variables are closely correlated with one another, and we will select one to include in the model. Like Ridge Regression, we can find the optimal value of a using the following cross validation commands:

```
>>> lmodel_lasso = linear_model.LassoCV(max_iter=10000).fit(news_
features_train, news_shares_train)
>>> lmodel_lasso.alpha_
```

Which suggests an optimal a value of *6.25e-5*.

In this case, there does not seem to be much value in applying this kind of penalization to the model, as the optimal a is near zero. Taken together, the analyses above suggest that modifying the coefficients themselves is not helping our model.

What might help us decide whether we would use Ridge or Lasso, besides the improvement in goodness of fit? One tradeoff is that while Lasso may generate a sparser model (more coefficients set to 0), the values of the resulting coefficients are hard to interpret. Given two highly correlated variables, Lasso will select one, while shrinking the other to 0, meaning with some modification to the underlying data (and thus bias to select one of these variables) we might have selected a different variable into the model. While Ridge regression does not suffer from this problem, the lack of sparsity may make it harder to interpret the outputs as well, as it does not tend to remove variables from the model.

A balance between these two choices is provided by Elastic Net Regression (Zou, Hui, and Trevor Hastie. "Regularization and variable selection via the elastic net." *Journal of the Royal Statistical Society: Series B (Statistical Methodology) 67.2 (2005): 301-320.)*. In Elastic Net, our penalty term becomes a blend of Ridge and Lasso, with the optimal β minimizing:

$$L(\beta) = \sum_{i=1}^{n}(y_i - x_i\beta)^2 + \alpha_1\sum_{j=1}^{m}\beta_j^2 + \alpha_2\sum_{i=1}^{n}|\beta|$$

Because of this modification, Elastic Net can select groups of correlated variables, while still shrinking many to zero. Like Ridge and Lasso, Elastic Net has a CV function to choose the optimal value of the two penalty terms α using:

```
>>> from sklearn.linear_model import ElasticNetCV

>>> lmodel_enet = ElasticNetCV().fit(news_features_train, news_shares_train)

>>> lmodel_enet.score(news_features_test, news_shares_test)
```

However, this still is not significantly improving the performance of our model, as the test *R2* is still unmoved from our original least squares regression. It may be the response is not captured well by a linear trend involving a combination of the inputs. There may be interactions between features that are not represented by coefficients of any single variable, and some variables might have nonlinear responses, such as:

- Nonlinear trends, such as a logarithmic increase in the response for a linear increase in the predictor

- Non-monotonic (increasing or decreasing) functions such as a parabola, with a lower response in the middle of the range of predictor values and higher values at the minimum and maximum

- More complex multi-modal responses, such as cubic polynomials

While we could attempt to use generalized linear models, as described above, to capture these patterns, in large datasets we may struggle to find a transformation that effectively captures all these possibilities. We might also start constructing "interaction features" by, for example, multiplying each of our input variables to generate *N(N-1)/2* additional variables (for the pairwise products between all input variables). While this approach, sometimes called "polynomial expansion," can sometimes capture nonlinear relationships missed in the original model, with larger feature sets this can ultimately become unwieldy. Instead, we might try to explore methods that can efficiently explore the space of possible variable interactions.

Tree methods

In many datasets, the relationship between our inputs and output may not be a straight line. For example, consider the relationship between hour of the day and probability of posting on social media. If you were to draw a plot of this probability, it would likely increase during the evening and lunch break, and decline during the night, morning and workday, forming a sinusoidal wave pattern. A linear model cannot represent this kind of relationship, as the value of the response does not strictly increase or decrease with the hour of the day. What models, then, could we use to capture this relationship? In the specific case of time series models we could use approaches such as the Kalman filter described above, using the components of the structural time series equation to represent the cyclical 24-hour pattern of social media activity. In the following section we examine more general approaches that will apply both to time series data and to more general non-linear relationships.

Decision trees

Consider a case where we assign a probability of posting on social media when hour `> 11 am` and `< 1 pm`, `> 1 pm` and `< 6 pm`, and so forth. We could visualize these as the branches of a tree, where at each branch point we have a condition (such as hour `< 6 pm`), and assign our input data to one branch or another. We continue this sort of branching until we reach the end of a series of such selections, called a "leaf" of the tree; the predicted response for the tree is then the average of the value of training data points in this last group. To predict the response of new data points, we follow the branches of the tree to the bottom. To compute a decision tree, then, we need the following steps:

1. Start with a training set of features X and responses y.

2. Find the column of X, along with the dividing point, which optimizes the split between the data points. There are several criteria we could optimize, such as the variance of the target response on each side of the decision boundary (see split functions, later). (Breiman, Leo, et al. Classification and regression trees. CRC press, 1984.). We assign training data points to two new branches based on this rule.

3. Repeat step 2 until a stopping rule is reached, or there is only a single value in each of the final branches of the tree.

4. The predicted response is then given by the average response of the training points that end up in a particular branch of the tree.

As mentioned previously, every time we select a split point in the tree model, we need a principled way of determining whether one candidate variable is better than another for dividing the data into groups that have more correlated responses. There are several options.

Variance Reduction measures weather the two groups formed after splitting the data have lower variance in the response variable y than the data as a whole, and is used in the **Classification and Regression Trees** (CART) algorithm for decision trees (Breiman, Leo, et al. Classification and regression trees. CRC press, 1984.). It may be calculated by:

$$VR(L,R) = \frac{1}{|A^2|}\sum_{i \in A}\sum_{j \in A}\frac{1}{2}(y_i - y_j)^2 - \left(\frac{1}{|L^2|}\sum_{i \in L}\sum_{j \in L}\frac{1}{2}(y_i - y_j)^2 + \frac{1}{|R^2|}\sum_{i \in R}\sum_{j \in R}\frac{1}{2}(y_i - y_j)^2 \right)$$

Where A is the set of all data points before the split, L is the set of values that fall to the left side of the split, and R is the set of points that falls to the right side. This formula is optimized when the combined variance of the two sides of the split point are less than the variance in the original data.

Variance reduction will work best for problems like the one we are examining in this chapter, where the output is a continuous variable. However, in classification problems with categorical outcomes, such as we will examine in *Chapter 5, Putting Data in its Place – Classification Methods and Analysis* the variance becomes less meaningful because the data can only assume fixed number of values (1 or 0 for a particular class). Another statistic we might optimize is the "information gain," which is used in the Iterative Dichotomiser 3 (ID3) and C4.5 algorithms for building decision trees (Quinlan, J. Ross. *C4. 5: programs for machine learning.* Elsevier, 2014; Quinlan, J. Ross. "Induction of decision trees." *Machine learning* 1.1 (1986): 81-106). The information gain statistic asks whether the data on the left and right sides of the decision split become more or less similar after being partitioned. If we considered the response y to be a probability, then the information gain is calculated as:

$$IG(L,R) = -\sum_{k=1}^{K} f_{A_k} \log_2 f_{A_k} - \left(-\alpha\sum_{k=1}^{K} f_{L_k} \log_2 f_{L_k} + (1-\alpha)\sum_{k=1}^{K} f_{R_k} \log_2 f_R \right)$$

$$GI(L,R) = 1 - \left(\alpha\sum_{k=1}^{K} f_{L_k}^2 + (1-\alpha)\sum_{k=1}^{K} f_{R_k}^2 \right)$$

Where α is the fraction of data that is divided to the left side of the split, and f_{Ak}, f_{Lk}, and f_{Rk} are the fraction of elements in class k among all data points, the Left side, and the Right side of the split. The three terms of this equation are known as Entropies (Borda, Monica. *Fundamentals in information theory and coding*. Springer Science & Business Media, 2011). Why does the entropy reflect a good split of the data? To see this, plot the values from 0 to 1 for the function `ylog2y` using the following:

```
>>> probs = np.arange(0.01,1,0.01)
>>> entropy = [ -1*np.log2(p)*p for p in probs]
>>> plt.plot(probs,entropy)
>>> plt.xlabel('y')
>>>plt.ylabel('Entropy')
```

Look at the result:

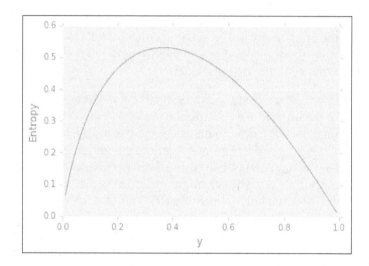

You can appreciate that the entropy drops as **y** approaches 0 or 1. This corresponds to a very high probability or low probability of a particular class in a classification problem, and thus trees which split data according to information gain will maximize the extent to which the left and right branches tend towards or against probability for a given class in the response.

Similarly, the CART algorithm (Breiman, Leo, et al. Classification and regression trees. CRC press, 1984.). Also use the *Gini impurity* to decide the split points, calculated as:

$$GI(L,R) = 1 - \left(\alpha \sum_{k=1}^{K} f_{L_k}^2 + (1-\alpha) \sum_{k=1}^{K} f_{R_k}^2 \right)$$

Inspecting this formula, you can see it will be maximized when one class is near a value of $f = 1$, while all others are 0.

How could we deal with null values and missing data in such a model? In scikit-learn, the current decision tree implementation does not accommodate missing values, so we either need to insert a placeholder value (such as -1), drop missing records, or impute them (for example, replacing with the column mean) (see Aside for more details). However, some implementations (such as the R statistical programming language's gbm package) treat missing data as a third branch into which to sort data.

Similar diversity is present in the treatment of categorical data. The current scikit-learn implementation expects only numerical columns, meaning that categorical features such as gender or country need to be encoded as binary indicators. However, other packages, such as the implementation in R, treat categorical data by assigning data into buckets based on their feature value, then sorting the buckets by average response to determine which buckets to assign to the left and right branches of a tree.

Aside: dealing with missing data

When dealing with missing values in data, we need to consider several possibilities. One is whether the data is *missing at random*, or *missing not at random*. In the first case, there is a correlation between the response variable and the fact that the data is missing. We could assign a dummy value (such as -1), remove the whole row with missing data from our analysis, or assign the column mean or median as a placeholder. We could also think of more sophisticated approaches, such as training a regression model that uses all the other input variables as predictors and the column with the missing data as the output response, and derive imputed values using the predictions from this model. If data is missing not at random, then simply encoding the data with a placeholder is probably not sufficient, as the placeholder value is correlated with the response. In this scenario, we may remove the rows with missing data, or if this is not possible, employ the model-based approach. This will be preferable to infer the value of the missing elements in the data as it should predict values that follow the same distribution as the rest of the column.

In practice, while constructing the tree, we usually have some stopping rule, such as the minimum number of observations that are needed to form a leaf node (otherwise the predicted response could come from a small number of data points, which usually increases the error of the predictions).

It is not clear at the outset how many times the tree should branch. If there are too few splits (decision points), then few rules can be applied to subdivide the dataset and the resulting accuracy of the model may be low. If there are too many splits in a very deep tree, then the model may not generalize well to a new set of data. For our example, let us try fitting the tree to a number of different depths:

```
>>> from sklearn.tree import DecisionTreeRegressor
>>> max_depths = [2,4,6,8,32,64,128,256]
>>> dtrees = []
>>> for m in max_depths:
...     dtrees.append(DecisionTreeRegressor(min_samples_leaf=20,max_
depth=m).\
...     fit(news_features_train, news_shares_train))
```

Now, we can evaluate the results by plotting the R2 against the tree depth for each model:

```
>>> r2_values = []
>>> for d in dtrees:
...     r2_values.append(d.score(news_features_test, news_shares_test))
>>> plt.plot(max_depths,r2_values,color='red')
>>> plt.xlabel('maximum depth')
>>> plt.ylabel('r-squared')
```

Looking at the performance on the test set, we can see that the gains in performance drop quickly once we make the tree too deep:

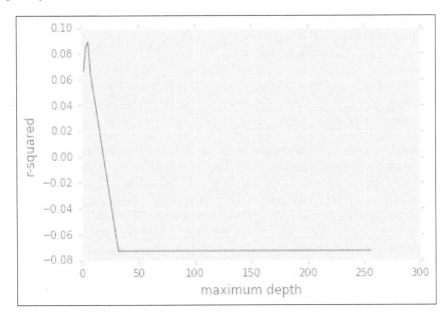

Unfortunately, the tree model is still not performing much better than our basic linear regression. To try and improve this, we can try to increase the number of trees rather than the depth of the trees. The intuition here is that a set of shallower trees may in combination capture relationships that it is difficult for a single deep tree to approximate. This approach, of using a combination of smaller models to fit complex relationships, is used both in the Random Forest algorithm discussed in the following section, and in Gradient Boosted Decision Trees (*Chapter 5, Putting Data in its Place – Classification Methods and Analysis*) and, in a sense, in the deep learning models we will discuss in *Chapter 7, Learning from the Bottom Up – Deep Networks and Unsupervised Features*.

Random forest

While the idea of capturing non-linear relationships seems reasonable, it is possible that it is difficult to construct a single tree that captures such complex relationships between input and output. What if we were to average over many simpler decision trees? This is the essence of the Random Forest algorithm (Ho, Tin Kam. "Random decision forests." *Document Analysis and Recognition, 1995., Proceedings of the Third International Conference on*. Vol. 1. IEEE, 1995.; Breiman, Leo. "Random forests." *Machine learning* 45.1 (2001): 5-32.), in which we construct several trees to try and explore the space of possible nonlinear interactions.

Random Forests are an innovation on the concept of Bootstrap Aggregation (Bagging) for tree models (Breiman, Leo. "Bagging predictors." *Machine learning* 24.2 (1996): 123-140.). In the generic Bagging algorithm, we construct a large number of trees by sampling, with replacement from the training data a small number of data points and building a tree only on this subset of data. While individual trees will be relatively weak models, by averaging over a large number of trees we can often achieve better prediction performance. Conceptually this is because instead of trying to fit a single model (such as a single line) through the response, we are approximating the response using an ensemble of small models that each fit a single simpler pattern in the input data.

Random Forests are a further development on the idea of Bagging by randomizing not just the data used to build each tree, but the variables as well. At each step we also only consider a random subset (for example, of size equal to the square root of the total number of columns) of the columns of X while constructing the splits in the tree (Hastie, Trevor, et al. "The elements of statistical learning: data mining, inference and prediction." *The Mathematical Intelligencer* 27.2 (2005): 83-85.). If we used all input columns at each round of training, we would tend to select the same variables that are most strongly correlated with the response. By instead randomly selecting a subset of variables, we can also find patterns among weaker predictors and more widely cover the space of possible feature interactions. As with Bagging, we follow this process of random data and variable selection many times, and then average together the predictions of all trees to reach an overall prediction. Again, we can explore whether varying a parameter (the number of trees) improves performance on the test set:

```
>>> from sklearn import ensemble
>>> rforests = []
>>> num_trees = [2,4,6,8,32,64,128,256]
>>> for n in num_trees:
...     rforests.\
...     append(ensemble.RandomForestRegressor(n_estimators=n,min_samples_
leaf=20).\
...     fit(news_features_train, news_shares_train))
```

Finally, we can start to see some increases in the accuracy of the model when we plot the results using the following code:

```
>>> r2_values_rforest = []
>>> for f in rforests:
...    r2_values_rforest.append(f.score(news_features_test, news_shares_
test))
>>> plt.plot(num_trees,r2_values_rforest,color='red')
>>> plot.xlabel('Number of Trees')
>>> plot.ylabel('r-squared')
```

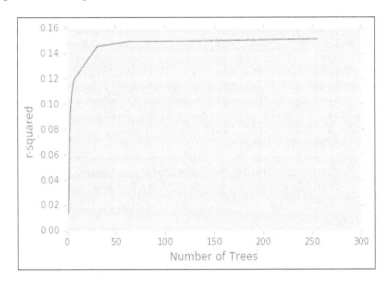

Like the linear regression model, we can get a ranking of feature importance. While for the linear regression, it is simply the magnitude of the slopes, in the random forest model the importance of features is determined in a more complex manner. Intuitively, if we were to shuffle the values of a particular column among the rows in the dataset, it should decrease the performance of the model if the column is important. By measuring the average effect of this permutation across all trees and dividing by the standard deviation of this effect, we can get can a ranking of the magnitude and consistency of the impact of a variable on the performance of the model. By ranking variables by the degree this randomization has on accuracy, we can derive a measure of feature significance. We can examine the important variables using the following commands to select the feature importance values of the largest random forest. Since the np.argsort command will by default return a list in ascending order, we use the [::-1] slice to invert the list order to place the large coefficient values at the beginning.

```
>>> ix = np.argsort(abs(f[5].feature_importances_))[::-1]
>>> news_trimmed_features.columns[ix]
```

This gives the following result:

```
Index(['kw_avg_avg', 'self_reference_avg_sharess', 'timedelta',
'LDA_01',          'kw_max_avg', 'n_unique_tokens', 'data_channel_is_
tech', 'LDA_02',          'self_reference_min_shares', 'n_tokens_content',
'LDA_03', 'kw_avg_max',          'global_rate_negative_words', 'avg_
negative_polarity',          'global_rate_positive_words', 'average_
token_length', 'num_hrefs',          'is_weekend', 'global_subjectivity',
'kw_avg_min',          'n_non_stop_unique_tokens', 'kw_min_max', 'global_
sentiment_polarity',          'kw_max_min', 'LDA_04', 'kw_min_avg', 'min_
positive_polarity',          'num_self_hrefs', 'avg_positive_polarity',
'self_reference_max_shares',          'title_sentiment_polarity', 'max_
positive_polarity', 'n_tokens_title',          'abs_title_sentiment_
polarity', 'abs_title_subjectivity',          'title_subjectivity',
'min_negative_polarity', 'num_imgs',          'data_channel_is_socmed',
'rate_negative_words', 'num_videos',          'max_negative_polarity',
'rate_positive_words', 'kw_min_min',          'num_keywords', 'data_
channel_is_entertainment', 'weekday_is_wednesday',          'data_channel_
is_lifestyle', 'weekday_is_friday', 'weekday_is_monday',          'kw_max_
max', 'data_channel_is_bus', 'data_channel_is_world',          'n_non_stop_
words', 'weekday_is_saturday', 'weekday_is_tuesday',          'weekday_is_
thursday'],          dtype='object')
```

Interestingly, if you compare this list with the linear regression model, the order is quite different. Promisingly, this suggests that the random forest was able to incorporate patterns that a linear regression cannot capture, resulting in the gains in R^2 seen in this section.

There is also a somewhat subtle problem in this dataset, in the sense that all the categorical variables have been encoded using a binary flag. The variable importance is thus applied individually to each member of a category. If one member of a category is highly correlated with the response while another is not, these individual variables' importance measures give an inaccurate picture of the true variable importance. One solution is to average the resulting values over all categories, a correction which we will not apply for now but raise as a consideration for your future analyses.

Here we provide a visual flowchart illustrating many of the tradeoffs we have discussed in this chapter on regression analysis. While it is difficult to provide comprehensive rules-of-thumb for all scenarios, it can serve as a starting point for diagnosing which method to apply for a given problem:

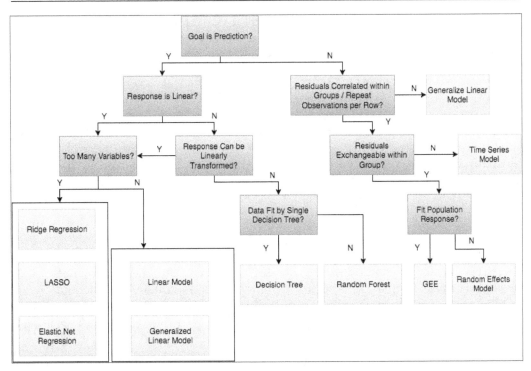

Flowchart for regression analysis

Scaling out with PySpark – predicting year of song release

To close, let us look at another example using PySpark. With this dataset, which is a subset of the Million Song dataset (Bertin-Mahieux, Thierry, et al. "The million song dataset." *ISMIR 2011: Proceedings of the 12th International Society for Music Information Retrieval Conference, October 24-28, 2011, Miami, Florida*. University of Miami, 2011), the goal is to predict the year of a song's release based on the features of the track. The data is supplied as a comma-separated text file, which we can convert into an RDD using the Spark `textFile()` function. As before in our clustering example, we also define a parsing function with a `try...catch` block so that we do not fail on a single error in a large dataset:

```
>>> def parse_line(l):
...     try:
...             return l.split(",")
...     except:
...         print("error in processing {0}".format(l))
```

We then use this function to map each line to the parsed format, which splits the comma delimited text into individual fields and converts these rows into a Spark DataFrame:

```
>>> songs = sc.textFile('/Users/jbabcock/Downloads/YearPredictionMSD.
txt').\
map(lambda x : parse_line(x)).\
toDF()
```

Since we convert the resulting RDD into a DataFrame, so that we can access its elements like a list or vector in Python. Next, we want to turn this into a LabeledPoint RDD, just as we did with the Streaming K-Means example in the previous chapter:

```
>>> from pyspark.mllib.regression import LabeledPoint
>>> songs_labeled = songs.map( lambda x: LabeledPoint(x[0],x[1:]) )
```

As part of the documentation for this dataset, we assume that the training data (excluding tracks from artists appearing in the test set) is contained in the first 463,715 rows, while the rest is the test data. To split it, we can use the zipWithIndex function, which assigns an index to each element in a partition, and across partitions:

```
>>> songs_train = songs_labeled.zipWithIndex().\
filter( lambda x: x[1] < 463715).\
map( lambda x: x[0] )
>>> songs_test = songs_labeled.zipWithIndex().\
filter( lambda x: x[1] >= 463715).\
map( lambda x: x[0] )
```

Finally, we can train a random forest model on this data using the following commands:

```
>>> from pyspark.mllib.tree import RandomForest
>>> rf = RandomForest.trainRegressor(songs_train,{},50,"auto","varian
ce",10,32)
>>> prediction = rf.predict(songs_test.map(lambda x: x.features))
>>> predictedObserved = songs_test.map(lambda lp: lp.label).
zip(prediction)
```

To evaluate the accuracy of the resulting model, we can use the RegressionMetrics module:

```
>>> from pyspark.mllib.evaluation import RegressionMetrics
>>> RegressionMetrics(predictedObserved).r2
```

The distributed nature of PySpark means that this analysis will run on both the single example file on your computer, and on a much larger dataset (such as the full million songs), all using the same code. If we wanted to save the random forest model (for example, if we want to store a particular day's model for future reference in a database, or distribute this model across multiple machines where it will be loaded from a serialized format), we can use to the `toString()` function, which can be potentially compressed using gzip.

Summary

In this chapter, we examined the fitting of several regression models, including transforming input variables to the correct scale and accounting for categorical features correctly. In interpreting the coefficients of these models, we examined both cases where the classical assumptions of linear regression are fulfilled and broken. In the latter cases, we examined generalized linear models, GEE, mixed effects models, and time series models as alternative choices for our analyses. In the process of trying to improve the accuracy of our regression model, we fit both simple and regularized linear models. We also examined the use of tree-based regression models and how to optimize parameter choices in fitting them. Finally, we examined an example of using random forest in PySpark, which can be applied to larger datasets.

In the next chapter, we will examine data that has a discrete categorical outcome, instead of a continuous response. In the process, we will examine in more detail how the likelihood functions of different models are optimized, as well as various algorithms for classification problems.

5
Putting Data in its Place – Classification Methods and Analysis

In the previous chapter, we explored methods for analyzing data whose outcome is a continuous variable, such as the purchase volume for a customer account or the expected number of days until cancellation of a subscription service. However, many of the outcomes for data in business analyses are discrete — they may only take a limited number of values. For example, a movie review can be 1–5 stars (but only integers), a customer can cancel or renew a subscription, or an online advertisement can be clicked or ignored.

The methods used to model and predict outcomes for such data are similar to the regression models we covered in the previous chapter. Moreover, sometimes we might want to convert a regression problem into a classification problem: for instance, rather than predicting customer spending patterns in a month, we might be more interested in whether it is above a certain threshold that is meaningful from a business perspective, and assign values in our training data as 0 (below the threshold) and 1 (above) depending upon this cutoff. In some scenarios, this might increase the noise in our classification: imagine if many customers' personal expenditures were right near the threshold we set for this model, making it very hard to learn an accurate model. In other cases, making the outcome discrete will help us hone in on the question we are interested in answering. Imagine the customer expenditure data is well separated above and below our threshold, but that there is wide variation in values above the cutoff. In this scenario, a regression model would try to minimize overall error in the model by fitting the trends in larger data points that disproportionately influence the total value of the error, rather than achieving our actual goal of identifying high- and low- spending customers.

In addition to these considerations, some data is inherently not modeled effectively by regression analyses. For instance, consider the scenario in which we are trying to predict which ad out of a set of five a customer is most likely to click. We could encode these ads with the numerical values ranging from 1 to 5, but they do not have a natural ordering that would make sense in a regression problem – 2 is not greater than 1, it is simply a label denoting which of the five categories an ad belongs to. In this scenario, it will make more sense to encode the labels of the dataset as a vector of length 5 and place a 1 in the column corresponding to the ad, which will make all labels equivalent from the perspective of the algorithm.

With these points in mind, in the following exercises, we will cover:

- Encoding data responses as categorical outcomes
- Building classification models with both balanced and skewed data
- Evaluating the accuracy of classification models
- Assessing the benefits and shortcomings of different classification methods

Logistic regression

We will start our exploration of classifier algorithms with one of the most commonly used classification models: logistic regression. Logistic regression is similar to the linear regression method discussed in *Chapter 4, Connecting the Dots with Models – Regression Methods*, with the major difference being that instead of directly computing a linear combination of the inputs, it compresses the output of a linear model through a function that constrains outputs to be in the range [0,1]. As we will see, this is in fact a kind of "generalized linear model that we discussed in the last *Chapter 4, Connecting the Dots with Models – Regression Methods*, recall that in linear regression, the predicted output is given by:

$$Y = X\beta^T$$

where Y is the response variable for all n members of a dataset, X is an n by m matrix of m features for each of the n rows of data, and βT is a column vector of m coefficients (Recall that the T operator represents the transpose of a vector or matrix. Here we transpose the coefficients so they are of dimension mx1, so that we can form a product with the matrix X with is nxm), which gives the change in the response expected for a 1-unit change in a particular feature. Thus, taking the dot product of X and β (multiplying each coefficient by its corresponding feature and summing over the features) gives the predicted response. In logistic regression, we begin instead with the formula:

$$Y = logistic\left(X\beta^T\right)$$

where the `logistic` function is:

$$logistic\left(X\beta^{T}\right) = logistic\left(z\right) = \frac{1}{1+e^{(-z)}}$$

You can see the behavior of the logistic function by plotting using the following code in a notebook session:

```
>>> %matplotlib inline
... import pandas as pd
... import matplotlib.pyplot as plt
... import numpy as np
... plt.style.use('ggplot')
>>> input = np.arange(-10,10,1)
>>> output = 1/(1+np.exp(-input))
>>> pd.DataFrame({"input":input,"output":output}).
plot(x='input',y='output')
```

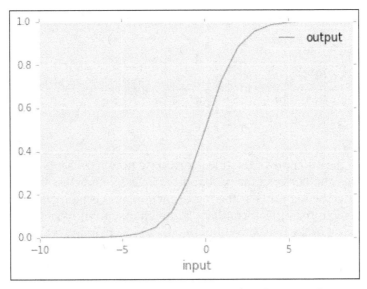

Figure 1: The Output of the Logistic Function for a Continuous Input

As you can see in Figure 1, the logistic function takes the output of the linear regression and transforms it using a sigmoid (an S-shaped function): as the linear regression value becomes larger, the exponential term tends toward 0, making the output 1. Conversely, as the linear regression value becomes negative, the exponential term becomes very large, and the output becomes 0.

How can we interpret the coefficients in this model, given that it is no longer modeling a simple linear trend? Because of the logistic transform, the coefficients no longer represent an expected increase in response per 1-unit increase in the predictor. To develop a similar interpretation, we start with the observation that the logistic regression equation represents the probability of a given observation, x, being a member of class 1 (assuming the response variable for the data falls into two classes — see the following for a discussion of cases where the number of classes is > 2). We could also write a similar equation to represent the probability of a given observation being class 0, which is given by:

$$Y = 1 - logistic(z) = 1 - \frac{1}{1+e^{(-z)}} = \frac{1+e^{(-z)}}{1+e^{(-z)}} - \frac{1}{1+e^{(-z)}} = \frac{e^{(-z)}}{1+e^{(-z)}}$$

Now, we can take the natural logarithm of these two probabilities get finally:

$$\log\left(\frac{P(Y=1)}{1-P(Y=1)}\right) = \log\left(\frac{\frac{1}{1+e^{(-z)}}}{\frac{e^{(-z)}}{1+e^{(-z)}}}\right) = \log(1) - \log(e^{(-z)}) = X\beta^T$$

In other words, the outcome of the linear response now represents the natural logarithm of the ratio between the probability of class 1 and class 0. This quantity is also referred to as the log-odds or the logit function, and is equivalent to the inverse of the logistic function. In this formula, a 1-unit change in the coefficient β will lead to a 1-unit increase in the log-odds, allowing us a way to interpret the coefficients in this model.

You may recall from *Chapter 4, Connecting the Dots with Models – Regression Methods*, that in **Generalized Linear Models (GLMs)**, link function transforms the linear response to a nonlinear range. In logistic regression, the logit function is the link function. While a full discussion of the various types of GLMs is outside the scope of this book, we refer the interested reader to more comprehensive treatments of this topic (Madsen, Henrik, and Poul Thyregod. *Introduction to general and generalized linear models*. CRC Press, 2010; Madsen, Henrik, and Poul Thyregod. Introduction to general and generalized linear models. CRC Press, 2010: Hardin, James William, Joseph M. Hilbe, and Joseph Hilbe. Generalized linear models and extensions. Stata press, 2007.).

If you have been reading carefully, you may realize that we have contradicted ourselves in the discussion above. On the one hand, we want to fit data in which the only allowable outcome is either a 0 or a 1. One the other hand, our logistic function (and the log-odds) can take a value between 0 and 1, continuously. Thus, to correctly apply this model, we will need to choose a threshold between 0 and 1 to classify the outputs of the regression: if a value is above this threshold, we consider the observation as class 1, otherwise 0. The simplest threshold to choose would be half, and indeed for balanced dataset with an equal number of positive and negative examples, this is a reasonable choice. However, in many cases that we encounter in the real world (such as ad clicks or subscriptions), the number of positive outcomes is much fewer than the negatives. If we optimize a logistic regression model using such an imbalanced dataset, the optimal parameters will identify few observations as positive. Thus, using half as a cutoff will inaccurately classify many negatives as class 1 (positive) and result in a high false positive rate.

We have a few options to address this problem of imbalanced classes in our data. The first is to simply tune the threshold for the logistic function to consider the outcome as 1, which we can do visually using the **receiver operator characteristic (ROC)** curve, described in more detail in the following exercises. We could also rebalance our training data such that half represents a reasonable value, by selecting an equal number of positive and negative examples. In case we were worried about making a biased choice among the many negative examples, we could repeat this process many times and average the results — this process is known as Bagging and was described in more detail in *Chapter 4, Connecting the Dots with Models – Regression Methods*, in the context of Random Forest regression models. Finally, we could simply penalize errors on the few positive examples by assigning a weight to them in the error function that is greater than the more numerous negative examples. More details on reweighting appear as follows.

Multiclass logistic classifiers: multinomial regression

While we have dealt thus far with the simple of example of a two-class problem , we could imagine scenarios in which there are multiple classes: for example, predicting which of a set of items a customer will select in an online store. For these sorts of problems, we can imagine extending the logistic regression to κ classes, where $K > 2$. Recall that taking e to the power of the logit function gives:

$$e^{logit(z)} = \frac{logisitic(z)}{1 - logisitic(z)} = \frac{\frac{1}{1 + e^{(-z)}}}{\frac{e^{(-z)}}{1 + e^{(-z)}}} = \frac{1}{e^{(-z)}} = e^{(z)} = e^{\left(X\beta^T\right)}$$

In a two-class problem, this value compares the ratio of the probability that $Y=1$ to all other values, with the only other value being 0. We could imagine running instead a series of logistic regression models for K classes, where `e(Logit(x))` gives the ratio of the probability of $Y = class\ k$ to any of other class. We would then up with a series of K expressions for `e(xβ)` with different regression coefficients. Because we want to constrain the outcome to be in the range 0 to -1, we can divide the output of any of the K models by the sum of all K models using the formula:

$$P\left(y_i = k\right) = \frac{e^{\left(x_i\beta_k^T\right)}}{\sum_{j=1}^{K} e^{\left(x_i\beta_j^T\right)}}$$

This equation also known as the `softmax` function. It is used extensively in neural network models (which we will cover in *Chapter 7, Learning from the Bottom Up – Deep Networks and Unsupervised Features*). It has the nice property that even for extreme values of `e(xβ)` for a given class k, the overall value of the function cannot go beyond 1. Thus, we can keep outliers in the dataset while limiting their influence on the overall accuracy of the model (since otherwise they would tend to dominate the overall value of an error function, such as the squared error we used in linear regression in *Chapter 4, Connecting the Dots with Models – Regression Methods*).

To keep the current presentation less complex, we will examine only a 2-class problem in the following exercises. However, keep in mind that as with logistic regression, the other methods discussed in the following can be extended to work with multiple classes as well. Additionally, we will demonstrate a full multiclass problem in *Chapter 7*, *Learning from the Bottom Up – Deep Networks and Unsupervised Features* using neural networks.

Now that we have covered what logistic regression is and the problem it is designed to solve, let us prepare a dataset for use with this and other classification methods. In addition to working through a practical example of fitting and interpreting a logistic regression model, we will use this a starting point to examine other classification algorithms.

Formatting a dataset for classification problems

In this example, we will use a census dataset with rows representing the characteristic of an adult US citizen (Kohavi, Ron. *Scaling Up the Accuracy of Naive-Bayes Classifiers: A Decision-Tree Hybrid*. KDD. Vol. 96. 1996). The objective is to predict whether an individual's income is above or below the average income of $55,000 a year. Let us start by loading the dataset into a pandas data frame and examining the first few rows using the following commands:

```
>>> census = pd.read_csv('census.data',header=None)
>>> census.head()
```

```
census = pd.read_csv('census.data',header=None)

census.head()
```

	0	1	2	3	4	5	6	7	8	9	10	11	12	13	14
0	39	State-gov	77516	Bachelors	13	Never-married	Adm-clerical	Not-in-family	White	Male	2174	0	40	United-States	<=!
1	50	Self-emp-not-inc	83311	Bachelors	13	Married-civ-spouse	Exec-managerial	Husband	White	Male	0	0	13	United-States	<=!
2	38	Private	215646	HS-grad	9	Divorced	Handlers-cleaners	Not-in-family	White	Male	0	0	40	United-States	<=!
3	53	Private	234721	11th	7	Married-civ-spouse	Handlers-cleaners	Husband	Black	Male	0	0	40	United-States	<=!
4	28	Private	338409	Bachelors	13	Married-civ-spouse	Prof-specialty	Wife	Black	Female	0	0	40	Cuba	<=!

Why did we use the argument (header = None) to load the data? Unlike some of the other datasets we have examined in previous chapters, the column names for the census data are contained in a separate file. These feature names will be helpful in interpreting the results, so let us parse them from the dataset description file:

```
>>> headers_file = open('census.headers')
>>> headers = []
>>> for line in headers_file:
>>>     if len(line.split(':'))>1: # colon indicates line is a column
description
>>>         headers.append(line.split(':')[0]) # the column name precedes
the colon
>>> headers = headers[15:] # the filter in the if (...) statement above is
not 100 percent accurate, need to remove first 15 elements
>>> headers.append('income') # add label for the response variable in the
last column
>>> census.columns = headers # set the column names in the dataframe to
be extracted names
```

Now that we have the column names appended to the dataset, we can see that the response variable, income, needs to be re-encoded. In the input data, it is coded as a string, but since scikit-learn is unable to take a string as an input, we need to convert it into a 0 or 1 label using the following code:

```
>>> census.income = census.income.map( lambda x: 0 if x==' <=50K' else 1)
```

Here, we have used a lambda expression to apply an anonymous function (a function without a name defined in the rest of the program) to the data. The conditional expression within the map (...) call takes x as an input and returns either 0 or 1. We could just as easily have formally defined such as function, but especially for expressions we do not intend to reuse, lambda expressions provide an easy way to specify such transformations without crowding our code with a lot of functions that do not have general utility.

Let us take a moment and look at the distribution of the different income classes by plotting a histogram with income as the value on the vertical axis:

```
>>> census.plot(kind='hist', y='income')
```

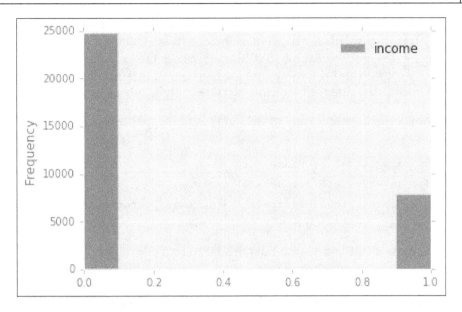

Notice that observations with the label 1 are about 50 percent less prevalent than those with a label of 0. As we discussed previously, this is a situation in which a simple threshold of half in evaluating the class probabilities will lead to an inaccurate model, and we should keep this data skew in mind as we evaluate the performance later.

In addition to our outcome variable, many of the features in this dataset are also categorical: we will need to re-encode them as well before fitting our model. We can do so in two steps: first, let us find the number of unique elements in each of these columns and map them to integer values using a dictionary. To begin, we check whether each column in the data frame is categorical (dtype equal to **object**), and, if so, we add its index into the list of columns we want to convert:

```
>>> categorical_features = [e for e,t in enumerate(census.dtypes) if
t=='object' ]
```

Now that we have the column numbers we want to convert, we need to make a mapping of each column from a string to a label from *1* to *k*, where *k* is the number of categories:

```
>>> categorical_dicts = []
>>> for c in categorical_features:
>>>     categorical_dicts.append(dict( (i,e) for (e,i) in
enumerate(census[headers[c]].unique()) ))
```

Notice that we first extract the unique elements of each column and then use the enumerate function on this list of unique elements to generate the labels we need. By converting this indexed list into a dictionary where the keys are the unique elements of a column and the values are the labels, we have exactly the mapping we need to re-encode the categorical string variables in this data as integers.

Now we can create a second copy of the data using the mapping dictionary we generated above:

```
>>> census_categorical = census
>>> for e,c in enumerate(categorical_features):
>>>     census_categorical[headers[c]] = \ census_categorical[headers[c]].\
map(categorical_dicts[e].get)
```

Now, we can use scikit-learn's one-hot encoder to transform these integer values into a series of columns, of which only one is set to 1, representing which of the k classes this row belongs to. To use the one-hot encoder, we also need to know how many categories each of the columns has, which we can do with the following command by storing the size of each mapping dictionary:

```
>>> n_values = [len(d) for d in categorical_dicts]
```

We then apply the one-hot encoder:

```
>>> from sklearn.preprocessing import OneHotEncoder
>>> census_categorical_one_hot = OneHotEncoder(categorical_
features=categorical_features, n_values=n_values).fit_transform(census_
categorical[headers[:-1]])
```

From here we have the data in the right format to fit our logistic regression. As with our examples in *Chapter 4, Connecting the Dots with Models – Regression Methods*, we need to split our data into training and test sets, specifying the fraction of data in the test set (*0.4*). We also set the random number generator seed to 0 so that we can replicate the analysis later by generating the same random set of numbers:

```
>>> from scipy import sparse
>>> from sklearn import cross_validation
>>> census_features_train, census_features_test, census_income_train,
census_income_test = \
>>> cross_validation.train_test_split(census_categorical_one_hot, \
>>> census_categorical['income'], test_size=0.4, random_state=0)
```

Now that we have prepared training and test data, we can fit a logistic regression model to the dataset. How can we find the optimal parameters (coefficients) of this model? We will examine two options.

The first approach, known as **stochastic gradient descent (SGD)**, calculates the change in the error function at a given data point and adjusts the parameters to account for this error. For an individual data point, this will result in a poor fit, but if we repeat this process over the whole training set several times, the coefficients will converge to the desired values. The term **stochastic** in this method's name refers to the fact that this optimization is achieved by following the gradient (first derivative) of the loss function with respect to a given data point in a random order over the dataset. Stochastic methods such as this one often scale well to large datasets because they allow us to only examine the data individually or in small batches rather than utilizing the whole dataset at once, allowing us to parallelize the learning procedure or at least not use all the memory on our machine to process large volumes of data.

In contrast, the optimization methods implemented by default for the logistic regression function in scikit-learn are known as **second-order methods**. SGD, because it adjusts the model parameter values using the first derivative of the error function, is known as a first-order method. Second-order methods can be beneficial in cases where the first derivative is changing very slowly, as we will see in the following, and to find the optimal value in cases where the error function follows complex patterns.

Let us look at each of these methods in more detail.

Learning pointwise updates with stochastic gradient descent

How do we find the optimal parameters for our logistic regression model using stochastic updates? Recall that we are trying to optimize the probabilities:

$$P\left(y_i = 1\right) = \frac{1}{1 + e^{(-z)}} = F\left(z_i\right)$$

$$P\left(y_i = 0\right) = \frac{e^{(-z)}}{1 + e^{(-z)}} = 1 - F\left(z_i\right)$$

f we want to optimize the probability of each individual point in our dataset, we want to maximize the value of the equation, known as the Likelihood as it scores the probability of given point being class 1 (or 0) based on the model;

$$L\left(y_i\right) = \left(F\left(z_i\right)\right)^{y_i} \left(1 - F\left(z_i\right)\right)^{1-y_i}$$

You can see that if the real label `yi` is `1`, and the model gives high probability of `1`, then we maximize the value of `F(zi)` (since the exponent of the second term is `0`, making it `1`, while the first term in the product is simply the value of `F(zi)`). Conversely, if the real label of `yi` is `0`, then we want the model to maximize the value of `(1-F(zi))`, which is the probability of class `0` under the model.

Thus, each point will contribute to the likelihood by the probability of its real class. It is usually easier to work with sums than products, so we can take the logarithm of the likelihood equation and sum over all elements in the data set using:

$$L(Y) = \sum_{i=1}^{n} \left(y_i \log\left(F(z_i)\right) + (1 - y_i) \log\left(1 - F(z_i)\right) \right)$$

To find the optimal value of the parameters, we just take the first partial derivative with respect to the parameters of this equation (the regression coefficients) and solve for the value of β that maximizes the likelihood equation by setting the derivative equal to 0 and finding the value of β as illustrated below:

$$\frac{\partial}{\partial \beta} \log\left(L(y_i)\right) = \frac{\partial}{\partial \beta} \left(y_i \log\left(F(z_i)\right) + (1 - y_i) \log\left(1 - F(z_i)\right) \right) = 0$$

$$= \frac{y_i}{F(z_i)} F'(z_i) + \frac{(1 - y_i)}{(1 - F(z_i))} F'(z_i)$$

$$= \left(\frac{y_i}{F(z_i)} - \frac{(1 - y_i)}{(1 - F(z_i))} \right) F'(z_i)$$

$$= \left(\frac{y_i}{F(z_i)} - \frac{(1 - y_i)}{(1 - F(z_i))} \right) \left(\frac{1}{1 + e^{(-x_i \beta^T)}} \right) \left(\frac{e^{(-x_i \beta^T)}}{1 + e^{(-x_i \beta^T)}} \right) (-x_i)$$

$$= \left(\frac{y_i}{\frac{1}{1 + e^{(-x_i \beta^T)}}} - \frac{(1 - y_i)}{\frac{e^{(-x_i \beta^T)}}{1 + e^{(-x_i \beta^T)}}} \right) \left(\frac{1}{1 + e^{(-x_i \beta^T)}} \right) \left(\frac{e^{(-x_i \beta^T)}}{1 + e^{(-x_i \beta^T)}} \right) (-x_i)$$

$$= \left(y_i \left(\frac{e^{(-x_i \beta^T)}}{1 + e^{(-x_i \beta^T)}} \right) - (1 - y_i) \left(\frac{1}{1 + e^{(-x_i \beta^T)}} \right) \right) (-x_i)$$

$$= \left(\frac{y_i \left(1 + e^{(-x_i \beta^T)} \right)}{1 + e^{(-x_i \beta^T)}} - \left(\frac{1}{1 + e^{(-x_i \beta^T)}} \right) \right) (-x_i)$$

$$= -(y_i - F(z_i)) x_i$$

This is the direction we want to update the coefficients β in order to move it closer to the optimum. Thus, for each data point, we can make an update of the following form:

$$\beta_t = \beta_{t-1} + \alpha\left(y_i - F\left(z_i\right)\right)x_i$$

where α is the learning rate (which we use to control the magnitude by which the coefficients can change in each step – usually a smaller learning rate will prevent large changes in value and converge to a better model, but will take longer), t is the current optimization step, and *t-1* is the previous step. Recall that in *Chapter 4, Connecting the Dots with Models – Regression Methods* we discussed the concept of regularization, in which we can use a penalty term λ to control the magnitude of our coefficients. We can do the same here: if the regularization term in our likelihood is given by (to penalize the squared sum of the coefficients, which is the *L2* norm from Ridge Regression in *Chapter 4, Connecting the Dots with Models – Regression Methods*):

$$\frac{1}{2}\lambda\beta\beta^T$$

Then once we take the first derivate, we have:

$$\lambda\beta$$

And the final update equation becomes:

$$\beta_t = \beta_{t-1} + \alpha\left(y_i - F\left(z_i\right)\right)x_i - \lambda\beta_{t-1}$$

We can see, this regularization penalty has the effect of shrinking the amount by which we modify the coefficients β at any given step.

As we mentioned previously, stochastic updates are especially efficient for large datasets as we only have to examine each data point one at a time. One downside of this approach is that we need to run the optimization long enough to make sure the parameters converge. For example, we could monitor the change in the coefficient values as we take the derivative with respect to each data point, and stop when the values cease changing. Depending upon the dataset, this could occur quickly or take a long time. A second downside is that following the gradient of the error function along the first derivative will not always lead to the fastest solution. Second-order methods allow us to overcome some of these deficits.

Jointly optimizing all parameters with second-order methods

In the case of logistic regression, our objective function is convex (see aside), meaning that whichever optimization method we choose should be able to converge to the global optimum. However, we could imagine other scenarios: for example, the surface of the likelihood equation plotted as a function of the inputs could vary slowly in a long ravine toward its global optimum. In such a case, we would like to find the direction to move the coefficients that is the optimal tradeoff between the rate of change and the **rate of the rate of change**, represented by the second derivative of the likelihood. Finding this tradeoff allows the optimization routine to traverse slowly varying regions quickly. This kind of strategy is represented by the class of so-called **Newton methods**, which minimizes equations of the following form:

$$f\left(x^*\right) = f\left(x_t + \Delta x\right)$$

Where f(x*) is the objective function we are trying to minimize, such as the logistic regression error, and x are the values (such as the model coefficients) that do minimize regression likelihood, x* are the inputs which optimize the value of the function (such as the optimal coefficients β), and xt are the value of these parameters at the current step of the optimization (there is admittedly some abuse of notation here: in the rest of the chapter, *x* are the input rows, where here we use *x* to represent a parameter value in a model). The name **Newton method** is due to the father of physics, Isaac Newton, who described an early version of this procedure (Ypma, Tjalling J. *Historical development of the Newton-Raphson method*. SIAM review 37.4 (1995): 531-551). The minimization involves finding the direction we should move the parameters at the current stage, xt, in order to find the minimal value of f. We can use a Taylor Expansion from Calculus to approximate the value of the preceding function:

$$f\left(x^*\right) = f\left(x_t\right) + f'\left(x_t\right)\Delta x + \frac{1}{2}f''\left(x_t\right)\left(\Delta x\right)^2$$

We want to find the value of Δx which maximizes the function, since this is the direction we wish to move the parameters, just as in gradient descent. We can obtain this optimal direction by solving for the point where the gradient of the function becomes 0 with respect to Δx, to give:

$$\frac{df(x^*)}{d\Delta x} = f'(x) + 2\left(\frac{1}{2}\right)f''(x)(\Delta x) = 0$$
$$-f'(x) = f''(x)(\Delta x)$$
$$\Delta x = -\frac{f'(x)}{f''(x)}$$

Thus, when f'(x) is changing slowly (small f"(x)), we take larger steps to change the value of the parameters, and vice versa.

One of the most commonly used second order methods for logistic regression is **iteratively reweighted least squares (IRLS)**. To show how it works let us translate the equations above to our logistic regression model. We already known f'(x), since this is just our formula from above used for stochastic gradient descent:

$$\left(y_i - F(z_i)\right)x_i - \lambda\beta_t$$

What about the second derivative of the likelihood? We can solve for it as well

$$\frac{\partial L(y_i)}{\partial\beta\partial\beta^T} = \frac{\partial}{\partial\beta}\left(\frac{\partial L(y_i)}{\beta^T}\right)$$
$$= \frac{\partial}{\partial\beta}\left(-\left(y_i - F(z_i)\right)x_i - \lambda\beta\right)$$
$$= \frac{\partial F(z_i)x_i}{\partial\beta} - \lambda = -\frac{\partial}{\partial\beta}\left(\frac{1}{1+e^{\left(-x_i\beta^T\right)}}\right)x_i - \lambda$$
$$= \left(\frac{1}{1+e^{\left(-x_i\beta^T\right)}}\right)\left(\frac{e^{\left(-x_i\beta^T\right)}}{1+e^{\left(-x_i\beta^T\right)}}\right)(x_i)(x_i)^T - \lambda$$
$$= (x_i)F(z_i)\left(1-F(z_i)\right)(x_i)^T - \lambda$$

Here we are still writing this equation as a solution for a single data point. In second order methods we are not usually going to use stochastic updates, so we need to apply the formula to all data points. For the gradient (first derivative), this gives the sum:

$$-\sum_{i=1}^{n} x_i \left(y_i - F\left(z_i\right)\right) - \lambda\beta$$

For second derivative, we can express the result as a matrix. The matrix of pairwise second derivatives is known also known as the Hessian matrix.

$$= \left(X\right)^T F\left(Z\right)\left(1 - F\left(Z\right)\right)\left(X\right) - I\lambda$$
$$= X^T A X - I\lambda$$

Where I is the identity matrix (a matrix with 1 on the diagonal and 0 elsewhere), and A contains the second derivative evaluated for each pair of points i and j. Thus, if we use these expressions to make a Newton update, we have:

$$\beta_t = \beta_{t-1} + \left(X^T A X - I\lambda\right)^{-1} \left(\sum_{i=1}^{n} x_i \left(y_i - F\left(z_i\right)\right) - \lambda\beta_t \right)$$

Because the second derivative appears in the denominator, we use a matrix inverse (given by the *-1* exponent) to perform this operation. If you look closely at the denominator, we have the product XT X weighted by the elements of A, and in the numerator we have X(Y-F(X)). This resembles the equation for ordinary linear regression that we saw in *Chapter 4, Connecting the Dots with Models – Regression Methods*! In essence, this update is performing a stepwise linear regression weighted at each pass by A (whose values change as we update the coefficients), thus giving the method its name. One of the shortcomings of IRLS is that we need to repeatedly invert a Hessian matrix that will become quite large as the number of parameters and data points grows. Thus, we might try to find ways to approximate this matrix instead of explicitly calculating it. One method commonly used for this purpose is the Limited Memory Broyden–Fletcher–Goldfarb–Shanno (L-BFGS) algorithm (Liu, Dong C., and Jorge Nocedal. *On the limited memory BFGS method for large scale optimization*. Mathematical programming 45.1-3 (1989): 503-528), which uses the last k updates of the algorithm to calculate an approximation of the Hessian matrix instead of explicitly solving for it in each stage.

In both SGD and Newton methods, we have theoretical confidence that both methods will eventually converge to the correct (globally optimal) parameter values due to a property of the likelihood function known as convexity. Mathematically, a convex function F fulfills the condition:

$$F\left(\alpha x_1 + (1-\alpha)x_2\right) \le \alpha F\left(x_1\right) + (1-\alpha)F\left(x_2\right)$$

Conceptually, this means that for two points x1 and x2, the value of F for points between them (the left-hand side of the equation) is less than or equal to the straight line between the points (the right-hand side of the equation, which gives a linear combination of the function value at the two points). Thus, a convex function will have a global minimum between the points x1 or x2. Graphically, you can see this by plotting the following in a python notebook

```
>>> input = np.arange(10)-5
>>> parabola = [a*a for a in input]
>>> line = [-1*a for a in input-10]
>>> plt.plot(input,parabola)
>>> plt.plot(input,line,color='blue')
```

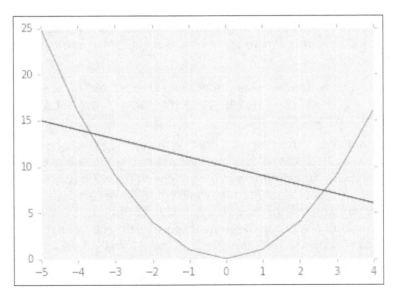

The parabola is a convex function because the values between x1 and x2 (the two points where the blue line intersects with the parabola) are always below the blue line representing $\alpha(F(x1))+(1-\alpha)\ (F(x2))$. As you can see, the parabola also has a global minimum between these two points.

When we are dealing with matrices such as the Hessian referenced previously, this condition is fulfilled by each element of the matrix being ≥ 0, a property known as positive semidefinite, meaning any vector multiplied by this matrix on either side (xTHx) yields a value ≥ 0. This means the function has a global minimum, and if our solution converges to a set of coefficients, we can be guaranteed that they represent the best parameters for the model, not a local minimum.

We noted previously that we could potentially offset imbalanced distribution of classes in our data by reweighting individual points during training. In the formulas for either SGD or IRLS, we could apply a weight wi for each data point, increasing or decreasing its relative contribution to the value of the likelihood and the updates made during each iteration of the optimization algorithm.

Now that we have described how to obtain the optimal parameters of the logistic regression model, let us return to our example and apply these methods to our data.

Fitting the model

We can use either the SGD or second-order methods to fit the logistic regression model to our data. Let us compare the results using SGD; we fit the model using the following command:

```
>>> log_model_sgd = linear_model.SGDClassifier(alpha=10,loss='log',
penalty='l2',n_iter=1000, fit_intercept=False).fit(census_features_
train,census_income_train)
```

Where the parameter log for loss specifies that this is a logistic regression that we are training, and n_iter specifies the number of times we iterate over the training data to perform SGD, alpha represents the weight on the regularization term, and we specify that we do not want to fit the intercept to make comparison to other methods more straightforward (since the method of fitting the intercept could differ between optimizers). The penalty argument specifies the regularization penalty, which we saw in *Chapter 4, Connecting the Dots with Models – Regression Methods*, already for ridge regression. As l2 is the only penalty we can use with second-order methods, we choose l2 here as well to allow comparison between the methods. We can examine the resulting model coefficients by referencing the coeff_ property of the model object:

```
>>> log_model_sgd.coef_
```

Compare these coefficients to the second-order fit we obtain using the following command:

```
>>> log_model_newton = linear_model.LogisticRegression(penalty='l2',solve
r='lbfgs', fit_intercept=False).fit(census_features_train,census_income_
train
```

Like the SGD model, we remove the intercept fit to allow the most direct comparison of the coefficients produced by the two methods., We find that the coefficients are not identical, with the output of the SGD model containing several larger coefficients. Thus, we see in practice that even with similar models and a convex objective function, different optimization methods can give different parameter results. However, we can see that the results are highly correlated based on a pairwise scatterplot of the coefficients:

```
>>> plt.scatter(log_model_newton.coef_,log_model_sgd.coef_)
>>> plt.xlim(-0.08,0.08)
>>> plt.ylim(-0.08,0.08)
>>> plt.xlabel('Newton Coefficent')
>>> plt.ylabel('SGD Coefficient')
```

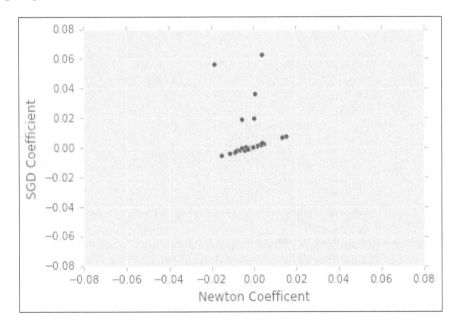

The fact that the SGD model has larger coefficients gives us a hint as to what might be causing the difference: perhaps SGD is more sensitive to differences in scale between features? Let us evaluate this hypothesis by using the **StandardScaler** introduced in *Chapter 3, Finding Patterns in the Noise – Clustering and Unsupervised Learning* in the context of K-means clustering to normalize the features before running the SGD model using the following commands:

```
>>> from sklearn.preprocessing import StandardScaler
>>> census_features_train_sc= StandardScaler().fit_transform(X=census_
features_train.todense())
```

Recall that we need to turn the features matrix to a dense format since StandardScaler does not accept a sparse matrix as input. Now, if we retrain the SGD using the same arguments and plot the result versus the Newton method, we find the coefficients are much closer:

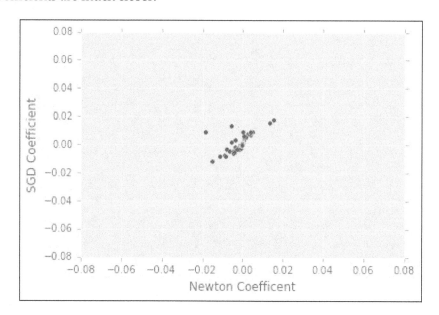

This example should underscore the fact that the optimizer is sometimes as important as the actual algorithm, and may determine what steps we should take in data normalization.

Evaluating classification models

Now that we have fit a classification model, we can examine the accuracy on the test set. One common tool for performing this kind of analysis is the **Receiver Operator Characteristic (ROC)** curve. To draw an ROC curve, we select a particular cutoff for the classifier (here, a value between 0 and 1 above which we consider a data point to be classified as a positive, or 1) and ask what fraction of 1s are correctly classified by this cutoff (true positive rate) and, concurrently, what fraction of negatives are incorrectly predicted to be positive (false positive rate) based on this threshold. Mathematically, this is represented by choosing a threshold and computing four values:

```
TP = true positives = # of class 1 points above the threshold

FP = false positives = # of class 0 points above the threshold

TN = true negatives = # of class 0 points below the threshold

FN = false negatives = # of class 1 points below the threshold
```

The **true positive rate (TPR)** plotted by the ROC is then $TP/(TP+FN)$, while the **false positive rate (FPR)** is $FP/(FP+TN)$.

If both rates are equal, then this is no better than random. In other words, at whatever cutoff we choose, a prediction of class 1 by the model is equally likely regardless if the point is actually positive or negative. Thus, a diagonal line from the lower left to the upper right hand represent the performance of a classifier made through randomly choosing labels for data points, since the true positive and false positive rates are always equal. Conversely, if the classifier exhibits better than random performance, the true positive rate rises much faster as correctly classified points are enriched above the threshold. Integrating the **area under the curve (AUC)** of the ROC curve, which has a maximum of 1, is a common way to report the accuracy of classifier methods. To find the best threshold to use for classification, we find the point on this curve where the ratio between true positive and false positive rates is maximal.

In our example, this is important because 1 is less frequent than 0. As we mentioned in the beginning of this chapter when we were examining the data set, this can cause problems in training a classification model. While the naïve choice would be to consider events with predicted probability above 0.5 as 1, in practice we find that due to this dataset imbalance, a lower threshold is optimal as the solution is biased toward the zeros. This effect can become even more extreme in highly skewed data: consider an example where only 1 in 1,000 points have label 1. We could have an excellent classifier that predicts that every data point is 0: it is 99.9% percent accurate! However, it would not be very useful in identifying rare events. There are a few ways we could counteract this bias besides adjusting the threshold in the AUC.

One way would be to rebalance the model by constructing a training set that is 50 percent 1s and 50 percent 0s. We can then evaluate the performance on the unbalanced test dataset. If the imbalance is very large, our rebalanced training set might contain only a small number of the possible variation in the 0s: thus, to generate a model representative of the entire dataset, we may want to construct many such datasets and average the results of the models generated from them. This approach is not dissimilar to the Bagging method used in constructing Random Forest models, as we saw in *Chapter 4, Connecting the Dots with Models – Regression Methods*.

Secondly, we can use our knowledge of the imbalance to change the contribution of each data point as we optimize the parameters. For example, in the SGD equations, we can penalize errors on 1s 1,000 times as much as errors on 0s. This weight will then correct the bias in the model.

Our interpretation of the AUC is also changed in very imbalanced datasets. While an overall AUC of 0.9 might be considered good, if the ratio between the TPR and FPR at a false positive rate of 0.001 (the fraction of data containing the rare class) is not > 1, it indicates we may have to search through a large amount of the head of the ranking to enrich the rare events. Thus, while the overall accuracy appears good, the accuracy in the range of data we most These scenarios are not uncommon in practice. For example, ad clicks are usually much less frequent than non-clicks, as are responses to sales inquiries. Visually, a classifier that is not well-fit to imbalanced data would be indicated by an ROC curve where the difference between TPR and FPR is greatest near the middle of the curve (~0.5). Conversely, in an ROC curve of a classifier that is appropriately adapted to rare events, most of the area is contained to the left hand side (rising sharply from a cutoff of 0 and leveling off to the right), representing enrichment of positives at high thresholds.

Note that false positive rate and false negative rate are just two examples of accuracy metrics we could compute. We may also be interested in knowing, above a given cutoff for model score, 1) how many of our positive examples are classified (recall) and what percentage of points above this threshold are actually positive 2) precision. These are calculated as:

Precision = TP/(TP+FP)

Recall = TP/(TP+FN)

In fact, recall is identical to the true positive rate. While the ROC curve allows us to evaluate whether the model generates true positive predictions at a greater rate than false positives, comparing precision versus recall gives a sense of how reliable and complete the predictions above a given score threshold are. We could have very high precision, but only be able to detect a minority of the overall positive examples. Conversely, we could have high recall at the cost of low precision as we incur false positives by lowering the score threshold to call positives in our model. The tradeoff between these can be application specific. For example, if the model is largely exploratory, such as a classifier used to generate potential sales leads for marketing, then we accept a fairly low precision since the value of each positive is quite high even if the true predictions are interspersed with noise. On the other hand, in a model for spam identification, we may want to err on the side of high precision, since the cost of incorrectly moving a valid business email to the user's trash folder may be higher than the occasional piece of unwanted mail that gets through the filter. Finally, we could also consider performance metrics that are appropriate even for imbalanced data, because they represent a tradeoff between the precision and recall for majority and minority classes. These include the F-measure:

$$F_1 = 2 \frac{(precision)(recall)}{(precision + recall)}$$

And Matthew's correlation coefficient (Matthews, Brian W. *Comparison of the predicted and observed secondary structure of T4 phage lysozyme*. Biochimica et Biophysica Acta (BBA)-Protein Structure 405.2 (1975): 442-451.):

$$MCC = \frac{TPxTN - FPxFN}{\sqrt{(TP + FP)(TP + FN)(TN + FP)(TN + FN)}}$$

Returning to our example, we have two choices in how we could compute the predictions from our model: either a class label (0 or 1) or a probability of a particular individual being class 1. For computing the ROC curve, we want the second choice, since this will allow us to evaluate the accuracy of the classifier over a range of probabilities used as a threshold for classification:

```
>>> train_prediction = log_model_newton.predict_proba(census_features_
train)
```

```
>>> test_prediction = log_model_newton.predict_proba(census_features_
test)
```

With this probability, we can we see visually that our model gives a subpar accuracy using the following code to plot the ROC curve for the training and test sets:

```
>>>   from sklearn import metrics
>>> fpr_train, tpr_train, thresholds_train = metrics.roc_curve(np.
array(census_income_train),\
   np.array(train_prediction[:,1]), pos_label=1)
>>> fpr_test, tpr_test, thresholds_test = metrics.roc_curve(np.
array(census_income_test),\
   np.array(test_prediction[:,1]), pos_label=1)
>>> plt.plot(fpr_train, tpr_train)
>>> plt.plot(fpr_test, tpr_test)
>>> plt.xlabel('False Positive Rate')
>>> plt.ylabel('True Positive Rate')
```

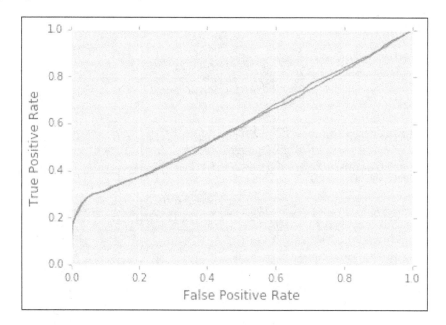

Numerically, we find that the AUC of the test and training set is little better than random (0.5), as both the commands:

```
>>> metrics.auc(fpr_train,tpr_train)
```

and

```
>>> metrics.auc(fpr_test,tpr_test)
```

give results of ~ 0.6.

If possible, we would like to improve the performance of our classified—how can we diagnose the problems with our existing logistic regression model and work toward a better prediction?

Strategies for improving classification models

Confronted with this less than desirable performance, we typically have a few options:

- Train with more data
- Regularize the model to reduce over-fitting
- Choose another algorithm

In our example with an under-performing logistic regression model, which option makes most sense?

Let us consider take the first option, that we simply need more data to improve performance. In some cases, we may not have enough data in our training set to represent the patterns we observe in the test set. If this were the case, we would expect to see our performance on the test set improve as we increase the size of the training set used to build the model. However, we do not always have the convenience of getting more data. In this example, we don't actually have more data to train with; even if is possible to collect more data in theory, in practice it may be too expensive to justify the cost, or we may need to make a decision before more data will be available.

What about over-fitting? In other words, perhaps our model is precisely tuned to the patterns in the training set, but does not generalize to the test set. Like the first option, we will observe better performance on the training set than the test set. However, the solution is not necessarily to add more data, but rather to prune features to make the model more general. In the preceding scenario, we see that the performance on both training and test is similar, so this does not seem like the most likely explanation.

Finally, we might try another algorithm. To do so, let us consider what the limitations of our current model are. For one, the logistic regression only incorporates single features: it has no way to represent interactions between them. For instance, it can only model the effect of marital status, not marital status conditional on education and age. It is perhaps not surprising that these factors probably in combination predict income, but not necessarily individually. It may help to look at the values of the coefficients, and to do so, we will need to map the original column headers to column names in our one-hot encoding, where each of the categorical features is now represented by several columns. In this format, the numerical columns are appended to the end of the data frame, so we need to add them last to the list of columns. The following code remaps the column headers using the mapping of category to one-hot position we calculated earlier:

```
>>> expanded_headers = []
>>> non_categorical_headers = []
>>> categorical_index = 0
>>> for e,h in enumerate(np.array(census.columns[:-1])):
...    if e in set(categorical_features):
...        unsorted_category = np.array([h+key for key in categorical_
dicts[categorical_index].keys()]) # appends the category label h to each
feature 'key'
...        category_indices = np.array(list(categorical_dicts[categorical_
index].values())) # gets the mapping from category label h to the
position in the one-hot array
...        expanded_headers+=list(unsorted_category[np.argsort(category_
indices)]) # resort the category values in the same order as they appear
in the one-hot encoding
...        categorical_index+=1 # increment to the next categorical feature
...    else:
...        non_categorical_headers+=[h]
... expanded_headers+=non_categorical_headers
```

We can check that the individual coefficient make sense: keep in mind that the sort function arranges items in ascending order, so to find the largest coefficients we sort by the negative value:

```
>>> expanded_headers[np.argsort(-1*log_model.coef_[0])]
array(['capital-gain', 'capital-loss', 'hours-per-week',
'age',         'education-num', 'marital-status Married-civ-spouse',
'relationship Husband', 'sex Male', 'occupation Exec-managerial',
'education Bachelors', 'occupation Prof-specialty',         'education
Masters', 'relationship Wife', 'education Prof-school',        'workclass
Self-emp-inc', 'education Doctorate',         'workclass Local-gov',
'workclass Federal-gov',        'workclass Self-emp-not-inc', 'race
White',         'occupation Tech-support', 'occupation Protective-serv',
'workclass State-gov', 'occupation Sales', …
```

Logically, the order appears to make sense, since we would expect age and education to be important predictors of income. However, we see that only *~1/3rd* of the features have a large influence on the model through the following plot:

```
>>> plt.bar(np.arange(108),np.sort(log_model_newton.coef_[0]))
```

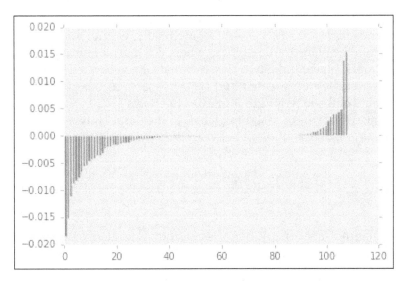

Thus, it looks like the model is only able to learn information from a subet of features. We could potentially try to generate interaction features by making combinatorial labels (for example, a binary flag representing married and maximum education level as Master's Degree) by taking the product of all features with each other. Generating potential nonlinear features in this way is known as polynomial expansion, since we are taking single coefficient terms and converting them into products that have squared, cubic, or higher power relationships. However, for the purposes of this example, will try some alternative algorithms.

Separating Nonlinear boundaries with Support vector machines

In our previous example of logistic regression, we assumed implicitly that every point in the training set might be useful in defining the boundary between the two classes we are trying to separate. In practice we may only need a small number of data points to define this boundary, with additional information simply adding noise to the classification. This concept, that classification might be improved by using only a small number of critical data points, is the key features of the **support vector machine (SVM)** model.

In its basic form, the SVM is similar to the linear models we have seen before, using the following equation:

$$F(X) = X\beta^T + b$$

where b is an intercept, and β is the vector of coefficients such as we have seen in regression models. We can see a simple rule that a point x is classified as class 1 if F(x) ≥ 1, and class -1 if F(x) ≤ -1. Geometrically, we can understand this as the distance from the plane to the point x, where β is a vector sitting orthogonal (at a right angle) to the plane. If the two classes are ideally separated, then the width between the two classes represented by $1/\|\beta\|$ is as large as possible; thus, in finding the optimal value of β, we would to minimize the norm $\|\beta\|$. At the same time, we want to minimize the error in assigning labels to the data. Thus, we can have a loss function that minimizes the tradeoff between these two objectives:

$$L(\beta, w, \alpha) = \frac{1}{2}\|B\|^2 - \sum_{i=1}^{n} \alpha_i \left(y_i \left(x_i \beta^T + b \right) - 1 \right)$$

where y is the correct label of x. When x is correctly classified, y(xβ+b) ≥ 1, and we overall subtract from the values of L. Conversely, when we incorrectly predict x.

Note that the | | here represent the Euclidean norm, or:

$$\|\beta\| = \sqrt{\beta_1^2 + \beta_2^2 + \ldots + \beta_m^2}$$

y(xβ+b) < 1, and we thus add to the value of L. If we want to minimize the value of L, we could find the optimal value of β and b by taking the derivative of this function and setting it to 0. Starting with β:

$$\frac{\partial L}{\partial \beta} = \beta - \sum_{i=1}^{n} \alpha_i y_i x_i = 0$$

$$\beta = \sum_{i=1}^{n} \alpha_i y_i x_i$$

Similarly, for b:

$$\frac{\partial L}{\partial b} = \sum_{i=1}^{n} \alpha_i y_i = 0$$

Plugging these back into the loss function equation we get:

$$L(\beta, w, \alpha) = \frac{1}{2} \sum_{i=1}^{n} \sum_{j=1}^{n} \alpha_i \alpha_j y_i y_j x_i x_j - \sum_{i=1}^{n} \alpha_i \left(y_i x_i \left(\sum_{i=1}^{n} \alpha_i y_i x \right) - 1 \right)$$

$$= \sum_{i=1}^{n} \alpha_i - \frac{1}{2} \sum_{i=1}^{n} \sum_{j=1}^{n} \alpha_i \alpha_j y_i y_j x_i x_j$$

Two things are important here. First, only some of the α need to be nonzero. The rest can be set to 0, meaning only a small number of points influence the choice of optimal model parameters. These points are the support vectors that give the algorithm its name, which lie along the boundary between the two classes. Note that in practice we would not use the above version of the error function, but rather a **soft-margin** formulation in which we use the **hinge loss**:

$$\max\left(0, 1 - y_i \left(x_i \beta + b_i\right)\right)$$

This means that we only penalize points if they are on the wrong side of the separating hyperplane, and then by the magnitude of their misclassification error. This allows the SVM to be applied even in cases where the data is not linearly separable by allowing the algorithm to make mistakes according to the hinge loss penalty. For full details please consult references (Cortes, Corinna, and Vladimir Vapnik. **Support-vector networks**. Machine learning 20.3 (1995): 273-297; Burges, Christopher JC. *A tutorial on support vector machines for pattern recognition*. Data mining and knowledge discovery 2.2 (1998): 121-167.).

Second, we now see that the solution depends on the inputs x only through the product of individual points. In fact, we could replace this product with any function `K(xi,xj)`, where `K` is a so-called **kernel function** representing the similarity between `xi` and `xj`. This can be particularly useful when trying to capture nonlinear relationships between data points. For example, consider data points along a parabola in two-dimensional space, where `x2` (the vertical axis) is the square of `x1` (the horizontal). Normally, we could not draw a straight line to separate points above and below the parabola. However, if we first mapped the points using the function `x1`, `sqrt(x2)`, we can now linearly separate them. We saw the effectiveness of this nonlinear mapping in *Chapter 3, Finding Patterns in the Noise – Clustering and Unsupervised Learning*, when we use the Gaussian Kernel to separate the nonlinear boundary between concentric circles using Spectral K-Means clustering.

Besides creating a linear decision boundary between data points that are not linearly separable in the input space, Kernel functions also allow us to calculate similarities between objects that have no vector representation, such as graphs (nodes and edges) or collections of words. The objects do not need to be the same length, either, as long as we can compute a similarity. These facts are due to a result known as Mercer's Theorem, which guarantees that Kernel functions which are >=0 for all pairs of inputs represent a valid inner product $< \varphi(x_i), \varphi(x_j) >$ between inputs x mapped into a linearly separable space using the mapping represented by φ (Hofmann, Thomas, Bernhard Schölkopf, and Alexander J. Smola. *Kernel methods in machine learning*. The annals of statistics (2008): 1171-1220). This mapping could be explicit, such as the square root function applied to the parabolic input in the example above. However, we do not actually need the mapping at all, since the kernel is guaranteed to represent the similarity between the mapped inputs. Indeed, the mapping could even be performed in an infinite-dimensional space that we can not explicitly represent, as is the case with the Gaussian kernel we will describe as follows.

Now that we have covered some of the intuition behind SVMs, let us see if it can improve the performance of our classification model by fitting an SVM to the data.

Fitting and SVM to the census data

For this example, we will try the default kernel function for the SVM model in scikit-learn, which is a Gaussian kernel, which you may recognize as the same equation used in a normal distribution function. We previously used the Gaussian Kernel in the context of Spectral Clustering in *Chapter 3, Finding Patterns in the Noise – Clustering and Unsupervised Learning*, as a reminder, the formula is:

$$K\left(x_i, x_j\right) = e^{\frac{-\left\|x_i - x_j\right\|^2}{2\gamma^2}}$$

In essence, this function translates the difference between two data points into the range 1 (when they are equal and the exponent becomes 0) and 0 (when the difference is very large and the exponent tends toward a very large negative number). The parameter γ represents the standard deviation, or bandwith, which controls how quickly the value of the function tends towards zero as the difference between the points increases. Small values of the bandwith will make the numerator a larger negative number, thus shrinking the kernel value to 0.

As we mentioned preceding, the Gaussian kernel represented mapping the inputs x into an infinite dimensional space. We can see this if we expand the value of the kernel function using an infinite series:

$$e^{\frac{-\|x_i-x_j\|^2}{2\gamma^2}} = e^{\frac{1}{2\gamma^2}(-x_i)^2(-x_j)^2} e^{2(x_ix_j)} = e^{\frac{1}{2\gamma^2}(-x_i)^2(-x_j)^2} \sum_{k=0}^{\infty} \frac{2^k x_i^k x_j^k}{k!}$$

Thus, the Gaussian kernel captures a similarity in an infinite dimensional features space.

We fit the SVM model to the training data using the following commands:

```
>>> from sklearn import svm
>>> svm_model = svm.SVC(probability=True,kernel='rbf').fit(census_
features_train.toarray(),census_income_train)
>>> train_prediction = svm_model.predict_proba(census_features_train.
toarray())
>>> test_prediction = svm_model.predict_proba(census_features_test.
toarray())
>>> fpr_train, tpr_train, thresholds_train = metrics.roc_curve(np.
array(census_income_train),\
   np.array(train_prediction[:,1]), pos_label=1)
>>> fpr_test, tpr_test, thresholds_test = metrics.roc_curve(np.
array(census_income_test),\
   np.array(test_prediction[:,1]), pos_label=1)
>>> plt.plot(fpr_train, tpr_train)
>>> plt.plot(fpr_test, tpr_test)
>>> plt.xlabel('False Positive Rate')
>>> plt.ylabel('True Positive Rate')
```

However, upon plotting the ROC curve for the results, we find that we have not improved very much over the logistic regression:

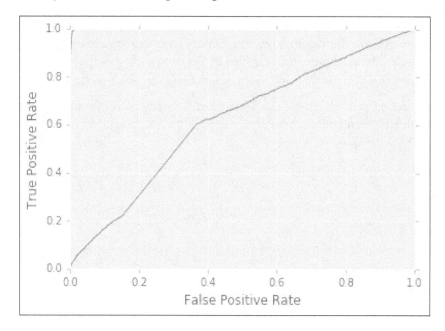

It may be difficult to see, but the red line in the upper left-hand corner of the image is the performance on the training set, while the blue line is the performance on the test set. Thus, we are in a situation such as we described previously, where the model almost perfectly predicts the training data but poorly generalizes to the test set.

In some sense, we were able to make progress because we used a nonlinear function to represent similarity within our data. However, the model now fits our data too well. If we wanted to experiment more with SVM models, we could tune a number of parameters: we could change kernel function, adjust the bandwidth of the Gaussian kernel (or the particular hyper parameters of whichever kernel function we chose), or tune the amount by which we penalize errors in classification. However, for our next step of algorithm optimization, we will instead switch gears and try to incorporate nonlinearity with many weak models instead of one overfit model, a concept known as boosting.

Boosting – combining small models to improve accuracy

In the previous examples, we have implicitly assumed that there is a single model that can describe all the patterns present in our data set. What if, instead, a different model were best suited for a pattern represented by a subset of data, and only by combining models representing many of these smaller patterns can we can get an accurate picture? This is the intuition behind boosting—we start with a weak individual model, determine which points it correctly classifies, and fit additional models to compensate for points missed by this first model. While each additional model is also relatively poor on its own, by successively adding these weak models that capture a certain subset of the data, we gradually arrive at an accurate prediction overall. Furthermore, because each of the models in this group is fit to only a subset of the data, we have to worry less about over-fitting. While the general idea of boosting can be applied to many models, let us look at an example using the decision trees we covered in *Chapter 4, Connecting the Dots with Models – Regression Methods*.

Gradient boosted decision trees

Recall that in *Chapter 4, Connecting the Dots with Models – Regression Methods*, we achieved greater predictive power in our regression task by averaging over a set of trees with random features. Gradient boosted decision trees (Breiman, Leo. Arcing the edge. Technical Report 486, Statistics Department, University of California at Berkeley, 1997; Friedman, Jerome H. *Greedy function approximation: a gradient boosting machine*. Annals of statistics (2001): 1189-1232; Friedman, Jerome H. *Stochastic gradient boosting*. Computational Statistics and Data Analysis 38.4 (2002): 367-378.) follow a similar strategy, but instead of choosing random features with each step, we greedily optimize at each point. The general algorithm is:

1. Start with a constant value, such as the average response across the input data. This is the baseline model, *F0*.

2. Fit a decision tree h to the training data, usually limiting it to have very shallow depth, with the target as the **pseudo-residuals** for each point i given by:

$$r_i = -\frac{\partial L\left(y_i, F\left(x_i\right)\right)}{\partial F\left(x_i\right)}$$

3. Conceptually, the pseudo-residual for a given loss function L (such as the squared error that we studied in *Chapter 4, Connecting the Dots with Models – Regression Methods* or the hinge loss for the SVM described above) is the derivative of the loss function with respect to the value of the current model *F* at a point `yi`. While a standard residual would just give the difference between the predicted and observed value, the pseudo-residual represents how rapidly the loss is changing at a given point, and thus in what direction we need to move the model parameters to better classify this point.

4. To step 1, add the value of the tree in step 2 multiplied by an optimal step γ and a learning rate α:

$$\gamma_t = \frac{\arg\min}{\gamma} \sum_{i=1}^{n} L\left(y_i, F_{t-1}(x_i) + h_t(x_i)\right)$$

$$F_t = F_{t-1}(X) + \alpha \gamma_t h_t(X)$$

5. We could either choose a γ that is optimal for the whole tree, or for each individual leaf node, and we can determine the optimal value using a method such as the Newton optimization we discussed above.

6. Repeat steps 1–3 until convergence.

The goal is that by fitting several weaker trees, in aggregate they make better predictions as they sequentially are fit to compensate for the remaining residuals in the model at each step. In practice, we also choose only a subset of the training data to fit the trees at each stage, which should further reduce the possibility of over-fitting. Let us examine this theory on our dataset by fitting a model with 200 trees with a maximum depth of 5:

```
>>> from sklearn.ensemble import GradientBoostingClassifier
>>> gbm = GradientBoostingClassifier(n_estimators=200, learning_
rate=1.0,\
... max_depth=5, random_state=0).fit(census_features_train.
toarray(),census_income_train)
>>> train_prediction = gbm.predict_proba(census_features_train.toarray())
>>> test_prediction = gbm.predict_proba(census_features_test.toarray())
>>> fpr_train, tpr_train, thresholds_train = metrics.roc_curve(np.
array(census_income_train),\
...    np.array(train_prediction[:,1]), pos_label=1)
>>>fpr_test, tpr_test, thresholds_test = metrics.roc_curve(np.
array(census_income_test),\
...    np.array(test_prediction[:,1]), pos_label=1)
```

Now, when we plot the results, we see a remarkable increase in accuracy on the test set:

```
>>> plt.plot(fpr_train, tpr_train)
>>> plt.plot(fpr_test, tpr_test)
>>> plt.xlabel('False Positive Rate')
>>> plt.ylabel('True Positive Rate')
```

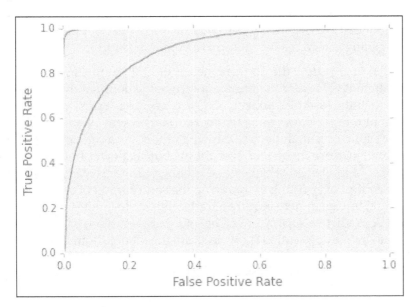

Similar to the random forest model, we can examine the importance of features as determined by the loss in accuracy upon shuffling their values among data points:

```
>>> np.array(expanded_headers)[np.argsort(gbm.feature_importances_)]
```

array(['native-country Outlying-US(Guam-USVI-etc)',   'native-
country Holand-Netherlands', 'native-country Laos',   'native-
country Hungary', 'native-country Honduras',   'workclass Never-
worked', 'native-country Nicaragua',   'education Preschool',
'marital-status Married-AF-spouse',   'native-country Portugal',
'occupation Armed-Forces',   'native-country Trinadad&Tobago',
'occupation Priv-house-serv',   'native-country Dominican-Republic',
'native-country Hong',   'native-country Greece', 'native-country
El-Salvador',   'workclass Without-pay', 'native-country Columbia',
'native-country Yugoslavia', 'native-country Thailand',   'native-
country Scotland', 'native-country Puerto-Rico',   'education 1st-
4th', 'education 5th-6th'

Note that this is not directly comparable to the same evaluation we performed for the logistic regression model as the importance here is not determined by whether the feature predicts positively or negatively, which is implicit in the sign of the coefficients in the logistic regression.

Also note that there is a subtler problem here with interpreting the output coefficients: many of our features are actually individual categories of a common feature, such as country of origin or education level. What we are really interested in is the importance of the overall feature, not the individual levels. Thus, to quantify feature importance more accurately, we could average the importance over all columns containing categories belonging to a common feature.

If we wanted to further tune the performance of the gbm model, we could perform a search of different values for the number of trees, the depth of those trees, the learning rate (α in the formulas above), and `min_samples_leaf` (which determines the minimum number of data points that need to be present to split the data form a bottom-most split, or leaf, in the tree), among others. As a rule of thumb, making deeper trees will increase the risk of over-fitting, but shallower trees will requires a larger number of models to achieve good accuracy. Similarly, a lower learning rate will also control over-fitting by reducing the contribution of any single tree to the model score, but again may require a tradeoff in more models to achieve the desired level of predictive accuracy. The balance between these parameters may be guided both by the application (how accurate the model should be to contribute meaningfully to a business problem) as well as performance considerations (if the model needs to run online in a website, for example, a smaller number of trees that occupy less memory may be beneficial and worth a somewhat reduced accuracy).

Comparing classification methods

In this chapter we have examined classification using logistic regression, support vector machines, and gradient boosted decision trees. In what scenarios should we prefer one algorithm over another?

For logistic regression, the data ideally will be linearly separable (the exponent in the formula for the logistic regression, after all, is essentially the same as the SVM equation for a separating hyperplane). If our goal is inference (producing a unit increase in response per 1-unit increase of input measurement, as we described in *Chapter 1, From Data to Decisions – Getting Started with Analytic Applications*) then the coefficients and log-odds values will be helpful. The stochastic gradient method can also be helpful in cases where we are unable to process all the data concurrently, while the second order methods we discussed may be easier to employ on un-normalized data. Finally, in the context of serializing model parameters and using these results to score new data, the logistic regression is attractive in that it is represented by a vector of numbers and is thus easily stored.

Support vector machines, as we discussed, can accommodate complex nonlinear boundaries between inputs. They can also be used on data without a vector representation, or data of different lengths, making them quite flexible. However, they require more computational resources for fitting as well as scoring.

Gradient boosted decision trees can fit nonlinear boundaries between inputs, but only certain kinds. Consider that a decision tree splits a dataset into two groups at each decision node. Thus, the resulting boundaries represent a series of hyperplanes in the m-dimensional space of the dataset, but only split along a particular dimension at each pass and only in a straight line. Thus, these planes will not necessarily capture the nonlinearity possible with the SVM, but if the data can be separated in this piecewise fashion a GBM may perform well.

The flowchart below gives a general overview from choosing among the classification methods we have discussed. Also, keep in mind that the Random Forest algorithm we discussed in *Chapter 4, Connecting the Dots with Models – Regression Methods* may also be applied for classification, while the SVM and GBM models describe in this chapter have forms that may be applied for regression.

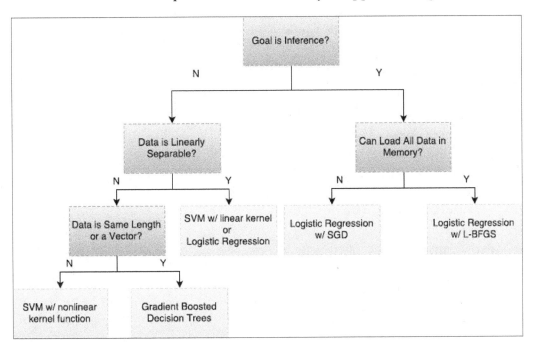

Case study: fitting classifier models in pyspark

Now that we have examined several algorithms for fitting classifier models in the scikit-learn library, let us look at how we might implement a similar model in PySpark. We can use the same census dataset from earlier in this chapter, and start by loading the data using a textRdd after starting the spark context:

```
>>> censusRdd = sc.textFile('census.data')
```

Next we need to split the data into individual fields, and strip whitespace

```
>>> censusRddSplit = censusRdd.map(lambda x: [e.strip() for e in
x.split(',')])
```

Now, as before, we need to determine which of our features are categorical and need to be re-encoded using one-hot encoding. We do this by taking a single row and asking whether the string in each position represent a digit (is not a categorical variable):

```
>>> categoricalFeatures = [e for e,i in enumerate(censusRddSplit.take(1)
[0]) if i.isdigit()==False]
>>> allFeatures = [e for e,i in enumerate(censusRddSplit.take(1)[0])]
```

Now, as before, we need to collect a dictionary representing the string-to-position mapping of each categorical label to a place in the one-hot-encoding vector:

```
>>> categoricalMaps = []
>>> for c in categoricalFeatures:
...     catDict = censusRddSplit.map(lambda x: x[c] if len(x) > c else
None).\
...     filter(lambda x: x is not None).\
...     distinct().\
...     zipWithIndex().\
...     collectAsMap()
...     censusRddSplit.map(lambda x: x[c]).take(1)
...     categoricalMaps.append(catDict)
```

Next, we calculate what the total length of the one-hot encoding vector should be to represent all the features. We subtract two from this value because the last categorical features is income, which has two values and which we use as the label for the data:

```
>>> expandedFeatures = 0
>>> for c in categoricalMaps:
...     expandedFeatures += len(c)
expandedFeatures += len(allFeatures)-len(categoricalFeatures)-2
```

Now, we use a map function to turn all of our data into labeled point objects for use in logistic regression. To do so, we extract the label for each row from the last element in the vector, then instantiate an empty vector using the length of the one-hot-encoded feature set we calculated preceding. We use two indices: one for which categorical variable we are accessing (to index the right dictionary to perform our mapping), and a second to record where in the feature vector we are (since for categorical variables we will skip over k spaces for a given variable, where k is the number of categories in that variable).

```
>>> def formatPoint(p):
...         if p[-1] == '<=50K':
...             label = 0
...         else:
...             label = 1
...         vector = [0.0]*expandedFeatures
...         categoricalIndex = 0
...         categoricalVariable = 0
...         for e,c in enumerate(p[:-1]):
...             if e in categoricalFeatures:
...                 vector[categoricalIndex + categoricalMaps[categoricalVariable][c]]=1
...                 categoricalIndex += len(categoricalMaps[categoricalVariable])
...                 categoricalVariable +=1
...             else:
...                 vector[e] = c
...                 categoricalIndex += 1
...         return LabeledPoint(label,vector)
```

We apply this function to all data points

```
>>> censusRddLabeled = censusRddSplit.map(lambda x: formatPoint(x))
```

Now that our data is in the right format, we can run logistic regression:

```
>>> from pyspark.mllib.classification import LogisticRegressionWithLBFGS
>>> censusLogistic = LogisticRegressionWithLBFGS.train(censusRddLabeled )
```

To access the weights from the resulting model, we can inspect the weights parameter:

```
>>> censusLogistic.weights
```

If we wanted to apply the generated model to a new dataset, we can use the `predict()` method of `censusLogistic` on a new feature vector. The steps described above are similar to the data processing we used for the scikit-learn example, but can ultimately scale to larger datasets.

Summary

In this chapter, you've examined how to use classification models and some of the strategies for improving model performance. In addition to transforming categorical features, you've looked at the interpretation of logistic regression accuracy using the ROC curve. In attempting to improve model performance, we demonstrated the use of SVMs and were able to increase performance on the training set the cost of overfitting. Finally, we were able to achieve good performance on the test set through gradient boosted decision trees. Taken together with the material in *Chapter 4, Connecting the Dots with Models – Regression Methods,* you should now have a full toolkit of methods for continuous and categorical outcomes, which you can apply to problems in main domains.

6
Words and Pixels – Working with Unstructured Data

Most of the data we have looked at thus far is composed of rows and columns with numerical or categorical values. This sort of information fits in both traditional spreadsheet software and the interactive Python notebooks used in the previous exercises. However, data is increasingly available in both this form, usually called structured data, and more complex formats such as images and free text. These other data types, also known as unstructured data, are more challenging than tabular information to parse and transform into features that can be used in machine learning algorithms.

What makes unstructured data challenging to use? It is challenging largely because images and text are extremely high dimensional, consisting of a much larger number of columns or features than we have seen previously. For example, this means that a document may have thousands of words, or an image thousands of individual pixels. Each of these components may individually or in complex combinations comprise a feature for our algorithms. However, to use these data types in prediction, we need to somehow distill this extremely complex data into common features or trends that might be used effectively in a model. This often involves both removing noise from these data types and finding simpler representations. At the same time, the greater inherent complexity of these data types potentially captures more information than available in tabular datasets, or may reveal information that is not available in any other source.

In this chapter, we will explore unstructured data by:

- Cleaning raw text through stemming, stop word removal, and other normalizations
- Using tokenization and n-grams to find common patterns in textual data
- Normalizing image data and removing noise
- Decomposing images into lower dimensional features through several common matrix factorization algorithms

Working with textual data

In the following example, we will consider the problem of separating text messages sent between cell phone users. Some of these messages are spam advertisements, and the objective is to separate these from normal communications (Almeida, Tiago A., José María G. Hidalgo, and Akebo Yamakami. *Contributions to the study of SMS spam filtering: new collection and results.* Proceedings of the 11th ACM symposium on Document engineering. ACM, 2011). By looking for patterns of words that are typically found in spam advertisements, we could potentially derive a smart filter that would automatically remove these messages from a user's inbox. However, while in previous chapters we were concerned with fitting a predictive model for this kind of problem, here we will be shifting focus to cleaning up the data, removing noise, and extracting features. Once these tasks are done, either simple or lower-dimensional features can be input into many of the algorithms we have already studied.

Cleaning textual data

Let us start by loading and inspecting the data using the following commands. Note that we need to supply column names for this data ourselves:

```
>>> spam = pd.read_csv('smsspamcollection/SMSSpamCollection',sep='\
t',header=None)
>>> spam.columns = ['label','text']
>>> spam.head()
```

This gives the following output:

	label	text
0	ham	Go until jurong point, crazy.. Available only ...
1	ham	Ok lar... Joking wif u oni...
2	spam	Free entry in 2 a wkly comp to win FA Cup fina...
3	ham	U dun say so early hor... U c already then say...
4	ham	Nah I don't think he goes to usf, he lives aro...

The dataset consists of two columns: the first contains the label (spam or ham) indicating whether the message is an advertisement or a normal message, respectively. The second column contains the text of the message. Right at the start, we can see a number of problems with using this raw text as input to an algorithm to predict the spam/nonspam label:

- The text of each message contains a mixture of upper and lower case letters, but this capitalization does not affect the meaning of a word.

- Many words (*to*, *he*, *the*, and so on) are common, but tell us relatively little about the message.

Other issues are subtler:

- When we compare words such as *larger* and *largest*, the most information about the meaning of the words is carried by the root, *large* — differentiating between the two forms may actually prevent us from capturing common information about the presence of the word *large* in a text, since the count of this stem in the message will be divided between the variants. Looking only at individual words does not tell us about the context in which they are used. Indeed, it may be more informative to consider sets of words.

- Even for words that do not fall into the common category, such as *and*, *the*, and *to*, it is sometimes unclear whether a word is present in a document because it is common across all documents or whether it contains special information about a particular document. For example, in a set of online movie reviews, words such as *character* and *film* will appear frequently, but do not help to distinguish one review from another since they are common across all reviews. Because the English language has a large vocabulary, the size of the resulting feature set could be enormous.

Let us start by cleaning up the text before delving into the other feature issues. We can base by lowercasing each word in the text using the following function:

```
>>> def clean_text(input):
...         return "".join([i.lower() for i in input])
```

We then apply this function to each message using the map function we have seen in previous examples:

```
>>> spam.text = spam.text.map(lambda x: clean_text(x))
```

Inspecting the resulting we can verify that all the letters are now indeed lowercase:

	label	text
0	ham	go until jurong point, crazy.. available only ...
1	ham	ok lar... joking wif u oni...
2	spam	free entry in 2 a wkly comp to win fa cup fina...
3	ham	u dun say so early hor... u c already then say...
4	ham	nah i don't think he goes to usf, he lives aro...

Next, we want to remove common words and trim the remaining vocabulary to just the stem portion of the word that is most useful for predictive modeling. We do this using the **natural language toolkit (NLTK)** library (Bird, Steven. *NLTK: the natural language toolkit*. Proceedings of the COLING/ACL on Interactive presentation sessions. Association for Computational Linguistics, 2006.). The list of stop words is part of the dataset associated for download with this library; if this is your first time opening NLTK, you can use the `nltk.download()` command to open a **graphical user interface (GUI)** where you can select the content you wish to copy to your local machine using the following commands:

```
>>> import nltk
>>> nltk.download()
>>> from nltk.corpus import stopwords
>>> stop_words = stopwords.words('english')
```

We then define a function to perform stemming:

```
>>> def stem_text(input):
...     return " ".join([nltk.stem.porter.PorterStemmer().stem(t) if t not in \
...         stop_words else for t in nltk.word_tokenize(input)])
```

Finally, we again use a lambda function to perform this operation on each message, and visually inspect the results:

```
>>> spam.text = spam.text.map(lambda x: stem_text(x))
```

	label	text
0	ham	go jurong point , crazy.. avail bugi n grea...
1	ham	ok lar ... joke wif u oni ...
2	spam	free entri 2 wkli comp win fa cup final tkt...
3	ham	u dun say earli hor ... u c alreadi say ...
4	ham	nah n't think goe usf , live around though

For example, you can see the stem *joke* has been extracted from *joking*, and *avail* from *available*.

Now that we have performed lower casing and stemming, the messages are in relatively cleaned up form, and we can proceed to generate features for predictive modeling from this data.

Extracting features from textual data

In perhaps the simplest possible feature for text data, we use a binary vector of *0s* and *1s* to simply record the presence or absence of each word in our vocabulary in each message. To do this we can utilize the CountVectorizer function in the scikit-learn library, using the following commands:

```
>>> from sklearn.feature_extraction.text import CountVectorizer
>>> count_vect_sparse = CountVectorizer().fit_transform(spam.text)
```

By default, the result is stored as a *sparse vector*, which means that only the non-zero elements are held in memory. To calculate the total size of this vector we need to transform it back into a *dense* vector (where all elements, even 0, are stored in memory):

```
>>> count_vect_sparse[0].todense().size
```

By checking the length of the feature vector created for the first message, we can see that it creates a vector of length 7,468 for each message with 1 and 0 indicating the presence or absence, respectively, of a particular word out of all words in this document list.

We can check that this length is in fact the same as the vocabulary (union of all unique words in the messages) using the following command to extract the `vocabulary_` element of the vectorizer, which also gives a value of 7,468:

```
>>> len(CountVectorizer().fit(spam.text).vocabulary_) Recall from the
earlier that individual words might not informative features if their
meaning is dependent upon the context given by other words in a sentence.
Thus, if we want to expand our feature set to potentially more powerful
features, we could also consider n-grams, sets of n co-occurring words
(for example, the phrase \the red house contains the n-grams the red,
and red house (2-grams), and the red house (3-gram)). These features are
calculated similarly as above, by supplying the argument ngram_range to
the CountVectorizer constructor:
```

```
>>> count_vect_sparse = CountVectorizer(ngram_range=(1, 3)).fit_
transform(spam.text)
```

We can see that this increases the size of the resulting feature by about 10-fold by again inspecting the length of the first row using:

```
>>> count_vect_sparse[0].todense().sizeInsert
```

However, even after calculating n-grams, we still have not accounted for the fact that some words or n-grams might be common across all messages and thus provide little information in distinguishing spam from nonspam. To account for this, instead of simply recording the presence or absence of a word (or n-gram), we might compare the frequency of words within a document to the frequency across all documents. This ratio, the **term-frequency-inverse document frequency (tf-idf)** is calculated in the simplest form as:

$$tf - idf\left(t_i, d_j\right) = \frac{\displaystyle\sum_{k=1}^{V_j} 1_{t_i=v_k}}{D} \bigg/ \frac{\displaystyle\sum_{j=1}^{D} 1_{t_i \in V_j}}{D}$$

Where *ti* is a particular term (word or n-gram), *dj* is a particular document, *D* is the number of documents, *Vj* is the set of words in document *j*, and *vk* is a particular word in document *j*. The subscripted 1 in this formula is known as an **Indicator Function**, which returns 1 if the subscripted condition is true, and 0 otherwise. In essence, this formula compares the frequency (count) of a word within a document to the number of documents that contain this word. As the number of documents containing the word decreases, the denominator decreases, and thus the overall formula becomes larger from dividing by a value much less than 1. This is balanced by the frequency of the word within a document in the numerator. Thus, the tf-idf score will more heavily weight words that are present at greater frequency within a document compared to those common among all documents and thus might be indicative of special features of a particular message.

Note that the formula above represents only the simplest version of this expression. There are also variants in which we might logarithmically transform the counts (to offset the bias from large documents), or scale the numerator by the maximum frequency found for any term within a document (again, to offset bias that longer documents could have higher term frequencies than shorter documents by virtue of simply having more words) (Manning, Christopher D., Prabhakar Raghavan, and Hinrich Schütze. *Scoring, term weighting and the vector space model.* Introduction to Information Retrieval 100 (2008): 2-4.). We can apply tf-idf to the spam data using the following commands:

```
>>> from sklearn.feature_extraction.text import TfidfVectorizer
>>> tf_idf = TfidfVectorizer().fit_transform(spam.text)
```

We can see the effect of this transformation by taking the maximum value across rows using:

```
>>> tf_idf.todense().max(1)
```

Where the '1' argument to max indicates that the function is applied along rows (instead of columns, which would be specified with '0'). When our features consisted only of binary values, the maximum across each rows would be 1, but we can see that it is now a float value.

The final text feature we will discuss is concerned with condensing our feature set. Simply put, as we consider larger and larger vocabularies, we will encounter many words that are so infrequent as to almost never appear. However, from a computational standpoint, even a single instance of a word in one document is enough to expand the number of columns in our text features for all documents. Given this, instead of directly recording whether a word is present, we might think of compressing this space requirement so that we use fewer columns to represent the same dataset. While in some cases, two words might map to the same column, in practice this happens infrequently enough due to the long-tailed distribution of word frequencies that it can serve as a handy way to reduce the dimensionality of our text data. To perform this mapping, we make use of a hash function that takes as input a word and outputs a random number (column location) that is keyed to the value of that string. The number of columns we ultimately map to in our transformed dataset is controlled by the n_features argument to the HashingVectorizer, which we can apply to our dataset using the following commands:

```
>>> from sklearn.feature_extraction.text import HashingVectorizer
>>> h = HashingVectorizer(n_features=1024).fit_transform(spam.text)
```

Using dimensionality reduction to simplify datasets

Even though using the HashingVectorizer allows us to reduce the data to a set of 1,024 columns from a feature set that was much larger, we are still left with many variables in our dataset. Intuition tells us that some of these features, either before or after the application of the HashingVectorizer, are probably correlated. For example, a set of words may co-occur in a document that is spam. If we use n-grams and the words are adjacent to one another, we could pick up on this feature, but not if the words are simply present in the message but separated by other text. The latter might occur, for example, if some common terms are in the first sentence of the message, while others are near the end.More broadly, given a large set of variables such as we have already seen for textual data, we might ask whether we could represent these data using a more compact set of features. In other words, is there an underlying pattern to the variation in thousands of variables that may be extracted by calculating a much smaller number of features representing patterns of correlation between individual variables? In a sense, we already saw several examples of this idea in *Chapter 3, Finding Patterns in the Noise – Clustering and Unsupervised Learning*, in which we reduced the complexity of a dataset by aggregating individual datapoints into clusters. In the following examples, we have a similar goal, but rather than aggregating individual datapoints, we want to capture groups of correlated variables.

While we might achieve this goal in part through the variable selection techniques such as regularization, which we discussed in the *Chapter 4, Connecting the Dots with Models – Regression Methods*, we do not necessarily want to remove variables, but rather capture their common patterns of variation.

Let us examine some of the common methods of dimensionality reduction and how we might choose between them for a given problem.

Principal component analysis

One of the most commonly used methods of dimensionality reduction is **Principal Component Analysis (PCA)**. Conceptually, PCA computes the axes along which the variation in the data is greatest. You may recall that in *Chapter 3, Finding Patterns in the Noise – Clustering and Unsupervised Learning*, we calculated the eigenvalues of the adjacency matrix of a dataset to perform spectral clustering. In PCA, we also want to find the eigenvalue of the dataset, but here, instead of any adjacency matrix, we will use the covariance matrix of the data, which is the relative variation within and between columns. The covariance for columns xi and xj in the data matrix x is given by:

$$Cov\left(x_i, x_j\right) = \frac{1}{n} \sum_{i,j=1}^{n} \left(x_i - \mu_i\right)\left(x_j - \mu_j\right)$$

This is the average product of the offsets from the mean column values. We saw this value before when we computed the correlation coefficient in *Chapter 3, Finding Patterns in the Noise – Clustering and Unsupervised Learning*, as it is the denominator of the Pearson coefficient. Let us use a simple example to illustrate how PCA works. We will make a dataset in which the six columns are derived from the same underlying normal distribution, one of which is given reversed in sign, using the following commands:

```
>>> syn_1 = np.random.normal(0,1,100)
>>> syn_2 = -1*syn_1
>>> syn_data = [ syn_1, syn_1, syn_1, syn_2, syn_2, syn_2]
```

Note that each of our columns has mean 0 and standard deviation 1. If this were not the case, we could use the scikit-learn utility StandardScaler as we discussed in *Chapter 3, Finding Patterns in the Noise – Clustering and Unsupervised Learning*, when we normalized data for use in k means clustering. We might simply center the variables at 0 and use the resulting covariance matrix if we believe that the differences in scale of the variables are important to our problem. Otherwise, differences in scale will tend to be reflected by the differing variance values within the columns of the data, so our resulting PCA will reflect not only correlations within variables but also their differences in magnitude. If we do not want to emphasize these differences and are only interested in the relative correlation among variables, we can also divide each column of the data by its standard deviation to give each column a variance of 1. We could also potentially run PCA not on the covariance matrix, but the Pearson correlation matrix between variables, which is already naturally scaled to 0 and a constant range of a values (from -1 to 1) (Kromrey, Jeffrey D., and Lynn Foster-Johnson. *Mean centering in moderated multiple regression: Much ado about nothing.* Educational and Psychological Measurement 58.1 (1998): 42-67.). For now, we can compute the covariance matrix of our data with the following command:

```
>>> syn_cov = np.cov(syn_data)
```

Recalling our discussion of spectral clustering in *Chapter 3, Finding Patterns in the Noise – Clustering and Unsupervised Learning*, if we consider the covariance matrix as a stretching operation on a vector, then, if we find the vectors that lie along these directions of distortion, we have in a sense found the axes that define the variation in the data. If we then compare the eigenvalues of these vectors, we could determine if one or more of these directions reflect a greater proportion of the overall variation of the data. Let us compute the eigenvalues and vectors of the covariance matrix using:

```
>>> [eigenvalues, eigenvectors] = np.linalg.eig(syn_cov)
```

This gives the following eigenvalue variable as:

```
array([  0.00000000e+00,   4.93682786e+00,   1.23259516e-32,
1.50189461e-16,   0.00000000e+00,  -9.57474477e-34])
```

You can see that most of the eigenvalues are effectively zero, except the second. This reflects the fact that the data we constructed, despite having six columns, is effectively derived from only one dataset (a normal distribution). Another important property of these eigenvectors is that they are orthogonal, which means that they are at right angles to each other in n-dimensional space: if we were to take a dot product between them, it would be 0, and they thus represent independent vectors that, when linearly combined, can be used to represent the dataset.

If we were to multiply the data by the eigenvector corresponding to this second eigenvalue, we would project the data from a six-dimensional to a one-dimensional space:

```
>>> plt.hist(np.dot(np.array(syn_data).transpose(),np.
array(eigenvectors[:,1])))
```

Note that we needed to transpose the data to have the 100 rows and 6 columns, as we initially constructed it as a list of 6 columns, which NumPy interprets as instead having 6 rows and 100 columns. The resulting histogram is as shown in the following:

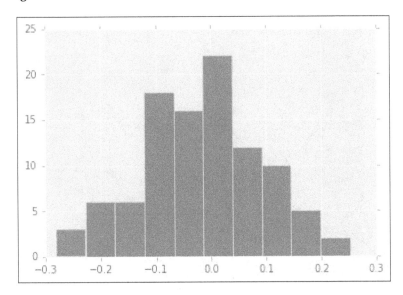

In other words, by projecting the data onto the axis of greatest variance, we have recovered that fact that this six-column data was actually generated from a single distribution. Now if we instead use the PCA command, we get a similar result:

```
>>> syn_pca = PCA().fit(np.array(syn_data))
```

When we extract the `explained_variance_ratio_`, the algorithm has effectively taken the preceding eigenvalues, ordered them by magnitude, and divided by the largest one, giving:

```
array([  1.00000000e+000,   6.38413622e-032,   2.02691244e-063,
2.10702767e-094,   3.98369984e-126,   5.71429334e-157])
```

If we were to plot these as a barplot, a visualization known as a `scree plot` could help us determine how many underlying components are represented in our data:

```
>>> scree, ax = plt.subplots()
>>> plt.bar(np.arange(0,6),syn_pca.explained_variance_ratio_)
>>> ax.set_xlabel('Component Number')
>>> ax.set_ylabel('Variance Explained')
>>> plt.show()
```

This generates the following plot:

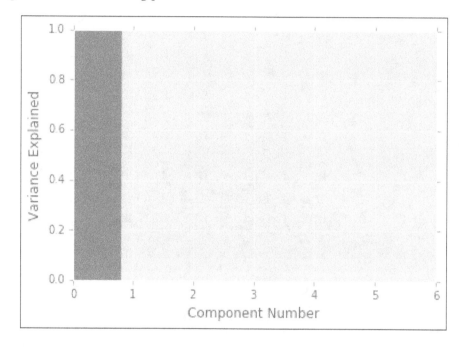

Evidently, only the first component carries any variance, represented by the height of the bar, with all other components being near 0 and so not appearing in the plot. This sort of visual analysis is comparable to how we looked for an elbow in the inertia function for k-means in *Chapter 3, Finding Patterns in the Noise – Clustering and Unsupervised Learning*, as a function of k to determine how many clusters were present in the data.We can also extract the data projected onto the first principal components and see a similar plot as shown previously when we projected the data onto an eigenvector of the covariance matrix:

```
>>> plt.hist(syn_pca.components_[0])
```

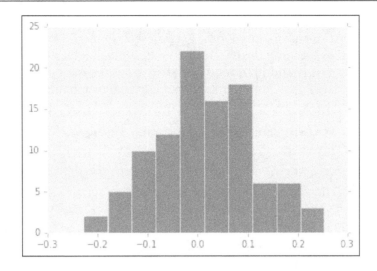

Why are they not exactly identical? While conceptually PCA computes the eigenvalues of the covariance matrix, in practice most packages do not actually implement the calculation we illustrated previously for purposes of numerical efficiency. Instead, they employ a matrix operation known as the **Singular Value Decomposition (SVD)**, which seeks to represent a covariance matrix of X as a set of lower dimensional row and column matrices:

$$X^T X = W^T \sigma W$$

Where if X is an n by m, W may be n by k, where $k << m$. Here, σ represents a matrix with 0 everywhere but the diagonal, which contains non-zero entries. Thus, the covariance matrix is represented as the product of two smaller matrices and a scaling factor given by the diagonal elements in σ. Instead of calculating all eigenvectors of the covariance matrix, as we did previously, we can ask only for the k columns or W^T we think are likely to be significant judged by the sort of scree plot analysis we demonstrated above. However, when we project the data onto the principal components we obtain through this method, the calculation of the SVD can potentially give different signs to the projection of the data on the principal components, even if the relative magnitude and signs of these components remains the same. Thus, when we look at the scores assigned to a given row of data after projecting it onto the first k principal components, we should analyze them relative to other values in the dataset, just as when we examined the coordinates produced by Multidimensional Scaling in *Chapter 3, Finding Patterns in the Noise – Clustering and Unsupervised Learning*. Details of the SVD calculation used by the default scikit-learn implementation of PCA are given in (Tipping, Michael E., and Christopher M. Bishop. *Probabilistic principal component analysis*. Journal of the Royal Statistical Society: Series B (Statistical Methodology) 61.3 (1999): 611-622.).

Now that we have examined conceptually what PCA calculates, let us see if it can help us reduce the dimensionality of our text dataset. Let us run PCA on the n-gram feature set from above, asking for 100 components. Note that because the original dataset is a sparse matrix and PCA requires a dense matrix as an input, we need to convert it using `toarray()`. Also, to retain the right dimensionality for use with the PCA fit function, we need to transpose the result:

```
>>> pca_text = PCA(num_components=10).fit(np.transpose(count_vect_
sparse.toarray()))
```

If we make a scree plot of total variance explained by the first 10 principal components of this dataset, we see that we will probably require a relatively large number of variables to capture the variation in our data since the upward trend in variance explained is relatively smooth:

```
>>> scree, ax = plt.subplots()
>>> plt.bar(np.arange(0,10),pca_text.explained_variance_ratio_)
>>>ax.set_xlabel('Component Number')
>>>ax.set_ylabel('Variance Explained')
>>> plt.show()
```

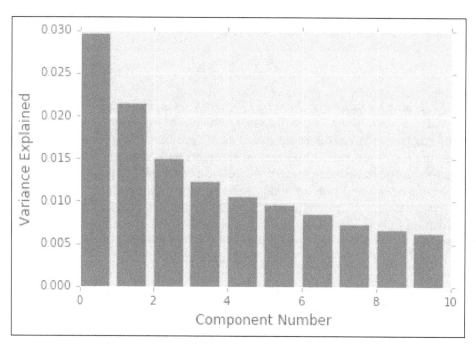

We could also visualize this by looking at the cumulative variance explained using *k* components using the following curve:

```
>>> scree, ax = plt.subplots()
>>> plt.plot(pca_text.explained_variance_ratio_.cumsum())
>>> ax.set_xlabel('Number of Components')
>>> ax.set_ylabel('Cumulative Variance Explained')
>>> plt.show()
```

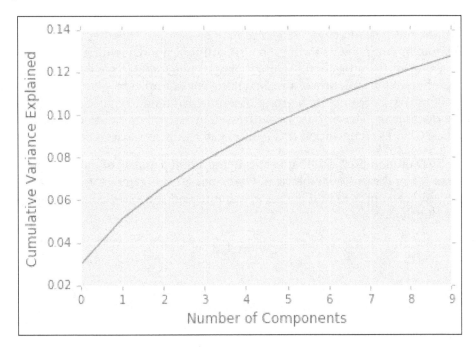

A word on normalization: in practice, for document data, we might not want to scale the data by subtracting the mean and dividing by the variance as the data is mostly binary. Instead, we would just apply the SVD to a binary matrix or perhaps the tF-idf scores we computed previously, an approach also known as **Latent Semantic Indexing (LSI)** (Berry, Michael W., Susan T. Dumais, and Gavin W. O'Brien. *Using linear algebra for intelligent information retrieval.* SIAM review 37.4 (1995): 573-595; Laham, T. K. L. D., and Peter Foltz. *Learning human-like knowledge by singular value decomposition: A progress report.* Advances in Neural Information Processing Systems 10: Proceedings of the 1997 Conference. Vol. 10. MIT Press, 1998.). CUR decomposition and nonnegative matrix factorization

What drawbacks might there be to using PCA to reduce the dimensionality of a dataset? For one, the components (covariance matrix eigenvectors) generated by PCA are still essentially mathematical entities: the patterns in variables represented by these axes might not actually correspond to any element of the data, but rather a linear combination of them. This representation is not always easily interpretable, and can particularly difficult when trying to convey the results of such analyses to domain experts to generate subject-matter specific insights. Second, the fact that PCA produces negative values in its eigenvectors, even for positive-only data such as text (where a term cannot be negatively present in a document, just 0, 1, a count, or a frequency), is due to the fact that the data is linearly combined using these factors. In other words, positive and negative values may be summed together when we project the data onto its components through matrix multiplication, yielding an overall positive value for the projection. Again, it may be preferable to have factors that give some insight into the structure of the data itself, for example, by giving a factor that consists of binary indicators for a group of words that tend to co-occur in a particular group of documents. These goals are addressed by two other matrix factorization techniques: CUR Decomposition and Non-negative Matrix Factorization.

Like the SVD used in PCA, CUR attempts to represent a matrix of data X as a product of lower dimensional matrices. Here, instead of eigenvectors, the CUR decomposition attempts to find the set of columns and rows of the matrix that best represent the dataset as:

$$X = CUR$$

Where C is a matrix of c columns of the original dataset, R is a set of r rows from the original dataset, and U is a matrix of scaling factors. The c columns and r rows used in this reconstruction are sampled from the columns and rows of the original matrix, with probability proportional to the `leverage score`, given by:

$$lv_j = \frac{1}{k}\sum_{i=1}^{k}\left(v_j^i\right)^2$$

Where lv_j is the statistical leverage for column (row) j, k is the number of components in the SVD of X, and v_j are the jth elements of these k component vectors. Thus, columns (rows) are sampled with high probability if they contribute significantly to the overall norm of the matrix's singular values, meaning they are also have a major influence on the reconstruction error from the SVD (for example, how well the SVD approximates the original matrix) (Chatterjee, Samprit, and Ali S. Hadi. Sensitivity analysis in linear regression. Vol. 327. John Wiley & Sons, 2009; Bodor, András, et al. *rCUR: an R package for CUR matrix decomposition*. BMC bioinformatics 13.1 (2012): 1).

While this decomposition is not expected to approximate the original dataset with the same accuracy as the SVD approach used in PCA, the resulting factors may be easier to interpret since they are actual elements of the original dataset.

 Please note that while we use SVD to determine sampling probabilities for the columns and rows, the final factorization of CUR does not.

There are many algorithms for generating a CUR decomposition (Mahoney, Michael W., and Petros Drineas. *CUR matrix decompositions for improved data analysis. Proceedings of the National Academy of Sciences 106.3 (2009): 697-702. Boutsidis, Christos, and David P. Woodruff. Optimal cur matrix decompositions.* Proceedings of the 46th Annual ACM Symposium on Theory of Computing. ACM, 2014). CUR decomposition is implemented in the `pymf` library, and we can call it using the following commands:

```
>>> cur = pymf.CUR(count_vect_sparse.toarray().transpose(),crank=100,rra
nk=100)
>>> cur.factorize() >>> cur.factorize()
```

The `crank` and `rrank` parameters indicate how many rows and columns, respectively, should be chosen from the original matrix in the process of performing the decomposition. We can then examine which columns (words from the vocabulary) were chosen in this reconstruction using the following commands to print these significant words whose indices are contained in the cur object's `._cid` (column index) element. First we need to collect a list of all words in the vocabulary of our spam dataset:

```
>>> vocab = CountVectorizer().fit(spam.text).vocabulary_
>>> vocab_array = ['']*len(vocab.values())
>>> for k,v in vocab.items():
...       vocab_array[v]=k
>>>vocab_array = np.array(vocab_array)
```

Since the `vocabulary_` variable returned by the `CountVectorizer` is a dictionary giving the positions of terms in the array to which they are mapped, we need to construct our array by placing the word at the position given by this dictionary. Now we can print the corresponding words using:

```
>>> for i in cur._cid:
... print(vocab_array[i])
```

Like CUR, nonnegative matrix factorization attempts to find a set of positive components that represents the structure of a dataset (Lee, Daniel D., and H. Sebastian Seung. *Learning the parts of objects by non-negative matrix factorization.* Nature 401.6755 (1999): 788-791; Lee, Daniel D., and H. Sebastian Seung. *Algorithms for non-negative matrix factorization.* Advances in neural information processing systems. 2001.; P. Paatero, U. Tapper (1994). Paatero, Pentti, and Unto Tapper. *Positive matrix factorization: A non-negative factor model with optimal utilization of error estimates of data values.* Environmetrics 5.2 (1994): 111-126. Anttila, Pia, et al. *Source identification of bulk wet deposition in Finland by positive matrix factorization.* Atmospheric Environment 29.14 (1995): 1705-1718.). Similarly, it tries to reconstruct the data using:

$$X = WH$$

Where W and H are lower dimensional matrices that when multiplied, reconstruct X; all three of W, H, and X are constrained to have no negative values. Thus, the columns of X are linear combinations of W, using H as the coefficients. For example, if the rows of X are words and the columns are documents, then each document in X is represented as a linear combination of underlying document types in W with weighted given by H. Like the elements returned by CUR decomposition, the components W from nonnegative matrix factorization are potentially more interpretable than the eigenvectors we get from PCA.

There are several algorithms to compute W and H, with one of the simplest being through multiplicative updates (Lee, Daniel D., and H. Sebastian Seung. *Algorithms for non-negative matrix factorization.* Advances in neural information processing systems. 2001). For example, if we want to minimize the Euclidean distance between X and WH:

$$\left\| X - WH \right\|_F^2 = \left(X - WH \right)\left(X - WH \right)^T$$

We can calculate the derivative of this value with respective to W:

$$\frac{\partial}{\partial W}\left(X - WH \right)\left(X - WH \right)^T \approx$$
$$-X^T H + WH^T H =$$
$$\frac{X^T H}{WH^T H}$$

Then to update W we multiply at each step by this gradient:

$$W \leftarrow W \frac{X^T H}{WH^T H}$$

And the same for H:

$$H \leftarrow H \frac{HX^T}{HH^T W^T}$$

These steps are repeated until the values of W and H converge. Let us examine what components we retrieve from our text data when we use NMF to extract components:

```
>>> from sklearn.decomposition import NMF
>>> nmf_text = NMF(n_components=10).fit(np.transpose(count_vect_sparse.toarray()))
```

We can then look at the words represented by the components in NMF, where the words have a large value in the components matrix resulting from the decomposition.

We can see that they appear to capture distinct groups of words, but are any correlated with distinguishing spam versus nonspam? We can transform our original data using the NMF decomposition, which will give the weights for linearly combining these features (for example, the weights to linearly combine the 10 basis documents we get from the decomposition to reconstruct the message) using the command:

```
>>> nmf_text_transform = nmf_text.transform(count_vect_sparse.toarray())
```

Now let us plot the average weight assigned to each of these `nmf` factors for the normal and spam messages. We can do this by plotting a bar chart where the x axis are the 10 `nmf` factors, and the y axis are the average weight assigned to this factor for a subset of documents:

```
>>> plt.bar(range(10),nmf_text_transform[spam.label=='spam'].mean(0))
```

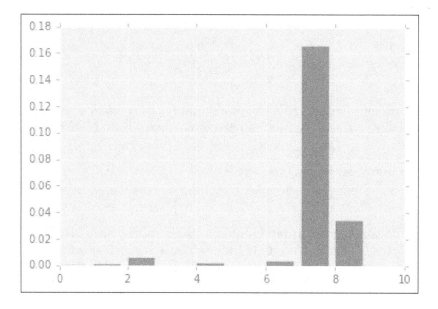

```
>>> plt.bar(range(10),nmf_text_transform[spam.label=='ham'].mean(0))
```

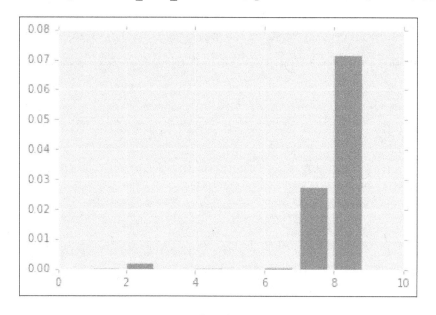

Promisingly, the factors 8 and 9 seem to have very different average weights between these two classes of messages. In fact, we may need fewer than 10 factors to represent the data, since these two classes may well correspond to the underlying spam versus nonspam messages.

Latent Dirichlet Allocation

A related method of decomposing data into an interpretable set of features is **Latent Dirichlet Allocation (LDA)**, a method initially developed for textual and genetics data that has since been extended to other areas (Blei, David M., Andrew Y. Ng, and Michael I. Jordan. *Latent dirichlet allocation*. the Journal of machine Learning research 3 (2003): 993-1022. Pritchard, Jonathan K., Matthew Stephens, and Peter Donnelly. *Inference of population structure using multilocus genotype data*. Genetics 155.2 (2000): 945-959.). Unlike the methods we looked at previously, where the data is represented as a set of lower dimensional matrices that, when multiplied, approximate the original data, LDA uses a probability model. This model is often explained using a plate diagram that illustrates the dependencies among the variables, as shown in the following diagram:

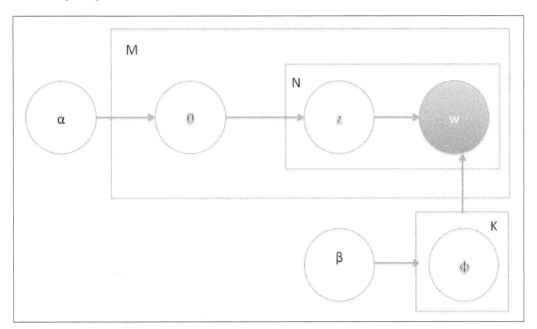

What exactly does this diagram describe? It is what is known as a generative model: a set of instructions by which to generate a probability distribution over documents. The idea is comparable to a distribution such as the Gaussian 'bell-curve' you are probably familiar with, except here instead of drawing real numbers from the distribution we sample documents. Generative models may be contrasted with the predictive methods which we have seen in previous chapters that attempts to fit the data to a response (as in the regression or classification models we have studied in *Chapters 4, Connecting the Dots with Models – Regression Methods*, and *Chapter 5, Putting Data in its Place – Classification Methods and Analysis*), instead of simply generate samples of the data according to a distribution. The plate diagram represents the components of this generative model, and we can think of this model as the following series of steps to generate a document:Initialize a Dirichlet distribution to choose from a set of topics. These topics are analogous to the components we found in NMF, and can be thought of as *basis documents* representing groups of commonly co-occurring words. The Dirichlet distribution is given by the following formula:

$$\frac{1}{B(\alpha)} \prod_{i=1}^{K} x_i^{\alpha_i - 1}$$

The preceding formula gives the probability of observing a given distribution of items (here topics) among K classes and can be used to sample a vector of K class memberships (for example, sample a random vector giving what fraction of documents in the collection belong to a given topic). The alpha parameter in the Dirichlet distribution is used as an exponent of the K category probabilities and increases the significance ascribed to a particular component (for example, a more frequent topic). The term B is the beta function, which is simply a normalization term. We use the Dirichlet distribution in step 1 to generate a per-topic probability distribution for a document i. This distribution would be, for example, a series of weights that sum to 1 giving the relative probability that a document belongs to a given topic. This is the parameter θ in the plate diagram. M represents the number of documents in our dataset.

1. For each of the N word positions in the document, choose a topic Z from the distribution θ. Each of the M topics has a Dirichlet distribution with parameter β instead of giving per word probabilities, given by ϕ. Use this distribution to choose word in each N position in a document.

2. Repeat steps 2–4 for each word position for each document in a dataset to generate a group of documents.

In the previous diagram, the numbers (**M**, **N**, **K**) inside the rectangles indicate the number of time that the variables represented by circles are generated in the generative model. Thus, the words w, being innermost, are generated $N \times M$ times. You can also notice that the rectangles enclose variables that are generated the same number of times, while arrows indicate dependence among variables during this data generation process. You can also now appreciate where the name of this model comes from, as a document is latently allocated among many topics, just as we used the factors in NMF to find linear combinations of 'basis documents' that could reconstruct our observed data.

This recipe can also be used to find a set of topics (for example word probability distributions) that fit a dataset, assuming the model described previously was used to generate the documents. Without going into the full details of the derivation, we randomly initialize a fixed number of K topics and run the model, as described previously, by always sampling a document's topic, given all other documents, and a word, given the probability of all other words in the document. We then update the parameters of the model based on the observed data and use the updated probabilities to generate the data again. Over many iterations, this process, known as Gibbs sampling, will converge from randomly initialized values to a set of model parameters that best fit the observed document data. Let us now fit an LDA model to the spam dataset using the following commands:

```
>>> lda = LatentDirichletAllocation(n_topics=10).fit(count_vect_sparse)
```

As with NMF, we can examine the highest probability words for each topic using:

```
>>> for i in range(10):
...     print(vocab_array[np.argsort(lda.components_[i])[1:10]])
```

Likewise, we can see if these topics represent a meaningful separation between the spam and nonspam messages. First we find the topic distribution among the 10 latent topics for each document using the following `transform` command:

```
>>> topic_dist = lda.transform(count_vect_sparse)
```

This is analogous to the weights we calculated in NMF. We can now plot the average topic weight for each message class as follows:

```
>>> plt.bar(range(10),topic_dist[spam.label=='ham'].mean(0))
```

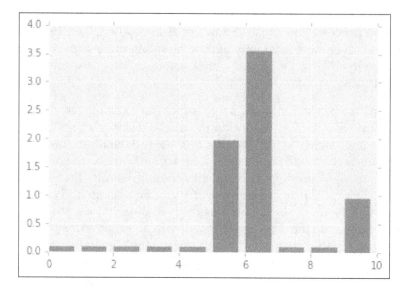

```
>>> plt.bar(range(10),topic_dist[spam.label=='spam'].mean(0))
```

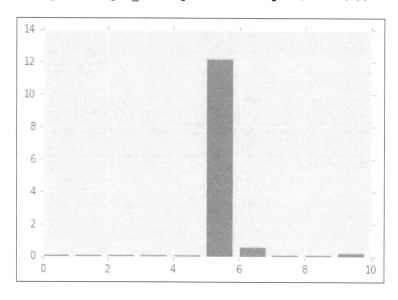

Again, promisingly, we find a different average weight for topic 5 for spam than nonspam, indicating that the LDA model has successfully separated out the axis of variation we are interested in for classification purposes.

Using dimensionality reduction in predictive modeling

The analysis we have outlined previously has been largely devoted to trying to extract a lower-dimensional representation of a text collection by finding a smaller set of components that capture the variation among individual documents. In some cases, this sort of analysis can be useful as an exploratory data analysis tool, which, like the clustering techniques we described in *Chapter 3, Finding Patterns in the Noise – Clustering and Unsupervised Learning*, allows us to understand the structure in a dataset. We might even combine clustering and dimensionality reduction, which is in essence the idea of spectral clustering as we examined in *Chapter 3, Finding Patterns in the Noise – Clustering and Unsupervised Learning* using SVD to reduce the adjacency matrix to a more compact representation and then clustering this reduced space to yield a cleaner separation between datapoints.

Like the groups assigned through clustering, we can also potentially use the components derived from these dimensionality reduction methods as features in a predictive model. For example, the NMF components we extracted previously could be used as inputs to a classification model to separate spam from nonspam messages. We have even seen this use earlier, as the online news popularity dataset we used in *Chapter 4, Connecting the Dots with Models – Regression Methods*, had columns derived from LDA topics. Like the regularization methods we saw in *Chapter 4, Connecting the Dots with Models – Regression Methods*, dimensionality reduction can help reduce overfitting by extracting the underlying correlations among variables since these lower-dimensional variables are often less noisy than using the whole feature space. Now that we have seen how dimensionality reduction could help us find structure in textual data, let us examine another class of potentially high-dimensional data found in images.

Images

Like textual data, images are potentially noisy and complex. Furthermore, unlike language, which has a structure of words, paragraphs, and sentences, images have no predefined rules that we might use to simplify raw data. Thus, much of image analysis will involve extracting patterns from the input's features, which are ideally interpretable to a human analyst based only on the input pixels.

Cleaning image data

One of the common operations we will perform on images is to enhance contrast or change their color scale. For example, let us start with an example image of a coffee cup from the `skimage` package, which you can import and visualize using the following commands:

```
>>> from skimage import data, io, segmentation
>>> image = data.coffee()
>>> io.imshow(image)
>>> plt.axis('off');
```

This produces the following image:

In Python, this image is represented as a three-dimensional matrix with the dimensions corresponding to height, width, and color channels. In many applications, the color is not of interest, and instead we are trying to determine common shapes or features in a set of images that may be differentiated based on grey scale alone. We can easily convert this image into a grey scale version using the commands:

```
>>> grey_image = skimage.color.rgb2gray(image)
>>> io.imshow(grey_image)
>>> plt.axis('off');
```

A frequent task in image analysis is to identify different regions or objects within an image. This can be made more difficult if the pixels are clumped into one region (for example, if there is very strong shadow or a strong light in the image), rather than evenly distributed along the intensity spectrum. To identify different objects, it is often desirable to have these intensities evenly distributed, which we can do by performing histogram equalization using the following commands:

```
>>> from skimage import exposure
>>> image_equalized = exposure.equalize_hist(grey_image)
>>> io.imshow(image_equalized)
>>> plt.axis('off');
```

To see the effect of this normalization, we can plot the histogram of pixels by intensity before and after the transformation with the command:

```
>>> plt.hist(grey_image.ravel())
```

This gives the following pixel distribution for the uncorrected image:

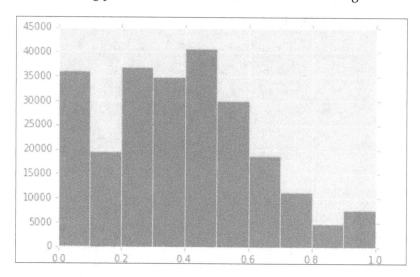

The `ravel()` command used here is used to flatten the 2-d array we started with into a single vector that may be input to the histogram function. Similarly, we can plot the distribution of pixel intensities following normalization using:

```
>>> plt.hist(image_equalized.ravel(),color='b')
```

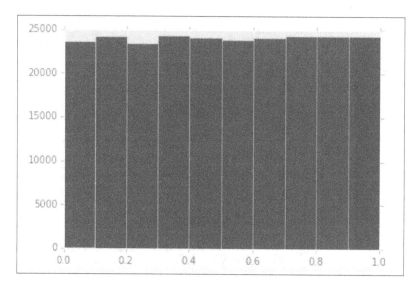

Thresholding images to highlight objects

Another common task for image analysis is to identify individual objects within a single image. To do so, we need to choose a threshold to binarize an image into white and black regions and separate overlapping objects. For the former, we can use thresholding algorithms such as Otsu thresholding (Otsu, Nobuyuki. *A threshold selection method from gray-level histograms.* Automatica 11.285-296 (1975): 23-27), which uses a *structuring element* (such as disk with n pixels) and attempts to find a pixel intensity, which will best separate pixels inside that structuring element into two classes (for example, black and white). We can imagine rolling a disk over an entire image and doing this calculation, resulting in either a local value within the disk or a global value that separates the image into foreground and background. We can then turn the image into a binary mask by thresholding pixels above or below this value.

To illustrate, let us consider a picture of coins, where we want to separate the coins from their background. We can visualize the histogram-equalized coin image using the following commands:

```
>>> coins_equalized = exposure.equalize_hist(skimage.color.rgb2gray(data.coins()))
>>> io.imshow(coins_equalized)
```

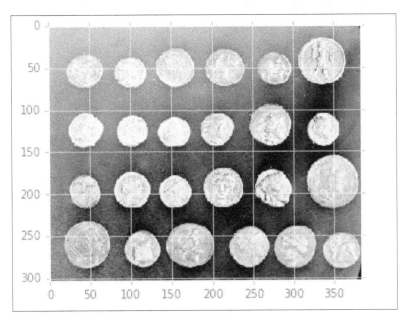

One problem we can see is that the background has a gradient of illumination increasing toward the upper left corner of the image. This difference doesn't change the distinction between background and objects (coins), but because part of the background is in the same intensity range as the coins, it will make it difficult to separate out the coins themselves. To subtract the background, we can use the closing function, which sequentially erodes (removes white regions with size less than the structuring element) and then dilates (if there is a white pixel within the structuring element, all elements within the structuring element are flipped to white). In practice, this means we remove small white specks and enhance regions of remaining light color. If we then subtract this from the image, we subtract the background, as illustrated here:

```
>>> from skimage.morphology import opening, disk
>>> d=disk(50)
>>> background = opening(coins_equalized,d)
>>> io.imshow(coins_equalized-background)
```

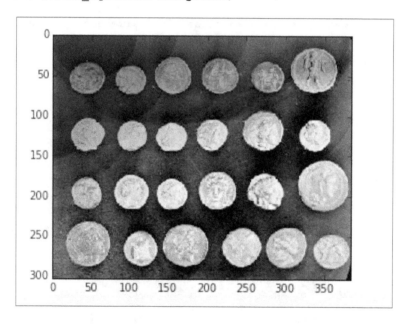

Now that we have removes the background, we can apply the Otsu thresholding algorithm mentioned previously to find the ideal pixel to separate the image into background and object using the following commands:

```
>>> from skimage import filter
>>> threshold_global_otsu = filter.threshold_otsu(coins_equalized-background)
>>> global_otsu = (coins_equalized-background) >= threshold_global_otsu
>>> io.imshow(global_otsu)
```

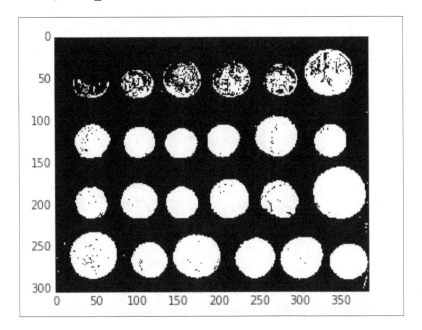

The image has now been segmented into coins and non-coin regions. We could use this segmented image to count the number coins, to highlight the coins in the original image using the regions obtained above as a *mask*, for example if we want to record pixel data only from the coin regions as part of a predictive modeling feature using image data.

Dimensionality reduction for image analysis

Once we have our images appropriately cleaned, how can we turn them into more general features for modeling? One approach is to try to capture common patterns of variation between a group of images using the same dimensionality reduction techniques as we used previously for document data. Instead of words in documents, we have patterns of pixels within an image, but otherwise the same algorithms and analysis largely apply. As an example, let us consider a set of images of faces (http://www.geocities.ws/senthilirtt/Senthil%20Face%20Database%20Version1) which we can load and examine using the following commands:

```
>>> faces = skimage.io.imread_collection('senthil_database_version1/S1/*.
tif')
>>> io.imshow(faces[1])
```

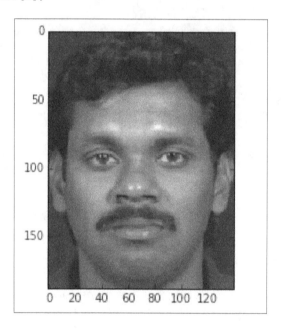

For each of these two-dimenional images, we want to convert it into a vector just as we did when we plotted the pixel frequency histograms during our discussion of normalization. We will also construct a set where the average pixel intensity across faces has been subtracted from each pixel, yielding each face as an offset from the *average face* in the data through the following commands:

```
>>> faces_flatten = [f.ravel() for f in faces]
>>> import pylab
>>> faces_flatten_demean = pylab.demean(faces_flatten,axis=1)
```

We consider two possible ways to factor faces into a more general features. The first is to use PCA to extract the major vectors of variation in this data — these vectors happen to also look like faces. Since they are formed from the eigenvalues of the covariance matrix, these sorts of features are sometimes known as eigenfaces. The following commands illustrate the result of performing PCA on the face dataset:

```
>>> from sklearn.decomposition import PCA
>>> faces_components = PCA(n_components=3).fit(faces_flatten_demean)
>>> io.imshow(np.reshape(faces_components.components_[1],(188,140)))
```

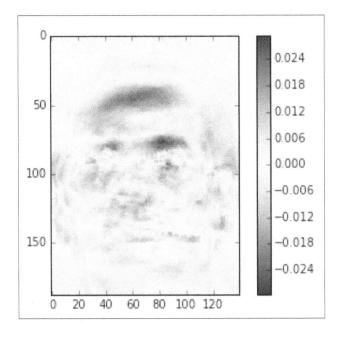

How much variation in the face data is captured by the principal components? In contrast to the document data, we can see that using PCA even with only three components allows to explain around two-thirds of the variation in the dataset:

```
>>> plt.plot(faces_components.explained_variance_ratio_.cumsum())
```

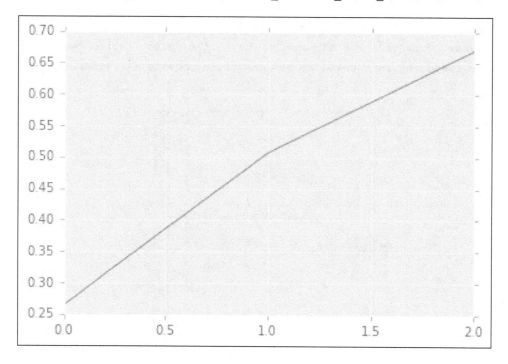

We could also apply NMF, as we described previously, to find a set of basis faces. You can notice from the preceding heatmap that the eigenfaces we extracted can have negative values, which highlights one of the interpretational difficulties we mentioned previously: we cannot really have negative pixels (since , so a latent feature with negative elements is hard to interpret. In contrast, the components we extract using NMF will look much more like elements of the original dataset, as shown below using the commands:

```
>>> from sklearn.decomposition import NMF
>>> faces_nmf = NMF(n_components=3).fit(np.transpose(faces_flatten))
>>> io.imshow(np.reshape(faces_nmf.components_[0],(188,140)))
```

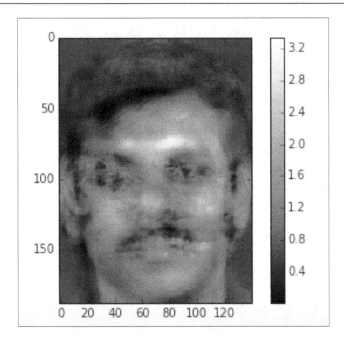

Unlike the eigenfaces, which resemble averaged versions of many images, the NMF components extracted from this data look like individual faces. While we will not go through the exercise here, we could even apply LDA to image data to find topics represented by distributions of pixels and indeed it has been used for this purpose (Yu, Hua, and Jie Yang. *A direct LDA algorithm for high-dimensional data – with application to face recognition.* Pattern recognition 34.10 (2001): 2067-2070; Thomaz, Carlos E., et al. *Using a maximum uncertainty LDA-based approach to classify and analyse MR brain images.* Medical Image Computing and Computer-Assisted Intervention–MICCAI 2004. Springer Berlin Heidelberg, 2004. 291-300.).

While the dimensionality reduction techniques we have discussed previously are useful in the context of understanding datasets, clustering, or modeling, they are also potentially useful in storing compressed versions of data. Particularly in model services such as the one we will develop in *Chapter 8, Sharing Models with Prediction Services*, being able to store a smaller version of the data can reduce system load and provide an easier way to process incoming data into a form that can be understood by a predictive model. We can quickly extract the few components we need, for example, from a new piece of text data, without having to persist the entire record.

Case Study: Training a Recommender System in PySpark

To close this chapter, let us look at an example of how we might generate a large-scale recommendation system using dimensionality reduction. The dataset we will work with comes from a set of user transactions from an online store (Chen, Daqing, Sai Laing Sain, and Kun Guo. *Data mining for the online retail industry: A case study of RFM model-based customer segmentation using data mining.* Journal of Database Marketing & Customer Strategy Management 19.3 (2012): 197-208). In this model, we will input a matrix in which the rows are users and the columns represent items in the catalog of an e-commerce site. Items purchased by a user are indicated by a 1. Our goal is to factorize this matrix into 1 x k *user factors* (row components) and k x 1 *item factors* (column components) using k components. Then, presented with a new user and their purchase history, we can predict what items they are like to buy in the future, and thus what we might recommend to them on a homepage. The steps to do so are as follows:

1. Consider a user's prior purchase history as *a* vector *p*. We imagine this vector is the product of an unknown *user factor* component *u* with the item factors *i* we obtained through matrix factorization: each element of the vector *p* is then the dot product of this unknown user factor with the item factor for a given item. Solve for the unknown user factor *u* in the equation:

$$p = ui$$

Given the item factors *i* and the purchase history *p*, using matrix.Use the resulting user factor *u*, take the dot product with each item factor to obtain and sort by the result to determine a list of the top ranked items.

Now that we have described what is happening *under the hood* in this example, we can begin to parse this data using the following commands. First, we create a parsing function to read the 2nd and 7th columns of the data containing the item ID and user ID, respectively:

```
>>> def parse_data(line):
...     try:
...         line_array = line.split(',')
...         return (line_array[6],line_array[1]) # user-term pairs
...     except:
...         return None
```

Next, we read in the file and convert the user and item IDs, which are both string, into a numerical index by incrementing a counter as we add unique items to a dictionary:

```
>>> f = open('Online Retail.csv',encoding="Windows-1252")
>>> purchases = []
>>> users = {}
>>> items = {}
>>>user_index = 0
>>>item_index = 0
>>>for index, line in enumerate(f):
...     if index > 0: # skip header
...             purchase = parse_data(line)
...             if purchase is not None:
...                 if users.get(purchase[0],None) is not None:
...                     purchase_user = users.get(purchase[0])
...                 else:
...                     users[purchase[0]] = user_index
...                     user_index += 1
...                     purchase_user = users.get(purchase[0])
...                 if items.get(purchase[1],None) is not None:
...                     purchase_item = items.get(purchase[1])
...                 else:
...                     items[purchase[1]] = item_index
...                     item_index += 1
...                     purchase_item = items.get(purchase[1])
...                 purchases.append((purchase_user,purchase_item))>>>f.close()
```

Next, we convert the resulting array of purchase into an `rdd` and convert the resulting entries into Rating objects -- a (user, item, rating) tuple. Here, we will just indicate that the purchase occurred by giving a rating of 1.0 to all observed purchases, but we could just as well have a system where the ratings indicate user preference (such as movie ratings) and follow a numerical scale.

```
>>> purchasesRdd = sc.parallelize(purchases,5).map(lambda x:
Rating(x[0],x[1],1.0))
```

Now we can fit the matrix factorization model using the following commands:

```
>>> from pyspark.mllib.recommendation import ALS,
MatrixFactorizationModel, Rating


>>> k = 10
>>> iterations = 10
>>> mfModel = ALS.train(purchasesRdd, k, iterations)
```

The algorithm for matrix factorization used in PySpark is **Alternating Least Squares (ALS)**, which has parameters for the number of row (column) components chosen (k) and a regularization parameter λ which we did not specify here, but functions similarly to its role in the regression algorithms we studied in *Chapter 4, Connecting the Dots with Models – Regression Methods,* by constraining the values in the row (column) vectors from becoming too large and potentially causing overfitting.

We could try several values of k and λ, and measure the mean squared error between the observed and predicted matrix (from multiplying the row factors by the column factors) to determine the optimal values.

Once we have obtained a good fit, we can use the `predict` and `predictAll` methods of the model object to obtain predictions for new users, and the persist it on disk using the `save` method.

Summary

In this chapter, we have examined complex, unstructured data. We cleaned and tokenized text and examined several ways of extracting features from documents in a way that could be incorporated into predictive models such as n-grams and tf-idf scores. We also examined dimensionality reduction techniques, such as the HashingVectorizer, matrix decompositions, such as PCA, CUR, NMF, and probabilistic models, such as LDA. We also examined image data, including normalization and thresholding operations, and how we can use dimensionality reduction techniques to find common patterns among images. Finally, we used a matrix factorization algorithm to prototype a recommender system in PySpark.

In the next section, you will also look at image data, but in a different context: trying to capture complex features from these data using sophisticated deep learning models.

7
Learning from the Bottom Up – Deep Networks and Unsupervised Features

Thus far, we have studied predictive modeling techniques that use a set of features (columns in a tabular dataset) that are pre-defined for the problem at hand. For example, a user account, an internet transaction, a product, or any other item that is important to a business scenario are often described using properties derived from domain knowledge of a particular industry. More complex data, such as a document, can still be transformed into a vector representing something about the words in the text, and images can be represented by matrix factors as we saw in *Chapter 6, Words and Pixels – Working with Unstructured Data*. However, with both simple and complex data types, we could easily imagine higher-level interactions between features (for example, a user in a certain country and age range using a particular device is more likely to click on a webpage, while none of these three factors alone are predictive) as well as entirely new features (such as image edges or sentence fragments) that would be difficult to construct without subject-area expertise or extensive trial and error.

Ideally, we could automatically find the best features for a predictive modeling task using whatever raw inputs we have at hand, without the effort of testing a vast number of transformations and interactions. The ability to do this—automatically determine complex features from relatively raw inputs—is an attractive property of *deep learning* methods, a class of algorithms commonly applied to neural network models that have enjoyed much recent popularity. In this chapter, we will examine the following topics:

- How a basic neural network is fit to data
- How deep learning methods improve the performance of classical neural networks
- How to perform image recognition with deep learning

Learning patterns with neural networks

The core building blocks for the deep learning algorithms we will examine are *Neural Networks*, a predictive model that simulates the way cells inside the brain fire impulses to transmit signals. By combining individual contributions from many inputs (for example, the many columns we might have in a tabular dataset, words in a document, or pixels in an image), the network integrates signals to predict an output of interest (whether it is price, click through rate, or some other response). Fitting this sort of model to data therefore involves determining the best parameters of the neuron to perform this mapping from input data to output variable.

Some common features of the deep learning models we will discuss in this chapter are the large number of parameters we can tune and the complexity of the models themselves. Whereas the regression models we have seen so far required us to determine the optimal value of ~50 coefficients, in deep learning models we can potentially have hundreds or thousands of parameters. However, despite this complexity, deep learning models are composed of relatively simple units, so we will start by examining these building blocks.

A network of one – the perceptron

The simplest neural network we could imagine is composed of a single linear function, and is known as a perceptron (Rosenblatt, Frank. The perceptron, a perceiving and recognizing automaton Project Para. Cornell Aeronautical Laboratory, 1957):

$$F(x) = \begin{cases} 1 \, if \; wx > b \\ 0 \, otherwise \end{cases}$$

Here, w is a set of weights for each of the input features in the column vector x, and b is the intercept. You may recognize this as being very similar to the formula for the SVM we examined in *Chapter 5, Putting Data in its Place – Classification Methods and Analysis*, when the kernel function used is linear. Both the function above and the SVM separates data into two classes depending upon whether a point is above or below the hyperplane given by w. If we wanted to determine the optimal parameters for this perceptron using a dataset, we could perform the following steps:

1. Set all weights w to a random value. Instead of using a fixed b as on offset, we will append a column of *1s* to the data set matrix represented by the $n \, x \, m$ matrix X (n data points with m features each) to represent this offset, and learn the optimal value along with the rest of the parameters.

2. Calculate the output of the model, *F(xi)*, for a particular observation *x*, in our dataset.

3. Update the weights using a learning rate *a* according to the formula:

$$\Delta w = \alpha \left(y_i - F\left(x_i \right) \right) x_i$$

4. Here, y_i is the target (the real label 0 or 1 for x_i). Thus, if $F(x_i)$ is too small, we increase the weights on all features, and vice versa.

5. Repeat steps 2 and 3 for each data point in our set, until we reach a maximum number of iterations or the average error given by:

$$\frac{1}{n}\sum_{i=1}^{n}\left| y_i - F\left(x_i \right) \right|$$

6. over the *n* data points drops below a given threshold ε (for example, *1e-6*).

While this model is easy to understand, it has practical limitations for many problems. For one, if our data cannot be separated by a hyperplane (they are not linearly separable), then we will never be able to correctly classify all data points. Additionally, all the weights are updated with the same rule, meaning we need to learn a common pattern of feature importance across all data points. Additionally, since the outputs are only 1 or 0, the Perceptron is only suitable for binary classification problems. However, despite these limitations, this model illustrates some of the common features of more complex neural network models. The training algorithm given above adjusts the model weights based on the error of classification tuned by a learning rate, a pattern we will see in more complex models as well. We will frequently see a thresholded (binary) function such as the preceding one, though we will also relax this restriction and investigate the use of other functions.

How can we develop this simple Perceptron into a more powerful model? As a first step, we can start by combining inputs from many individual models of this kind.

Combining perceptrons – a single-layer neural network

Just as a biological brain is composed of individual neuronal cells, a neural network model consists of a collection of functions such as the Perceptron discussed previously. We will refer to these individual functions within the network as **neurons** or **units**. By combining the inputs from several functions, blended using a set of weights, we can start to fit more complex patterns. We can also capture nonlinear patterns by using other functions than the linear decision boundary of the Perceptron. One popular choice is the logistic transform we previously saw in *Chapter 5, Putting Data in its Place – Classification Methods and Analysis*. Recall that the logistic transform is given by:

$$F(z) = \frac{1}{1 + e^{(-wx+b)}} = \frac{1}{1 + e^{(-z)}}$$

Here, w is a set of weights on the elements of the vector x, and b is an offset or bias, just as in the Perceptron. This bias serves the same role as in the Perceptron model, increasing or decreasing the score calculated by the model by a fixed amount, while the weights are comparable to regression coefficients we have seen in models from *Chapter 4, Connecting the Dots with Models – Regression Methods*. For simpler notation in the following derivation, we can represent the value $wx+b$ as a single variable z. As in the logistic regression model from *Chapter 5, Putting Data in its Place – Classification Methods and Analysis*, this function maps the input x into the range *[0,1]* and can be visually represented (**Figure 1**) as an input vector x (consisting of three green units) connected by lines (representing the weights W) to a single blue unit (the function $F(z)$).

In addition to increasing the flexibility with which we can separate data through this nonlinear transformation, let us also adjust our definition of the target. In the Perceptron model, we had a single output value 0 or 1. We could also think of representing this as a two-unit vector (shown in red in Figure 1), in which one element is set to 1 and the other 0, representing which of the two categories a data point belongs to. This may seem like an unnecessary complication, but it will become very useful as we build increasingly complex models.

With these modifications, our model now consists of the elements show in Figure 1. The logistic function takes input from the three features of *x* represented by the vector at the top of the diagram, combines them using the logistic function with the weights for each element of *x* given by *W1*, and returns an output. This output is then used by two additional logistic functions downstream, represented by the red units at the bottom of the diagram. The one on the left uses the output of the first function to give a score for the probability of class 1. On the right, a second function uses this output to give the probability of class 0. Again, the input from the blue unit to the red units is weighted by a vector *W2*. By tuning the value of *W2* we can increase or decrease the likelihood of *activting* one of the red nodes and setting its value to 1. By taking the maximum over these two values, we get a binary classification.

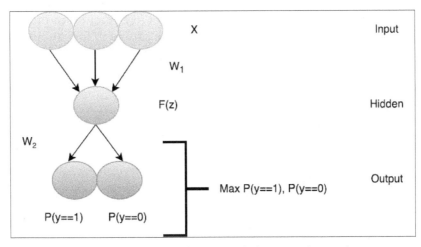

Figure 1: Architecture of a basic single-layer neural network

This model is still relatively simple, but has several features that will also be present in more complex scenarios. For one, we now actually have multiple layers, since the input data effectively forms the top layer of this network (green nodes). Likewise, the two output functions form another layer (red nodes). Because it lies between the input data and the output response, the middle layer is also referred to as the *hidden layer* of the network. In contrast, the bottom-most level is called the *visible layer*, and the top the *output layer*.

Right now, this is not a very interesting model: while it can perform a nonlinear mapping from the input x using the logistic function, we only have a single set of weights to tune from the input, meaning we can effectively only extract one set of patterns or features from the input data by reweighting it. In a sense, it is very similar to the Perceptron, just with a different decision function. However, with only a few modifications, we can easily start to create more complex mappings that can accommodate interactions between the input features. For example, we could add two more neurons to this network in the hidden layer, as shown in the **Figure 2**. With these new units, we now have three potentially different sets of weights for the elements of the input (each representing different weighting of the inputs), each of which could form a different signal when integrated in the hidden layer. As a simple example, consider if the vector represented an image: the hidden neurons on the right and left could receive weights of $(1,0,0)$ and $(0,0,1)$, picking up the edges of the image, while the middle neuron could receive weight $(0,1,0)$ and thus only consider the middle pixel. The output probabilities of the two classes in the output layer now receive contributions from all three hidden neurons. As a result, we could now adjust the weight parameters in the vector $W2$ to pool contributions from the three hidden units to decide the probability of the two classes

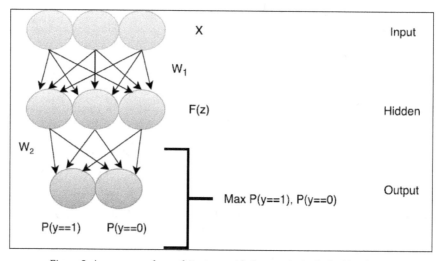

Figure 2: A more complex architecture with three units in the hidden layer

Even with these modifications, the **Figure 2** represents a relatively simple model. To add more flexibility to the model we could add many more units to the hidden layer. We could also extend this approach to a problem with more than two classes by adding more units to the output layer at the bottom of the diagram. Also, we have only considered linear and logistic transformations thus far, but as we will see later in this, chapter there are a wide variety of functions we could choose.

However, before we consider more complex variations on this design, let us examine the methodology to determine the proper parameters for this model. The insertion of the intermediate layers means we can no longer rely on the simple learning training algorithm that we used for the Perceptron model. For example, while we still want to adjust the weights between the input and hidden layer to optimize the error between the prediction and the target, the final prediction is now not given by the output of the hidden layer, but the output layer below it. Thus, our training procedure needs to incorporate errors from the output layer in tuning hidden levels of the network.

Parameter fitting with back-propagation

Given the three layer network shown in Figure 2, how can we determine the best set of **weights (W)** and **offsets (b)** that map our input data to the output? As with the Perceptron algorithm, we can initially set all our weights to random numbers (a common strategy is to sample them from a normal distribution with mean of 0 and standard deviation of 1). We then follow the flow of the arrows in the network from top to bottom, computing the logistic transform for each node at each stage until we arrive at the probabilities of each of the two classes.

To adjust our randomly chosen parameters to better fit the output, we can calculate what direction the weights should move to reduce the error between the predicted and observed response y, just as with the Perceptron learning rule. In **Figure 2** we can see two sets of weights we need to adjust: those between the input and hidden layer (W1) and those between the hidden layer and the output (W2).

Let us start with the simpler case. If we are tuning the bottom-most weights (between the output and the hidden layer), then we want to find the change in the errors (the difference between the prediction and the real value of the output) as we alter the weights. For now, we will use a squared error function to illustrate:

$$E(x_i) = \frac{1}{2}\left(F(z_i) - y_i\right)^2$$

Here, y_i is the actual value of the label, and `F(zi)` represents one of the red neurons in the output layer (in this example, a logistic function). We want to calculate the change in this error function when we adjust the weight (one of the lines connecting the hidden blue and output red neurons in the Figure 2), represented by the variable `Wij`, where `i` and `j` are indices for the red and blue neurons connected by a given weight. Recall that this weight is actually an argument of the variable z (since `z=wx+b`), representing the input to the function logistic F. Because the variable w is nested inside the logistic function, we cannot calculate the partial derivative the error function with respect to this weight directly to determine the weight update Δw.

We want to calculate a partial derivative because the error is a function of all input weights, but we want to update each weight independently

To see this, recall an example from calculus if we wanted to find the derivative of the function with respect to x:

$$F(x) = e^{x^2}$$

We would need to first take the derivative with respect to ez, then multiply by the derivative of z with respect to x, where z=x2, giving a final value of $e^{x^2} 2x$. This pattern, given more generally by:

$$\frac{\partial F}{\partial x} = \frac{\partial F \partial z}{\partial z \partial x}$$

This is known as the *chain rule*, since we *chain* together derivatives in calculations with nested functions. In fact, though are example was for only a single level of nesting, we could extend this to an arbitrary number, and would just need to insert more multiplication terms in the formula above.

Thus, to calculate the change in the error function *E* when we change a given weight wij, we need to take the derivative of the error function with respect to *F(z)* first, followed by the derivative of *F(z)* with respect to *z*, and finally the derivative of *z* with respect to the weight wij. When we multiply these three partial derivatives together and cancel terms in the numerator and denominator, we obtain the derivative of the error function with respect to the weight. This, the partial derivative of this error with respect to a particular weight *w* between one the outputs *i* and one of the hidden neurons *j* is given using the chain rule described previously:

$$\frac{\partial E}{\partial w_{ij}} = \frac{\partial E}{\partial F(z)_i} \frac{\partial F(z)_i}{z} \frac{\partial z}{\partial w_{ij}}$$

Now that we have the formula to determine the derivative of the error function with respect to the weight, let us determine the value of each of these three terms. The derivative for the first term is simply the difference between the prediction and the actual response variable:

$$\frac{\partial E}{\partial F(z)_i} = 2\frac{1}{2}\left(F(z)_i - y\right)(1) = F(z)_i - y$$

 Please note that the subscript i here refers to the index of the output neuron, not the data point i as it has been used previously.

For the second term, we find that the partial derivative of the logistic function has a convenient form as a product of the function and 1 minus the function:

$$\frac{\partial F(z)_i}{z} = \frac{(0)\left(1+e^{-z}\right)-(1)\left(-e^{-z}\right)}{\left(1+e^{-z}\right)^2} =$$

$$\frac{1}{\left(1+e^{-z}\right)}\frac{1-1+e^{-z}}{\left(1+e^{-z}\right)} = F(z)_i\left(1-F(z)_i\right)$$

Finally for the last term we have simply,

$$\frac{\partial z}{\partial w_{ij}} = F(z)_j$$

Here, $F(z)_j$ is the output of the hidden layer neuron j. To adjust the weight w_{ij}, we want to move in the opposite direction to which the error is increasing, just as in the stochastic gradient descent algorithm we described in *Chapter 5, Putting Data in its Place – Classification Methods and Analysis*. Thus, we update the value of the weight using the following equation:

$$w_{ij-new} = w_{ij-old} - \alpha\frac{\partial E}{\partial w_{ij}}$$

Where α is a learning rate. For the first set of weights (between the input and the hidden layer), the calculation is slightly more complicated. We start again with a similar formula as previously:

$$\frac{\partial E}{\partial w_{jk}} = \frac{\partial E}{\partial F(z)_j} \frac{\partial F(z)_j}{z} \frac{\partial z}{\partial w_{jk}}$$

Where wjk is the weight between a hidden neuron j and a visible neuron k. Instead of the output, F(z)i, the partial derivative of the error with respect to the weight is now calculated with respect to the hidden neuron's output F(z)j. Because the hidden neuron is connected to several output neurons, in the first term we cannot simply use the derivative of the error with respect to the output of the neuron, since F(z)j receives error inputs from all these connections: there is no direct relationship between F(z)j and the error, only through the F(z)i of the output layer. Thus, for hidden to visible layer weights we need to calculate the first term of this partial derivative by summing the results of applying the chain rule for the connection from each output neuron i:

$$\frac{\partial E}{\partial F(z)_j} = \sum_{i=1}^{n} \left(\frac{\partial E}{\partial z} \frac{\partial z}{\partial F(z)_i} \right) =$$

$$\sum_{i=1}^{n} \left(\frac{\partial E}{\partial F(z)_i} \frac{\partial F(z)_i}{\partial z} w_{ij} \right)$$

In other words, we sum the partial derivatives along all the arrows connecting wjk to the output layer. For the hidden to visible weights, this means two arrows (from each output to the hidden neuron j).

Since the input to the hidden neuron is now the data itself in the visible layer, the third term in the equation becomes:

$$\frac{\partial z}{\partial w_{jk}} = x_k$$

This is simply an element of the data vector x. Plugging in these values for the first and third terms, and using the gradient descent update given previously, we now have all the ingredients we need to optimize the weights in this network. To train the network, we repeat the following steps:

1. Randomly initialize the weights (again, using samples from the standard normal is a common approach).

2. From the input data, follow the arrows in **Figure 2** forward through the network (from top to bottom) to calculate the output in the bottom layer.

3. Using the difference between the calculated result in step 2 and the actual value of the output (such as a class label), use the preceding equations to calculate the amount by which to change each weight.

4. Repeat steps 1–3 until the weights have reached a stable value (meaning the difference between the old and new values is less than some small numerical cutoff such as *1e-6*).

This process is known as back-propagation (Bryson, Arthur E., Walter F. Denham, and Stewart E. Dreyfus. Optimal programming problems with inequality constraints. *AIAA journal 1.11 (1963): 2544-2550; Rumelhart, David E., Geoffrey E. Hinton, and Ronald J. Williams. Learning representations by back-propagating errors.* Cognitive modeling 5.3 (1988): 1; Bryson, Arthur Earl. Applied optimal control: optimization, estimation and control. CRC Press, 1975; Alpaydin, Ethem. Introduction to machine learning. MIT press, 2014.) because visually the errors in prediction flow backward through the network to the connection weights w from the input. In form, it is quite similar to the Perceptron learning rule that we discussed at the beginning of this chapter, but accommodates the complexity of relating the prediction error to the weights between the hidden and visible layers, which depend on all output neurons in the example we have illustrated.

Discriminative versus generative models

In the examples described previously and illustrated in Figures 1 and 2, the arrows always point exclusively forward from the input data to the output target. This is known as a feed-forward network, since the movement of information is always in one direction (Hinton, Geoffrey, et al. *Deep neural networks for acoustic modeling in speech recognition: The shared views of four research groups.* IEEE Signal Processing Magazine 29.6 (2012): 82-97). However, this is not a hard requirement—if we had a model in which arrows moved both forward and backward in the visible layer (Figure 3), we could in a sense have a generative model not unlike the LDA algorithm discussed in *Chapter 6, Words and Pixels – Working with Unstructured Data*:

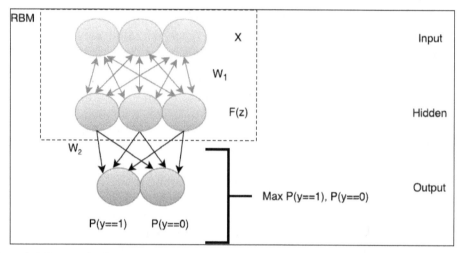

Figure 3: A Restricted Boltzman Machine (RBM) as the top two levels of the neural network from Figure 2

Instead of simply generating a predicted target in the output layer (a discriminative model), such a model could be used to draw samples from the presumed distribution of the input data. In other words, just as we could generate documents using the probability model described in LDA, we could draw samples from the visible layer using the weights from the hidden to the visible layer as inputs to the visible neurons. This kind of neural network model is also known as a belief network, since it can be used to simulate the 'knowledge' represented by the network (in the form of the input data) as well as perform classification. A visible and hidden layer in which there is a connection between each neuron in both layers is a kind of model known more generally as a Restricted Boltzman Machine (RBM) (Smolensky, Paul. Information processing in dynamical systems: Foundations of harmony theory. No. CU-CS-321-86. COLORADO UNIV AT BOULDER DEPT OF COMPUTER SCIENCE, 1986; Hinton, Geoffrey E., James L. Mcclelland, and David E. Rumelhart. *Distributed representations, Parallel distributed processing: explorations in the microstructure of cognition, vol. 1: foundations.* (1986).).

In addition to providing a way for us to understand the distribution of the data by simulating samples from the space of possible input data points that the network has been exposed to, RBMs can form useful building blocks in the deep networks that we will construct using additional hidden layers. However, we are presented with a number of challenges in adding these additional layers.

Vanishing gradients and explaining away

Even the architecture shown in Figures 2 and 3 is not the most complex neural network we could imagine. The extra hidden layer means we can add an additional interaction between the input features, but for very complex data types (such as images or documents), we could easily imagine cases where capturing all interactions of interests might require more than one layer of blending and recombination to resolve. For example, one could imagine a document dataset where individual word features captured by the network are merged into sentence fragments features, which are further merged into sentence, paragraph, and chapter patterns, giving potentially 5+ levels of interaction. Each of these interactions would require another layer of hidden neurons, with the number of connections (and weights which need to be tuned) consequently rising. Similarly, an image might be resolved into grids of different resolution that are merged into smaller and larger objects nested within each other. To accommodate these further levels of interaction by adding additional hidden layers into our network (Figure 4), we would end up creating an increasingly *deep* network. We could also add additional RBM layers like we described . Would this increased complexity help us learn a more accurate model? Would we still be able to compute the optimal parameters for such a system using the back-propagation algorithm?

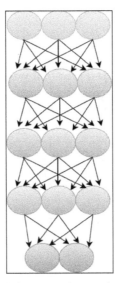

Figure 4: Multilayer neural network architecture

Let us consider what happens in back-propagation when we add an extra layer. Recall that when we derived the expression for the change in the error rate as a function of the weights in the first layer (between visible and the first hidden layer), we ended up with an equation that was a product of the weights between the output and hidden layer, as well as the weights in the first layer:

$$\frac{\partial z}{\partial w_{jk}} = \frac{\partial E}{\partial F(z)_j} \frac{\partial F(z)_j}{z} \frac{\partial z}{\partial w_{jk}}$$

$$= \left(\sum_{i=1}^{n} \frac{\partial E}{\partial F(z)_i} \frac{\partial F(z)_i}{\partial z} w_{ij} \right) F(z)_j \left(1 - F(z)_j \right) x_k$$

Let us consider what happens when the first term (the sum over the errors from the output layer) is <1. Since this formula is a product, the value of the entire expression also decreases, meaning we will change the value of wjk by very small steps. Now recall that to calculate the change in the error with respect to a visible to hidden connection wjk we needed to sum over all the connections from the output to this weight. In our example, we had just two connections, but in deeper networks we would end up with extra terms such as the first to capture the error contribution from all the layers between the hidden and output. When we multiply by more terms with value < 1, the value of the total expressions will increasingly shrink towards 0, meaning the value of the weight will get updated hardly at all during the gradient step. Conversely, if all these terms have value > 1, they will quickly inflate the value of the whole expression, causing the value of the weight to change wildly between gradient update steps.

Thus, the change in error as a function of the hidden to visible weights tends to approach 0 or increase in an unstable fashion, causing the weight to either change very slowly or oscillate wildly in magnitude. It will therefore take a longer time to train the network, and it will be harder to find stable values for weights closer to the visible layer. As we add more layers, this problem becomes worse as we keep adding more error terms that make it harder for the weights to converge to a stable value, as increasing the number of terms in the product representing the gradient has a greater likelihood of shrinking or exploding the value.

Because of this behavior adding more layers and using back-propagation to train a deep network are not sufficient for effectively generating more complex features by incorporating multiple hidden layers in the network. In fact, this problem also known as vanishing gradients due to the fact that the gradients have a greater chance of shrinking to zero and disappearing as we add layers, was one of the major reasons why multilayer neural network remained practically infeasible for many years (Schmidhuber, Jürgen. *Deep learning in neural networks: An overview*. Neural Networks 61 (2015): 85-117.). In a sense, the problem is that the outer layers of the network 'absorb' the information from the error function faster than the deeper layers, making the rate of learning (represented by the weight updates) extremely uneven.

Even if we were to assume that we are not limited by time in our back-propagation procedure and could run the algorithm until the weights finally converge (even if this amount of time were impractical for real-world use), multilayer neural networks present other difficulties such as explaining away.

The explaining away effect concerns the tendency for one input unit to overwhelm the effect of another. A classic example (Hinton, Geoffrey E., Simon Osindero, and Yee-Whye Teh. *A fast learning algorithm for deep belief nets*. Neural computation 18.7 (2006): 1527-1554) is if our response variable is a house jumping off the ground. This could be explained by two potential inputs piece of evidence, whether a truck has hit the house and whether an earthquake has occurred nearby (Figure 5):

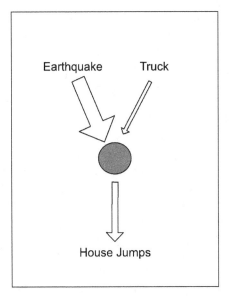

Figure 5: Explaining away causes imbalanced weighting in deep networks

If an earthquake has occurred, then the evidence for this being the cause of the house's movement is so strong that the truck collision evidence is minimized. Simply put, knowing that an earthquake has occurred means we no longer need any additional evidence to explain the house moving, and thus the value of the truck evidence becomes negligible. If we are optimizing for how we should weight these two sources of evidence (analogous to how we might weight the inputs from hidden neurons to an output unit), the weight on the truck collision evidence could be set to 0, as the earthquake evidence explains away the other variable. We could turn on both inputs, but the probability of these two co-occurring is low enough that our learning procedure would not optimally do so. In effect, this means that the value of the weights are correlated with whether the hidden neurons (represented by each evidence type) are turned on (set to 1). Thus, it is difficult to find a set of parameters that does not saturate one weight at the expense of the other. Given the problem of vanishing gradients and explaining away, how could we hope to find the optimal parameters in a deep neural network composed of many layers?

Pretraining belief networks

Both the vanishing gradient and explaining away effects are in a sense are caused by the fact that it is difficult to find an optimal set of weights for large networks if we start from a set of random values and perform back-propagation. Unlike the logistic regression objective function we saw in *Chapter 5, Putting Data in its Place – Classification Methods and Analysis*, the optimal error in a deep learning network is not necessarily convex. Thus, following gradient descent through back-propagation for many rounds is not guaranteed to converge to globally optimal value. Indeed, we can imagine the space of the Error function as a multidimensional landscape, where the elevation represents the value of the error function and the coordinates represent different values of the weight parameters. Back-propagation navigates through different parameter values by moving up or down the slopes of this landscape, which are represented by the *steps* taken with each weight update. If this landscape consisted of a single steep *peak* located at the optimal value of the weights, back-propagation might quickly converge to this value. More often, though, this multidimensional space could have many *ravines* and *valleys* (where the error functions dips and rises in irregular ways with particular set of weights), such that it is difficult for a first-order method such as back-propagation to navigate out of local minima/maxima. For example, the first derivative of the error function could change slowly over a valley in the error function landscape, as the error only gradually increases or decreases as we move in or around the valley. Starting in a random location in this landscape through the standard random initialization of the weight variables might leave us in a place where we are unlikely to ever navigate to the optimal parameter values. Thus, one possibility would be to initialize the weights in the network to a more favorable configuration before running back-propagation, giving us a better chance of actually finding the optimal weight values.

Indeed, this is the essence of the solution proposed by research published in 2006 (Hinton, Geoffrey E., Simon Osindero, and Yee-Whye Teh. *A fast learning algorithm for deep belief nets*. Neural computation 18.7 (2006): 1527-1554). Instead of fitting a multi-layer neural network directly to the response variable for a dataset (in this case, the digits represented by a set of images of hand-drawn numbers) after random initialization of the weight variables, this study suggested that the network weights could be initialized through a pre-training phase that would move them closer to the correct values before running back-propagation. The networks used in this study contained several RBM layers, and the proposed solution was to optimize one RBM at a time through the following steps, which are illustrated in **Figure 6**:

1. First, the visible layer is used to generate a set of values for the hidden neurons, just as in back-propagation.

2. However, the process is then inverted, with the hidden unit values in the uppermost RBM being used as the starting point and the network run backward to recreate the input data (as in Figure 3).

3. The optimal weights between the layers are then calculated using the difference of the input data and the data sample generated by running the model backwards from the hidden layer.

4. This process is iterated several times, until the inferred weights stop changing.

5. This process is then repeated with successive layers, with each deeper hidden layer forming the new input. Additionally, a constraint is enforced that the weights between the visible and first hidden layer and the weights between the first and second hidden layer are matrix transposes: this is known as *tied weights*. This condition is enforced for every pair of weights between adjacent hidden layers:

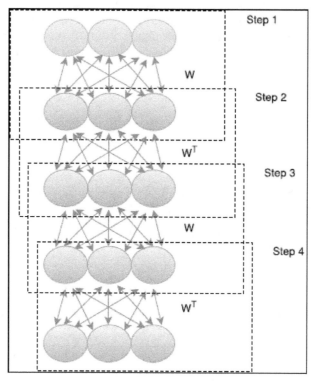

Figure 6: Pre-training algorithm for deep belief networks

This pre-training procedure has the practical effect that the network is initialized with weights that are in the general *shape* of the input data. The fact that this procedure is employed on a single layer at a time avoids some of the vanishing gradient problems discussed previously, since only a single set of weights is considered in each step. The problem of explaining away is also minimized due to the matching of weights as described in step 5. Going back to our example of house movement, the relative strength of the earthquake and truck weights would be represented in the first layer of the deep belief network. In the next phase of pre-training, these weights would be inverted through the matrix transpose, *undoing* the explaining away effect in the higher layer. This pattern is repeated in sequential layers, systematically removing the correlation between the value of the weights and the likelihood of the connected hidden unit being activated.

Once this pretraining is complete, a back-propagation-like approach is used as described for simpler networks, but the weights now converge much quicker to stable values because they have started at a more optimal, instead of random, value.

Using dropout to regularize networks

Even using the pretraining approach described previously, it can be computationally expensive to optimize a large number of parameters in deep networks. We also potentially suffer from the same problem as regression models with large numbers of coefficients, where the large number of parameters leads the network to overfit the training data and not generalize well to data it has not previously seen.

While in the case of regression, we used approaches such as Ridge, Lasso, and Elastic Net to regularize our models, for deep networks we can use an approach known as Dropout to reduce overfitting (Srivastava, Nitish, et al. *Dropout: a simple way to prevent neural networks from overfitting.* Journal of Machine Learning Research 15.1 (2014): 1929-1958.). The idea is relatively is simple: at each stage of tuning the weights, we randomly remove some neuron units along with their connections from the network and only update the remaining weights. As we repeat this process, we effectively average over many possible network structures. This is because with a 50% probability of dropping any given neuron at each stage from the network, each stage of our training effectively samples from 2n possible network structures. Thus, the model is regularized because we are only fitting a subsample of parameters at each stage, and similar to the random forest we examined in *Chapter 5, Putting Data in its Place – Classification Methods and Analysis*, we average over a larger number of randomly constructed networks. Even though dropout can reduce over fitting, it could potentially make the training process longer, since we need to average over more networks to obtain an accurate prediction.

Convolutional networks and rectified units

Even though the pre-training procedure provides a way to initialize network weights, as we add layers the overall model complexity increases. For larger input data (for example, large images), this can lead to increasing numbers of weights along with each additional layer, and thus the training period may take longer. Thus, for some applications, we might accelerate the training process by intelligently simplifying the structure of our network by (1) not making a connection between every single neuron in every layer and (2) changing the functions used for neurons.

These kinds of modifications are common in a type of deep network also known as a Convotional Network (LeCun, Yann, et al. *Gradient-based learning applied to document recognition*. Proceedings of the IEEE 86.11 (1998): 2278-2324; Krizhevsky, Alex, Ilya Sutskever, and Geoffrey E. Hinton. *Imagenet classification with deep convolutional neural networks*. Advances in neural information processing systems. 2012). The name convolution comes from image analysis, where a convolution operator such as the opening and dilation operations we used in *Chapter 6, Words and Pixels – Working with Unstructured Data* are applied to overlapping areas of an image. Indeed, convolutional Networks are commonly applied to tasks involving image recognition. While the number of potential configurations is large, a potential structure of a convolutional network might be the following (see Figure 7):

- **The visible, input layer, with width w and height h**: For color images, this input can be three-dimensional, with one depth layer for each of the red, green, and blue channels.

- **A convolutional layer**: Here, a single neuron could be connected to a square region through all three color channels (*nxnx3*). Each of these nxnx3 units has a weight connecting it to a neuron in the convolutional layer. Furthermore, we could have more than one neuron in the convolutional layer connected to each of these *nxnx3* units, but each with a different set of weights.

- **A rectifying layer**: Using the **Rectified Linear Unit (ReLU)** discussed later in this chapter, each of the neurons outputs in the convolutional layer are thresholded to yield another set of neurons of the same size.

- **A downsampling layer**: This type of layer averages over a subregion in the previous layer to produce a layer with a smaller width and height, while leaving the depth unchanged.

- **A fully connected layer**: In this layer each unit in the downsampling layer is connected to a vector of output (for example, a 10 unit vector representing 10 different class labels).

This architecture exploits the structure of the data (examining local patterns in images), and training is faster because we only make selective connections between neurons in each layer, leading to fewer weights to optimize. A second reason that this structure can train more rapidly is due to the activation functions used in the rectification and pooling layers. A common choice of pooling function is simply the maximum of all inputs, also known as a **Rectified Linear Unit (ReLU)** (Nair, Vinod, and Geoffrey E. Hinton. *Rectified linear units improve restricted boltzmann machines.* Proceedings of the 27th International Conference on Machine Learning (ICML-10). 2010). which is:

$$F(z) = max(z, 0)$$

Here, z is the input to a given neuron. Unlike the logistic function described previously, the ReLU is not bounded by the range [0,1], meaning that the values to neurons following it in the network can change more rapidly than is possible with logistic functions. Furthermore, the gradient of the ReLU is given by:

$$\frac{\partial F(z)}{\partial z} = \begin{cases} 1 \, if \, z > 0 \\ else \, 0 \end{cases}$$

This means that gradients do not tend to vanish (unless the neuron inputs drop very low such that it is always off) or explode, as the maximum change is 1. In the former case, to prevent the ReLU from turning permanently off, the function could be modified to be leaky:

$$F(z) = max(z, \alpha z)$$
$$\frac{\partial F(z)}{\partial z} = \begin{cases} 1 \, if \, z > 0 \\ else \, \alpha \end{cases}$$

Here, α is a small value such a `0.01`, preventing the neuron from ever being set to 0.

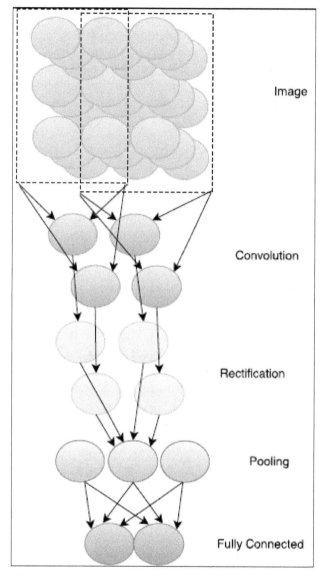

Figure 7: Convolutional neural network architecture. For clarity, connections in convolutional layer are represented to highlighted region rather than all wxhxd neurons, and only a subset of the network converging to a pooling layer neuron is shown.

Aside: Alternative Activation Functions

In addition to the linear, sigmoid, and ReLU functions discussed previously, other activation functions are also used in building deep networks. One is the hyperbolic tangent function, also known as the tanh function, given by:

$$\tanh(x) = \frac{e^{2x}-1}{e^{2x}+1} = \frac{1-e^{-2x}}{1+e^{-2x}}$$

The output of this function is in the range $[-1,1]$, unlike the sigmoid or ReLU, which are in the range $[0,1]$, and some evidence suggests that this could accelerate training of networks by allowing the average output of neurons to be zero and thus reduce bias (LeCun, Yann, Ido Kanter, and Sara A. Solla. "Second order properties of error surfaces: Learning time and generalization." Advances in neural information processing systems 3 (1991): 918-924.). Similarly, we could imagine using a Gaussian function such as the kernels we saw in *Chapters 3, Finding Patterns in the Noise – Clustering and Unsupervised Learning*, and *Chapter 5, Putting Data in its Place – Classification Methods and Analysis*, in the context of spectral clustering and SVMs, respectively. The softmax function used for multinomial regression in *Chapter 5, Putting Data in its Place – Classification Methods and Analysis*, is also a candidate; the number of potential functions increases the flexibility of deep models, allowing us to tune specific behavior according to the problem at hand.

Compressing Data with autoencoder networks

While most of our discussion in this chapter involves the use of deep learning for classification tasks, these models can also be used for dimensionality reduction in a way comparable to the matrix factorization methods we discussed in *Chapter 6, Words and Pixels – Working with Unstructured Data*. In such an application, also known as an *auto-encoder* network (Hinton, Geoffrey E., and Ruslan R. Salakhutdinov. *Reducing the dimensionality of data with neural networks*. Science 313.5786 (2006): 504-507), the objective is not to fit a response (such as binary label), but to reconstruct the data itself. Thus, the visible and output layers are always the same size (Figure 8), while the hidden layers are typically smaller and thus form a lower-dimensional representation of the data that can be used to reconstruct the input. Thus, like PCA or NMF, autoencoders discover a compact version of the input that can approximate the original (with some error). If the hidden layer was not smaller than the visible and output, the network might well just optimize the hidden layer to be identical to the input; this would allow the network to perfectly reconstruct the input, but at the expense of any feature extraction or dimensionality reduction.

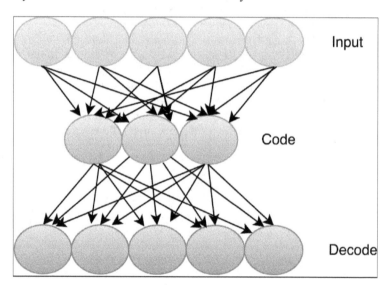

Figure 8: Autoencoder network architecture

Optimizing the learning rate

In the examples we have discussed above, the learning rate for the parameters at each stage is always a fixed value α. Intuitively, it makes sense that for some parameters we may want to adjust the value more aggressively, while others less. Many optimizations have been proposed for this sort of tuning. For example, Adative Gradient (AdaGrad) (Duchi, John, Elad Hazan, and Yoram Singer. *Adaptive subgradient methods for online learning and stochastic optimization*. Journal of Machine Learning Research 12.Jul (2011): 2121-2159.) uses a learning rate for each parameter based on the past history of gradients for a given parameter:

$$w_t = w_{t-1} - \frac{\alpha}{\sqrt{G_t + \varepsilon}} \frac{\partial E}{\partial w}$$

Where *Gt* represents the sum of squares of all gradients of a particular parameter, gt is the gradient at the current step, and ε is a smoothing parameter. Thus, the learning rate at each stage is the global value α, multiplied by a fraction that the current gradient represents of the historic variation. If the current gradient is high compared to historical updates, then we change the parameter more. Otherwise, we should change it less. Over time, most the learning rates will shrink toward zero, accelerating convergence.

A natural extension of this idea is used in AdaDelta (Zeiler, Matthew D. *ADADELTA: an adaptive learning rate method*. arXiv preprint arXiv:1212.5701 (2012)), where instead of using the full history of gradient updates G, we, at each step, replace this value with the average of the current gradient and the historical average gradient:

$$\frac{1}{T}\left(\frac{\partial E}{\partial w}\right)_t^2 = \gamma \frac{1}{T}\left(\frac{\partial E}{\partial w}\right)_{t-1}^2 + (1-\gamma)\left(\frac{\partial E}{\partial w}\right)_t^2$$

The expression for Adagrad then uses the above formula in the denominator instead of *Gt*. Like Adagrad, this will tend to reduce the learning rate for parameters that are not changing significantly relative to their history.

The `TensorFlow` library we will examine in the following also provides the Adaptive Moment Estimation (ADAM) method for adjusting the learning rate (Kingma, Diederik, and Jimmy Ba. *Adam: A method for stochastic optimization.* arXiv preprint arXiv:1412.6980 (2014).). In this method, like AdaDelta, we keep an average of the squared gradient, but also of the gradient itself. The update rule is then as follows:

$$w_t = w_{t-1} - \frac{\alpha}{\sqrt{\frac{1}{T}\left(\frac{\partial E}{\partial w}\right)_t^2 \left(\frac{1}{1-\beta_1}\right)} + \varepsilon} \frac{\partial E}{\partial w}\left(\frac{1}{1-\beta_2}\right)$$

Here, the weighted averages as in `AdaDelta`, normalized by dividing by a decay parameter $(1-\beta)$. Many other algorithms have been proposed, but the sample of methods we have described should give you an idea of how the learning rate may be adaptively tuned to accelerate training of deep networks.

Aside: alternative network architectures

In addition to the Convolutional, Feed Forward, and Deep Belief Networks we have discussed, other network architectures are tuned for particular problems. **Recurrent Neural Networks (RNNs)** have sparse two-way connections between layers, allowing units to exhibit reinforcing behavior through these cycles (Figure 9). Because the network has a memory from this cycle, it can be used to process data for tasks as speech recognition (Graves, Alex, et al. "A novel connectionist system for unconstrained handwriting recognition." IEEE transactions on pattern analysis and machine intelligence 31.5 (2009): 855-868.), where a series of inputs of indeterminate length is processed, and at each point the network can produce a predicted label based on the current and previous inputs. Similarly, **Long Short Term Memory Networks (LSTM)** (*Hochreiter, Sepp, and Jürgen Schmidhuber. Long short-term memory. Neural computation 9.8 (1997): 1735-1780*). have cyclic elements that allow units to remember input from previously input data. In contrast to RNNs, they also have secondary units that can erase the values in the cyclically activated units, allowing the network to retain information from inputs over a particular window of time (see **Figure 9**, the loop represents this `forgetting` function which may be activated by the inputs) .

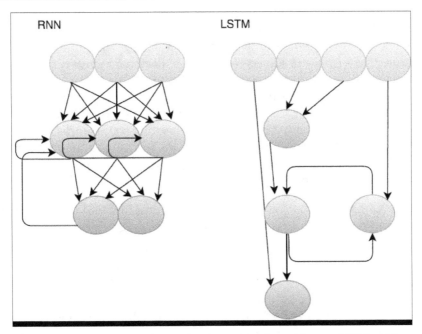

Figure 9: Recurrent Neural Network (RNN) and Long Short Term Memory (LSTM) architectures.

Now that we have seen how a deep learning network is constructed, trained, and tuned through a variety of optimizations, let's look at a practical example of image recognition.

The TensorFlow library and digit recognition

For the exercises in this chapter, we will be using the `TensorFlow` library open-sourced by Google (available at `https://www.tensorflow.org/`). Installation instructions vary by operating system. Additionally, for Linux systems, it is possible to leverage both the CPU and **graphics processing unit** (**GPU**) on your computer to run deep learning models. Because many of the steps in training (such as the multiplications required to update a grid of weight values) involve matrix operations, they can be readily parallelized (and thus accelerated) by using a GPU. However, the `TensorFlow` library will work on CPU as well, so don't worry if you don't have access to an Nvidia GPU card.

The MNIST data

The data we will be examining in this exercise is a set of images of hand-drawn numbers from 0 to 9 from the **Mixed National Institute of Standards and Technology (MNIST)** database (LeCun, Yann, Corinna Cortes, and Christopher JC Burges. *The MNIST database of handwritten digits.* (1998)). Similar to the Hello World! program used to introduce basic programming techniques, or the word count example used for demonstrating distributed computing frameworks, the MNIST data is a common example used to demonstrate the functions of neural network libraries. The prediction task associated with this data is to assign a label (digit from 0 to 9) for an image, given only the input pixels.

The `TensorFlow` library provides a `convenient` library function to load this data using the commands:

```
>>> from tensorflow.examples.tutorials.mnist import input_data
>>> mnist = input_data.read_data_sets('MNIST_data', one_hot=True)
```

Note that along with specifying that we wish to load the MNIST data, we have indicated that the target variable (the digit represented by the image) should be encoded in a binary vector (for example, the number 3 is indicated by placing a 1 in the fourth element of this vector, since the first element encodes the digit 0). Once we have loaded the data, we can start examining the images themselves. We can see that the data has already been conveniently divided into a training and test set using a 4:1 split by examining the length of the training and test sets using the commands:

```
>>> len(mnist.train.images)
>>> len(mnist.test.images)
```

Each of these images is a *28*28* pixel image. In the data, these are stored as a one-dimensional vector of length 784, but we can use the `skimage` library from the previous chapter to visualize the images once we have reshaped the array into its original dimensions using the commands.

```
>>> from skimage import io
>> io.imshow(np.reshape(mnist.train.images[0],(28,28)))
```

Which displays the first image in the set:

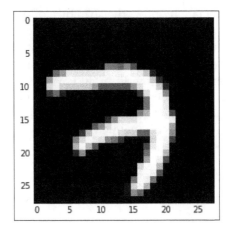

This looks like the number 7: to check the label assigned to this image, we can examine the labels element of the train object using:

```
>>> mnist.train.labels[0]
```

which gives

```
array([ 0.,   0.,   0.,   0.,   0.,   0.,   0.,   1.,   0.,   0.])
```

The label is a 10-element vector, representing (from left to right) the digits 0–9, with 1 in the position associated with the label for an image. Indeed, the label assigned to this image is 7. Note that the label array takes the same shape as the final layer of the neural network algorithms we have been examining, giving the convenient ability to directly compare the label to the output once we have calculated the prediction.

Now that we have examined the data, let us use the other utilities of the TensorFlow library to develop a neural network that can predict the label of an image.

Constructing the network

As you can probably appreciate by now, the structure of deep neural networks can be extremely complex. Thus, if we were to define variables for each layer of the network, we would end up with a long block of code that would need to be modified every time we changed the structure of the network. Because in practical applications we may want to experiment with many different variations of depth, layer size, and connectivity, we instead show in this exercise an example of how to make this structure generic and reusable. The key ingredients are functions to produce the layers, a list of the desired layers specified by these generator functions, and an outer process that links together the generated layers:

```python
>>> def weight_variable(dimensions,stddev):
...        return tf.Variable(tf.truncated_normal(dimensions, stddev=stddev))


>>> def bias_variable(dimensions,constant):
...        return tf.Variable(tf.constant(constant, shape=dimensions))


>>> def two_dimensional_convolutional_layer(x, W, strides, padding):
...        return tf.nn.conv2d(x, W, strides=strides, padding=padding)


>>> def max_pooling(x,strides,ksize,padding):
...     return tf.nn.max_pool(x, ksize=ksize,strides=strides,
padding=padding)


>>> def generate_network(weight_variables,\
                    bias_variables,\
                    relu_layers,\
                    pooling_layers,\
                    fully_connected_layers,\
                    inputs,\
                    conv_strides,\
                    pool_stries,\
                    ksize,\
                    output_channels,\
                    conv_field_sizes,\
                    conv_field_depths,\
                    sd_weights\
                    ,bias_mean,\
```

```
                            padding,\
                            conv_layers,\
                            fc_layers,\
                            fc_shape,\
                            keep_prob,\
                            class_num,\
                            dropouts):


     # add convolutional layers
     >>> for k in range(conv_layers):
     …        weight_variables.append(weight_variable([conv_field_sizes[k],
conv_field_sizes[k], conv_field_depths[k],output_channels[k]],sd_
weights))
             bias_variables.append(bias_variable([output_
channels[k]],bias_mean))
               relu_layers.append(tf.nn.relu(two_dimensional_
convolutional_layer(inputs[k],weight_variables[k],\

conv_strides,padding) + bias_variables[k]))
             pooling_layers.append(max_pooling(relu_layers[k],pool_
strides,ksize,padding))
             inputs.append(pooling_layers[k])


     # finally, add fully connected layers at end with dropout
     >>> for r in range(fc_layers):
             weight_variables.append(weight_variable(fc_shape,sd_weights))
             bias_variables.append(bias_variable([fc_shape[1]],bias_mean))
               pooling_layers.append(tf.reshape(pooling_layers[-1],[-1,fc_
shape[0]]))
             fully_connected_layers.append(tf.nn.relu(tf.matmul(pooling_
layers[-1], weight_variables[-1]) + bias_variables[-1]))
             dropouts.append(tf.nn.dropout(fully_connected_layers[-1],
keep_prob))


     # output layer
           weight_variables.append(weight_variable([fc_shape[1],class_
num],sd_weights))
             bias_variables.append(bias_variable([class_num],bias_mean))
           return tf.nn.softmax(tf.matmul(dropouts[-1],weight_variables[-
1])+bias_variables[-1])
```

This format thus allows us to template the construction of the network in a way that is easily reconfigured and reused.

This function constructs a series of `convolutional/max_pooling` layers, followed by one or more fully connected layers, whose output is used to generate a prediction. At the end, we simply return the final layer prediction from the `softmax` function as the output. Thus, we can configure a network by setting a few parameters:

```
>>> X = tf.placeholder("float", shape=[None, 784])
>>> observed = tf.placeholder("float", shape=[None, 10])
>>> images = tf.reshape(X, [-1,28,28,1])


# shape variables
>>> sd_weights = 0.1
>>> bias_mean = 0.1
>>> padding = 'SAME'
>>> conv_strides = [1,1,1,1]
>>> pool_strides = [1,2,2,1]
>>> ksize = [1,2,2,1]
>>> output_channels = [32,64]
>>> conv_field_sizes = [5,5]
>>> conv_field_depths = [1,32]
>>>fc_shape = [7*7*64,1024]
>>> keep_prob = tf.placeholder("float")
>>> class_num = 10
>>> conv_layers = 2
>>> fc_layers = 1


# layers variables
>>> weight_variables = []
>>> bias_variables = []
>>> relu_layers = []
>>> pooling_layers = []
>>> inputs = [images]
>>> fully_connected_layers = []
>>> dropouts = []


>>> prediction = generate_network(weight_variables,\
```

```
                     bias_variables,\
                     relu_layers,\
                     pooling_layers,\
                     fully_connected_layers,\
                     inputs,\
                     conv_strides,\
                     pool_strides,\
                     ksize,\
                     output_channels,\
                     conv_field_sizes,\
                     conv_field_depths,\
                     sd_weights\
                     ,bias_mean,\
                     padding,\
                     conv_layers,\
                     fc_layers,\
                     fc_shape,\
                     keep_prob,\
                     class_num,\
                     dropouts)
```

Note that the input (x) and the true labels (observed) are both placeholders, as is the probability of dropout in a layer (keep_prob) — they do not contain actual values, but will be filled in as the network is trained and we submit batches of data to the algorithm.

Now all we need to do is initialize a session and begin submitting batches of data using the following code:

```
>>> my_session = tf.InteractiveSession()
>>> squared_error = tf.reduce_sum(tf.pow(tf.reduce_sum(tf.
sub(observed,prediction)),[2]))
>>> train_step = tf.train.GradientDescentOptimizer(0.01).
minimize(squared_error)
>>> correct_prediction = tf.equal(tf.argmax(prediction,1),
tf.argmax(observed,1))
>>> accuracy = tf.reduce_mean(tf.cast(correct_prediction, "float"))
>>> my_session.run(tf.initialize_all_variables())
```

```
>>>for i in range(20000):
...    batch = mnist.train.next_batch(50)
 ...   if i%1000 == 0:
...        train_accuracy = accuracy.eval(feed_dict={X: batch[0], observed:
batch[1], keep_prob: 1.0})
   ...     print("step %d, training accuracy %g"%(i, train_accuracy))
...         train_step.run(feed_dict={X: batch[0], observed: batch[1], keep_
prob: 0.5})
...         print("test accuracy %g"%accuracy.eval(feed_dict={X: mnist.test.
images, observed: mnist.test.labels, keep_prob: 1.0}))
```

We can observe the progress of the algorithm as it trains, with the accuracy of every 1000th iteration printed to the console.

Summary

In this chapter, we introduced deep neural networks as a way to generate models for complex data types where features are difficult to engineer. We examined how neural networks are trained through back-propagation, and why additional layers make this optimization intractable. We discussed solutions to this problem and demonstrated the use of the `TensorFlow` library to build an image classifier for hand-drawn digits.

Now that you have covered a wide range of predictive models, we will turn in the final two chapters to the last two tasks in generating analytical pipelines: turning the models that we have trained into a repeatable, automated process, and visualizing the results for ongoing insights and monitoring.

8
Sharing Models with Prediction Services

Thus far, we have examined how to build a variety of models with data sources ranging from standard 'tabular' data to text and images. However, this only accomplishes part of our goal in business analysis: we can generate predictions from a dataset, but we cannot easily share the results with colleagues or with other software systems within a company. We also cannot easily replicate the results as new data becomes available without manually re-running the sorts of analyses discussed in previous chapters or scale it to larger datasets over time. We will also have difficulty to use our models in a public setting, such as a company's website, without revealing the details of the analysis through the model parameters exposed in our code.

To overcome these challenges, the following chapter will describe how to build 'prediction services', web applications that encapsulate and automate the core components of data transformation, model fitting, and scoring of new observations that we have discussed in the context of predicative algorithms in prior sections. By packaging our analysis into a web application, we can both easily scale the modeling system and change implementations in the underlying algorithm, all the while making such changes invisible to the consumer (whether a human or other software system), who interacts with our predictive models by making requests to our application through web URLs and a standard REST **application programmer interface (API)**. It also allows initialization and updates to the analysis to be automated through calls to the service, making the predictive modeling task consistent and replicable. Finally, by carefully parameterizing many of the steps, we can use the same service to interact with interchangeable data sources computation frameworks.

In essences, building a prediction service involves linking several of the components we have already discussed, such as data transformation and predictive modeling, with a set of new components that we will discuss in this chapter for the first time. To this end, we will cover the following topics:

- How to instrument a basic web application and server using the Cherrypy and Flask frameworks

- How to automate a generic modeling framework using a RESTful API

- Scaling our system using a Spark computation framework

- Storing the results of our predictive model in database systems for reporting applications we will discuss in *Chapter 9, Reporting and Testing – Iterating on Analytic Systems*

The architecture of a prediction service

Now with a clear goal in mind — to share and scale the results of our predictive modeling using a web application — what are the components required to accomplish this objective?

The first is the *client*: this could be either a web browser or simply a user entering a `curl` command in the terminal (see Aside). In either case, the client sends requests using **hypertext transfer protocol (HTTP)**, a standard transport convention to retrieve or transmit information over a network (Berners-Lee, Tim, Roy Fielding, and Henrik Frystyk. *Hypertext transfer protocol--HTTP/1.0*. No. RFC 1945. 1996). An important feature of the HTTP standard is that the client and server do not have to 'know' anything about how the other is implemented (for example, which programming language is used to write these components) because the message will remain consistent between them regardless by virtue of following the HTTP standard.

The next component is the *server*, which receives HTTP requests from a client and forwards them to the application. You can think of it as the gateway for the requests from the client to our actual predictive modeling application. In Python, web servers and applications each conform to the **Web Server Gateway Interface (WSGI)**, which specifies how the server and application should communicate. Like the HTTP requests between client and server, this standard allows the server and application to be modular as long as both consistently implement the interface. In fact, there could even be intervening middleware between the server and application that further modifies communication between the two: as long as the format of this communication remains constant, the details of each side of the interface are flexible. While we will use the Cherrypy library to build a server for our application, other common choices are Apache Tomcat and Nginx, both written in the Java programming language.

After the client request has been received and forwarded by the server, the application performs operations in response to the requests, and returns a value indicating the success or failure of the task. These requests could, for example, obtain for the predicted score for a particular user, update to the training dataset, or perform a round of model training.

Aside: The curl command

As part of testing our prediction service, it is useful to have a way to quickly issue commands to the server and observe the response we receive back. While we could do some of this interactively using the address bar of a web browser, it is not easy to script browser activities in cases where we want to run a number of tests or replicate a particular command. The `curl` command, found in most Linux command line terminals, is very useful for this purpose: the same requests (in terms of a URL) can be issued to the prediction service using the `curl` command as would be given in the browser, and this call can be automated using shell scripting. The `curl` application can be installed from `https://curl.haxx.se/`.

The web application relies upon server-side code to perform commands in response to requests from the web server. In our example, this server-side code is divided into several components: the first is a generic interface for the modeling logic, which specifies a standard way to construct predictive models, train them with an input dataset, and score incoming data. The second is an implementation of this framework using the logistic regression algorithm from *Chapter 5, Putting Data in its Place – Classification Methods and Analysis*. This code relies upon executing Spark jobs, which could be carried out either locally (on the same machine as the web application) or remotely (on a separate cluster).

The final piece of this chain is database systems that can persist information used by the prediction service This database could be as simple as file system on the same machine as the web server or as complex as a distributed database software. In our example we will use both Redis (a simple key-value store) and MongoDB (a NoSQL database) to store the data used in modeling, transient information about our application, and the model results themselves.

As we have emphasized, an important feature of these three components is that they are largely independent: because the WGSI standard defines how the web server and application communicate, we could change server and predictive model implementation, and as long as the commands used in the web application are the same, the code will still work since these commands are formatted in a consistent way.

Now that we have covered the basic components of a prediction service and how they communicate with one another, let us examine each in greater detail.

Clients and making requests

When a client issues requests to the server and the downstream application, we might potentially have a major design problem: how do we know in advance what kind of requests we might receive? If we had to re-implement a new set of standard requests every time we developed a web application, it would be difficult to reuse code and write generic services that other programs could call, since their requests would potentially have to change for every web application a client might interact with.

This is the problem solved by the HTTP standard, which describes a standard language and format in which requests are sent between servers and clients, allowing us to rely upon a common command syntax, which could be consumed by many different applications. While we could, in theory, issue some of these commands to our prediction service by pasting a URL into the address bar of our browser (such as GET, described below), this will only cover a subset of the kinds of requests we want to issue. The standard sorts of requests we typically implement in a web application are:

The GET requests

The GET requests only retrieve information, which will then be rendered in our web browser depending upon the kind of response. We could receive back an actual html page, or simply a piece of text. In order to specify what information we want to receive, a GET request will include variables in the URL in the form url?key1=value1&key2=value2. URL is the web address given to the prediction service, which in our example will just be the local machine, but could also be any valid IP address or URL. This URL is separated by a question mark (**?**) from the (key, value) pairs that define the parameters of our request for information. Multiple parameters may be specified: for example, we could indicate a pair of parameters for a user and item dataset using the string userid=12894&itemid=93819, with each key, value pair separated by the ampersand symbol (&).

We can directly issue a GET request by pasting the URL format described previously into the address bar of a browser or by issuing a curl command to the same address by typing the following into a terminal:

```
> curl <address>
```

We can also use the Python requests library (http://docs.python-requests.org/en/master/), which allows us to not worry about the details of formatting the URL. Using this library, the same GET request is called in the following way:

```
>>> r = requests.get(url,params)
```

Here, `params` is a dictionary of key-value pairs that we would have passed in the URL. The requests library performs this formatting for us, as we can see by printing the resulting URL:

```
>>> print(r.url)
```

Once we have issued the request, we can check the result using either of the following two commands:

```
>>> r.json()
```
```
>>> r.text
```

We can also check the status code of the response to see if there was an error or not (see aside on standard response codes):

```
>>> r.status_code
```

Aside: HTTP Status Codes

When we issue a request to a web application using the methods discussed in this chapter, one way to check the success of the request is to examine the response code, which gives a standard number corresponding to the response of the web application to the request. You may have even seen these codes before without realizing it, such as the 404 error that is returned when a webpage cannot be displayed in your browser. The standard codes to be aware of are:

200: success, we usually check this value to make sure we received a correct response.

404: not found, indicating that the web application could not find the resource we requested.

500: server error, which we will often receive if the code run by our web application runs into problems.

For a more comprehensive list please, see (Nottingham, Mark, and Roy Fielding. "Additional HTTP Status Codes." (2012); Berners-Lee, Tim, Roy Fielding, and Henrik Frystyk. Hypertext transfer protocol--HTTP/1.0. No. RFC 1945. 1996).

The POST request

Unlike the GET command, the POST request does not use data contained in the URL, but rather transmits information separate from the URL. If you have ever entered your credit card information in an online store, this information is probably transmitted using a POST request, which is fortunate since it then remains hidden. However, the fact that the information for the request is not contained in the URL means that we cannot simply paste the request into the address bar of our web browser: we would need a form on the webpage that issues the POST request or make the request programmatically ourselves. Without an actual form on a webpage, we can use a `curl` command to issue a POST request using the following syntax:

```
> curl -x POST  -d  <data> <url>
```

We can also use the Python requests library:

```
>>> r = requests.post(url,data)
```

In the preceding code, `data` is a Python dictionary of information that the web application can access in fulfilling the POST request.

The HEAD request

Like the GET request, HEAD retrieves information, but instead of the body of the response (such as a webpage or JSON), it only retrieves metadata about the response (such as the encoding). We can issue a HEAD request using the following:

```
> curl -i -X HEAD <url>
```

Note that we have added the `-i` flag to this request; normally, the `curl` command will not print header information without this option. Using the Python requests library we would use the command:

```
>>>   requests.head(url)
```

The PUT request

In cases where our web application has access to a database system, we issue PUT commands in order to store new information. Using `curl`, we make this request using the following:

```
> curl -X PUT -d key1=value1 -d key2=value2 <url>
```

We can also make this request using the requests library:

```
>>>  r = requests.put(url,data)
```

Here, data is a dictionary of the arguments we wish to place in the applications storage system.

The DELETE request

The opposite of the PUT command, DELETE requests are issued to remove a piece of data from the application's storage system. The curl command is as follows:

```
> curl -X DELETE -d key1=value1 -d key2=value2 <url>
```

While the same request using the requests library is as follows:

```
>>>  r = requests.delete(url,data)
```

Here, data is a dictionary of the arguments we wish to remove from the applications storage system.

While there are other requests types available, we will not cover them in this discussion; for more details please see (Berners-Lee, Tim, Roy Fielding, and Henrik Frystyk. Hypertext transfer protocol--HTTP/1.0. No. RFC 1945. 1996). Note that since we can issue these requests using the Python request library, we can actually test our web application in the Python notebooks we have been using in the exercises in this volume.

For our purposes, the client will be the Jupyter notebook itself or the command line of the terminal; however, we could imagine other cases where the client is actually another web application that issues these commands and acts on the response. Again, since the server only needs to guarantee a particular message format rather than the details of the sender, either option is interchangeable.

Now that we know how to issue HTTP requests to our service, let us look at the server.

Server – the web traffic controller

To run our prediction service, we need to communicate with external systems to receive requests to train a model, score new data, evaluate existing performance, or provide model parameter information. The web server performs this function, accepting incoming HTTP requests and forwarding them on to our web application either directly or through whatever middleware may be used.

Though we could have made many different choices of server in illustrating this example, we have chosen the CherryPy library because unlike other popular servers such as Apache Tomcat or Nginx, it is written in Python (allowing us to demonstrate its functionality inside a notebook) and is scalable, processing many requests in only a few milliseconds (`http://www.aminus.org/blogs/index.php/2006/12/23/ cherrypy_3_has_fastest_wsgi_server_yet.`). The server is attached to a particular port, or endpoint (this is usually given in the format `url:port`), to which we direct requests that are then forwarded to the web application. The use of ports means that we could in theory have multiple servers on a given URL, each listening to requests on a different endpoint.

As we discussed previously, the server uses the WGSI specification to communicate with the application itself. In concrete terms, the server has a function known as a callable (for example, any object with a `__call__` method) that is executed every time it receives a request, whose result is handed off to the application. In our example in this chapter, the WGSI is already implemented by CherryPy, and we will simply illustrate how it does so. Complete documentation of the interface is available at (`https://www.python.org/dev/peps/pep-0333/`). In a way, the WGSI solves the same problem as HTTP in the communication between servers and applications: it provides a common way in which the two systems exchange information, allowing us to swap the components or event place intervening components without altering the fundamental way in which information is transferred.

In cases where we might wish to scale the application to a larger load, we could imagine middleware such as a load balancer between the server and the application. The middleware would receive the callable output and pass it along to the web application. In the case of a load balancer, this could potentially redistribute requests to many separate instances of the same predictive service, allowing us to scale the service horizontally (see Aside). Each of these services would then return their response to the server before it is sent back to the client.

Aside: horizontal and vertical scaling

As the volume of data or computational complexity of our prediction services increases, we have two primary ways to increase the performance of the service. The first, known as horizontal scaling, might involve adding more instances of our application. Separately, we might also increase the number of resources in our underlying computing layer, such as Spark. In contrast, vertical scaling involves improving the existing resources by adding more RAM, CPU, or disk space. While horizontal scaling is more easily implemented using software alone, the right solution for such resources constraints will depend on the problem domain and organizational budget.

Application – the engine of the predictive services

Once a request has made its way from the client to the application, we need to provide the logic that will execute these commands and return a response to the server and subsequently client upstream. To do so, we must attach a function to the particular endpoint and requests we anticipate receiving.

In this chapter, we will be using the Flask framework to develop our web application (`http://flask.pocoo.org/`). While Flask can also support template generation of HTML pages, in this chapter we will be using it purely to implement various requests to the underlying predictive algorithm code through URL endpoints corresponding to the HTTP requests discussed previously. Implementing these endpoints allows a consistent interface through which many other software systems could interact with our application—they just need to point to the appropriate web address and process the response returned from our service. In case you are concerned we will not generate any actual 'webpages' in our application, do not be worried: we will use the same Flask framework in *Chapter 9, Reporting and Testing – Iterating on Analytic Systems*, to develop a dashboard system based on the data we will generate through the predictive modeling service in this chapter.

In writing the logic for our predictive modeling application, it is important to keep in mind that the functions that are called in response to client requests can themselves be interfaces specifying a generic, modular service. While we could directly implement a particular machine learning algorithm in the code for the web application itself, we have chosen to abstract this design, with the web application instead making a generic call to construct a model with some parameters, train, and score using an algorithm, regardless of the data or particular model used in the application. This allows us to reuse the web application code with many different algorithms while also affording the flexibility to implement these algorithms in different ways over time. It also forces us to determine a consistent set of operations for our algorithms since the web application will only interact with them through this abstraction layer.

Finally, we have the algorithm itself, which is called by the web application code. This program needs to implement functions, such as training a model and scoring records using a set of data, specified in the web application. The details can change substantially over time without need to modify the web application, allowing us to flexibly develop new models or experiment with different libraries.

Persisting information with database systems

Our prediction service will use data in a number of ways. When we start the service, we have standard configurations we would like to retrieve (for example, the model parameters), and we might also like to log records of the requests that the application responds to for debugging purposes. As we score data or prepare trained models, we would ideally like to store these somewhere in case the prediction service needs to be restarted. Finally, as we will discuss in more detail, a database can allow us to keep track of application state (such as which tasks are in progress). For all these uses, a number of database systems can be applied.

Databases are generally categorized into two groups: relational and non-relational. Relational databases are probably familiar to you, as they are used in most business data warehouses. Data is stored in the form of tables, often with facts (such as purchases or search events) containing columns (such as user account IDs or an item identifier) that may be joined to dimensional tables (containing information on an item or user) or relational information (such as a hierarchy of items IDs that define the contents of an online store). In a web application, a relational system can be used behind the scenes to retrieve information (for example, in response to a GET request for user information), to insert new information, or delete rows from the database. Because the data in a relational system is stored in tables, it needs to follow a common series of columns, and these sorts of systems are not designed with nested structures such as JSON in mind. If we know there are columns we will frequently query (such as an item ID), we can design indices on the tables in these systems that speed up retrieval. Some common popular (and open source) relational systems are MySQL, PostGreSQL, and SQLite.

Non-relational databases, also known as 'NoSQL', follow a very different data model. Instead of being formed of tables with multiple columns, these systems are designed as with alternative layouts such as key-value stores, where a row of information (such as a customer account) has a key (such as an item index) and an arbitrary amount of information in the value field. For example, the value could be a single item or a nested series of other key-values. This flexibility means that NoSQL databases can store information with diverse schema even in the same table, since the fields in the value do not need to be specifically defined. Some of these applications allow us to create indices on particular fields within the value, just as for relational systems. In addition to key-value databases (such as Redis) and document stores (such as MongoDB), NoSQL systems also include columnar stores where data are co-located in files based primarily on column chunks rather than rows (examples include Cassandra and Druid), and graph databases such as Neo4j which are optimized for data composed of nodes and edges (such as what we studied in the context of spectral clustering in *Chapter 3, Finding Patterns in the Noise – Clustering and Unsupervised Learning*). We will use MongoDB and Redis in our example in this chapter.

In addition to storing data with flexible schema, such as the nested JSON strings we might encounter in REST API calls, key-value stores can server another function in a web application by allowing us to persist the state of a task. For quickly answered requests such as a GET class for information, this is not necessary. However, prediction services might frequently have long-running tasks that are launched by a POST request and take time to compute a response. Even if the task is not complete though, we want to return an immediate response to the client that initiated the task. Otherwise, the client will stall waiting for the server to complete, and this can potentially affect performance of the client and is very much against the philosophy of decoupling the components of the system described previously. Instead, we want to return a task identifier to the client immediately, which will allow the client to poll the service to check on the progress of the task and retrieve the result when it is available. We can store the state of a task using a key-value database and provide both update methods to allow us to provide information on intermediate progress by editing the task records and GET methods to allow clients to retrieve the current status of the task. In our example, we will be using Redis as the backend to store task results for long-running applications, and also as the message queue by which tasks can communicate, a role known as a "broker".

Now that we have covered the basic structure of our prediction service, let us examine a concrete example that ties together many of the patterns we have developed in predictive modeling tasks over the previous sections.

Case study – logistic regression service

As an illustration of the architecture covered previously, let us look at an example of a prediction service that implements a logistic regression model. The model is both trained and scores new data using information passed through URLs (either through the web browser or invoking curl on the command line), and illustrates how these components fit together. We will also examine how we can interactively test these components using the same IPython notebooks as before, while also allowing us to seamlessly deploying the resulting code in an independent application.

Our first task is to set up the databases used to store the information used in modeling, as well as the result and model parameters.

Setting up the database

As a first step in our application, we will set up the database to store our training data and models, and scores obtained for new data. The examples for this exercise consist of data from a marketing campaign, where the objective was to convince customers to subscribe for a term deposit (Moro, Sérgio, Paulo Cortez, and Paulo Rita. "A data-driven approach to predict the success of bank telemarketing."Decision Support Systems 62 (2014): 22-31). Thus, the objective with this data is to predict based on a customer's feature variables whether they are likely to pay for this service. The data is contained in the `bank-full.csv` file, which we need to load into MongoDB (`https://www.mongodb.org/`).

After installing MongoDB for your system, you can test the database by running the following command in your terminal:

```
$ mongodb
```

The preceding command should start the database. Now, to import our training data, we can use the following command in a separate terminal window:

```
$ mongoimport -d datasets -c bank --type csv --file bank-full.csv —
headerline
```

This will allow us to import the data into a database called 'datasets', in a collection called bank. We can test if the data has been successfully loaded by opening a mongo client in the terminal:

```
$ mongo
```

If we run the following command, we should be able to see our dataset listed under the datasets database:

```
$ use datasets
$ show collections
```

We can verify that the data has been correctly parsed by examining one record:

```
$ db.bank.findOne()
```

 The code here is inspired by examples in `https://github.com/jadianes/spark-movie-lens` and `http://fgimian.github.io/blog/2012/12/08/setting-up-a-rock-solid-python-development-web-server`.

You can see that record appears like a Python dictionary. To retrieve elements with particular values, we can use findOne with key:values set to the filters we want to apply:

```
$ db.bank.findOne({},{key:value,..})
```

Now that we have the data loaded, we can interact with it through Python using the pymongo client. We initialize a client with access to the database we just created using the following:

```
>>> from pymongo import MongoClient
>>> MONGODB_HOST = 'localhost'
>>> MONGODB_PORT = 27017
>>> DBS_NAME = 'datasets'
>>> COLLECTION_NAME = 'bank'
>>> connection = MongoClient(MONGODB_HOST, MONGODB_PORT)
>>> collection = connection[DBS_NAME][COLLECTION_NAME]
>>> customers = collection.find(projection=FIELDS)
```

Note that the mongod command still needs to be running in a separate terminal window for you to access the database through Python. The customers object will then contain each customer's records. While for the current example we will primarily access MongoDB using the SparkConnector, the commands above will be useful in *Chapter 9, Reporting and Testing – Iterating on Analytic Systems* when we analyze the output of our model. Indeed, the MongoDB database allows us to store information used by our model service, but also can be a source of shared information for the reporting service we will build in *Chapter 9, Reporting and Testing – Iterating on Analytic Systems*, by visualizing the results of our modeling.

As we mentioned previously, we will also use the Redis (http://redis.io/) key-value store to log the intermediate state of long-running tasks, and also to store the serialized output from training models in Spark. After installing Redis DB on your system, you should be able to start the server by typing the following command in the terminal:

```
> redis-server
```

Which, if successful, should give and output like the following:

```
[45699] 19 Jul 00:35:48.207 * Increased maximum number of open files to 10032 (it was originally set to 4864)

                                              Redis 2.8.12 (00000000/0) 64 bit

                                              Running in stand alone mode
                                              Port: 7777
                                              PID: 45699


                                                    http://redis.io




[45699] 19 Jul 00:35:48.209 # Server started, Redis version 2.8.12
[45699] 19 Jul 00:35:48.212 * DB loaded from disk: 0.002 seconds
[45699] 19 Jul 00:35:48.212 * The server is now ready to accept connections on port 7777
```

The Python interface for Redis in the redis-py package (which, like many of the libraries we have seen in prior chapters, may be installed using `pip` or `easy_install`) is comparable to MongoDB. If we wanted to retrieve a record from our redis database, we could the following commands to start a client and issue a query or store data:

```
>>> import redis
>>> r = redis.StrictRedis(host='localhost', port=6379, db=1)
>>> r.get(key)
>>> r.set(key,value)
```

When we start a new client using 'StrictRedis', we specify the port the redis-server is listening on (default of 6379) and the database identifier. By issuing get and set commands, we can respectively retrieve prior results or update the database with new information. As with the Python mongo client, we will need to have the redis-server command running in a separate command line window to allow us to issue commands to the database in Python.

Now that we have our databases set up, let us look at the server that will manage requests for the applications using this data.

The web server

As described previously, the web server receives requests and forwards them to the web application. For our example, we start the server using the main function:

```
>>>if __name__ == "__main__":

    modelparameters = json.loads(open(sys.argv[1]).readline())

    service = modelservice(modelparameters)

    run_server(service)
```

There are three steps: we read the parameters for this service (here, just the name of the algorithm used), which is passed as command line argument, create the web application (using the same parameter file passed in during creation in the constructor), and then start the server. As you can see, the algorithm run by the prediction service is specified using a string argument. Later we will examine how this allows us to write a generic prediction service class, rather than a specific web application for each new algorithm we might use. When we start the server; it is registered on localhost on port 5000, as you can see by examining the body of the run_server function:

```
>>>  def run_server(app):
    import paste
    from paste.translogger import TransLogger
    app_ = TransLogger(app)
    cherrypy.tree.graft(app_, '/')
    cherrypy.config.update({
        'engine.autoreload.on': True,
        'log.screen': True,
        'server.socket_port': 5000,
        'server.socket_host': '0.0.0.0'
    })
    cherrypy.engine.start()
    cherrypy.engine.block()
```

There are a few key things happening in this function. Firstly, we see middleware in action since the TransLogger class from the paste library passes requests between the server and the application. The TransLogger object then represents a valid WGSI application since it has a callable (the application). We use the `tree.graft` command to attach the application (the model service itself) so that the object is called by the CherryPy modelserver whenever it receives an HTTP request.

When we start the cherrypy server, we provide a few configurations. The enable. autoreload.on parameter controls whether the application will refresh when we change the source files it is pointing to, in this case our Flask application. Log.screen directs the output of error and access message to the stdout, which is useful when we are still debugging. Finally, the last two settings specify the URL and endpoint where we will send requests to the application.

Once we start the application, we also set it to block, which means it must finish processing one request before considering another. If we want to tune performance, we could remove this configuration, which would allow the application to receive multiple requests without waiting for the first to finish. The URL for this server is thus accessed by `http://0.0.0.0:5000` once it is running—this is the address where we will send our various commands to the prediction service. To start the server, type the following in the command line:

```
> python modelserver.py parameters.json
```

The `parameters.json` file could contain parameters for the `modelservice` application that will be used when starting the modeling application, but for now we actually place nothing in this file. If successful, you should see the following output in the terminal:

```
[19/Jul/2016:00:52:46] ENGINE Bus STARTING
[19/Jul/2016:00:52:46] ENGINE Started monitor thread 'Autoreloader'.
[19/Jul/2016:00:52:46] ENGINE Started monitor thread '_TimeoutMonitor'.
[19/Jul/2016:00:52:47] ENGINE Serving on http://0.0.0.0:5000
[19/Jul/2016:00:52:47] ENGINE Bus STARTED
```

As we issue `curl` commands to the server, we will see the responses displayed in this output as well.

The web application

Now that we have started the server and can begin receiving commands from the client, let us look at the commands that will be executed by our application, such as HTTP requests issued through the Python notebook or curl commands. The code that is executed when we send requests to the CherryPy server is contained in the modelservice.py file.

The constructor for the application, called by the CherryPy server when we started it, returns an app object specified using the Flask framework:

```
>>> def modelservice(model_parameters):

  …return app
```

What is the definition of app? If we examine the beginning of the modelservice.py file, we see that app is defined using the Flask library:

```
>>> app = Flask(__name__)

… app.config.update(CELERY_BROKER_URL='redis://localhost:6379',CELERY_
RESULT_BACKEND='redis://localhost:6379')

… celery = Celery(app.import_name, backend=app.config['CELERY_RESULT_
BACKEND'],broker=app.config['CELERY_BROKER_URL'])

… celery.conf.update(app.config)
```

In addition to creating the Flask object app, we also generate a celery object. What is this celery object? As mentioned previously, we do not want to have our clients wait on long-running tasks to respond, as this would cause the client applications to potentially hang or timeout. Thus, our application needs to be non-blocking and return an immediate value for a long-running task, which is an ID that allows us to access the progress and results of the task through a REST API. We want to run the long-running task in a secondary process and have it report back the results or intermediate state as they become available. For our application, we will be using the Celery library (http://www.celeryproject.org/), an asynchronous task queuing system that is ideal for this sort of application. Celery consists of a client that submits jobs to a queue, and worker tasks, which read from this queue, perform work, and return the results to the client. The client and workers communicate via a messaging queue, such as the Redis key-value store we mentioned previously, and results are also persisted to this database. The arguments CELERY_BROKER_URL and CELERY_RESULT_BACKEND are used to specify, respectively, where the worker tasks retrieve information on scheduled tasks, and where we can look up information on the status of currently running tasks. In our example, both functions are served by Redis, but we could substitute other systems, such as the message queue system RabbitMQ (https://www.rabbitmq.com/).

In order for us to issue HTTP requests to the Celery worker tasks, we need to make sure that redis is already running, and then start the Celery workers using the following command:

```
> celery worker -A modelservice.celery
```

This starts celery worker processes with access to the commands specified in `modelservice.py` which we will cover below. If successful, you will see the following in your terminal.

```
-------------- celery@lgml-jbabcockH04 v3.1.22 (Cipater)
---- **** -----
--- * *** * -- Darwin-15.5.0-x86_64-i386-64bit
-- * - **** ---
- ** ---------- [config]
- ** ---------- .> app:         modelservice:0x110cc87d0
- ** ---------- .> transport:   redis://localhost:6379//
- ** ---------- .> results:     redis://localhost:6379/
- *** --- * --- .> concurrency: 4 (prefork)
-- ******* ----
--- ***** ----- [queues]
-------------- .> celery              exchange=celery(direct) key=celery

[2016-07-19 01:14:10,739: WARNING/MainProcess] celery@lgml-jbabcockH04 ready.
```

As we later send requests to the service which are passed off to the Celery workers, information (such as Spark outputs) will be printed in this window as well.

The flow of a prediction service – training a model

So now that we have the Celery process running along with the Flask application, how can we define the functions executed by the workers in response to our HTTP requests? How can we specify the URLs to which we will issue curl commands? We will illustrate the flow of events by showing how a call to the training function will kick off a series of Spark jobs to perform cross validation and store a LogisticRegression model.

We start by issuing a curl command to the `train` function with the following command:

```
curl -X POST http://0.0.0.0:5000/train/ -d @job.json --header "Content-
Type: application/json"
```

We could have similarly used the Python requests library to transmit the information in job.json to the model training task. The job.json file contains all the parameters we might need to use in the various stages of parsing the data and training the model, as we will see as we walk through the flow of this request through our application. When this command is received by the CherryPy modelserver, it is forwarded to the Flask app defined in modelservice.py. How can we make the Flask application respond to this request? It is as easy as providing a decorator specifying a function to run in response to requests to this URL:

```
>>> @app.route("/train/",methods=["POST"])
... def train():
...     try:
...             parsed_parameters = request.json
...             trainTask = train_task.apply_async(args=[parsed_parameters])
...             return json.dumps( {"job_id": trainTask.id } )
...     except:
...             print(traceback.format_exc())
```

The @app.route decorator indicates that the Flask object app listens for POST commands to a URL given as an argument to route. In responses, it extracts the dictionary of parameters from the POST request and passes them to a train_task, which will be run on a Celery worker process through the apply_async function. We then immediately return a task identifier associated with this task, which we can use to check the status or, as we will see, identify the output of the resulting model.

How do we specify the Celery task train_task? Similarly, we provide a decorator indicating that this function will be run on a worker process:

```
>>> @celery.task(bind=True)
... def train_task(self,parameters):
...     try:
...             spark_conf = start_conf(parameters)
...             model.set_model(parameters)
...             messagehandler = MessageHandler(self)
...             model.train(parameters,messagehandler=messagehandler,sc=spark_
conf)
...     except:
...             messagehandler.update('FAILURE',traceback.format_exc())
```

There are a few important details here. First, along with annotating the function with `@celery.task`, we provide the argument `bind=True`. This ensures that the function has a 'self' argument. Why would we need a self argument? In our example, we attach a `MessangeHandler` object to the training task using a reference to the function (self), allowing us to inject updates on the status of the task as it proceeds, and also retrieve the identifier for the task which was returned after we issued the POST request. The `MessageHandler` class is relatively simple and defined as follows in the `messagehandler.py` file in the code examples for this chapter:

```
>>> class MessageHandler:
    ...
    ...def __init__(self,parent):
    ...    self.parent = parent
    ...    self.task_id = parent.request.id
    ...
    ... def update(self,state,message):
    ...    self.parent.update_state(state=state,meta={"message": message})
    ...
    ...def get_id(self):
    ...return self.task_id
```

When we construct the `MessageHandler` object, we retrieve the ID associated with the tasks from the `request.id` field. If we had not used the `bind=True` argument above, we would not be able to access this field, since we would not have a reference (self) to the task object to pass to the `MessageHandler`. This is also needed for the `update` function, which allows us to inject status updates about the progress of the task using the reference to the train task above. Finally, if we need to access the training task identifier anywhere else in our application, we can do so using `get_id`.

How could we access the tasks status modified by update? If you recall, when we initialized the Celery application, we provided the Redis database as a storage location for task status information. Using the identifier returned in response to our POST request, we could use a GET method to look up the status of this task, which we specify through another Flask app endpoint:

```
>>> @app.route('/training/status/<task_id>')
... def training_status(task_id):
...     try:
...             task = train_task.AsyncResult(task_id)
...             message = ""
...             if task.state == 'PENDING':
```

```
...        response = {
...            'status': task.status,
...            'message': "waiting for job {0} to start".format(task_
id)
...        }
...    elif task.state != 'FAILED':
...        if task.info is not None:
...            message = task.info.get('message','no message')
...        response = {
...            'status': task.status,
...            'message': message
...        }
...    else:
...        if task.info is not None:
...            message = task.info.get('message','no message')
...        response = {
...            'status': task.status,
...            'message': message
...        }
...    return json.dumps(response)
... except:
...    print(traceback.format_exc())
```

Thus, using a `curl` command, we could issue a GET to obtain the status of our training task, either printing it to the console or, if we made this application more complex, using it to generate a dashboard of job states in a pipeline or system.

Now that we have a way to inject updates about the status of our tasks, let us return to the `train_task` definition. In addition to creating the `MessageHandler` for this task, we also generate a `SparkConfiguration` and initialize a model object. The SparkConfiguration will probably look familiar from some of the examples in previous chapters, and is returned from the following function:

```
>>> def start_conf(jobparameters):
...     conf = SparkConf().setAppName("prediction-service")
...     conf.set("spark.driver.allowMultipleContexts",True)
...     conf.set("spark.mongodb.input.uri",jobparameters.
get('inputCollection',\
...         "mongodb://127.0.0.1/datasets.bank?readPreference=primaryPreferr
ed"))
```

```
    … conf.set("spark.mongodb.output.uri",jobparameters.
get('outputCollection',\
    …      "mongodb://127.0.0.1/datasets.bankResults"))
    …return conf
```

> Note that the arguments to the SparkConfiguration are used by the Spark mongo connector. This connector is an external dependency that needs to be downloaded and added at runtime to the system path of our Spark application, which can be accomplished by adding the following to your system parameters (assuming a Linux command line environment):
>
> ```
> export PYSPARK_SUBMIT_ARGS="--packages org.mongodb.
> spark:mongo-spark-connector_2.10:1.0.0 pyspark-shell"
> ```

Here we set the application name by which we will identify the train task in the Spark UI on port 4040, and allow multiple contexts through "spark.driver. allowMultipleContexts" such that several Spark applications could be potentially run in parallel. Finally, we provide the mongodb input and output locations where Spark will read the data for training and store scored results. Note that these are both given as defaults, but could be changed by modifying parameters in the job.json file, allowing our application to operate on different inputs and store to different output locations by only changing the arguments to the POST request.

Now that we have the configuration to pass to the Spark job, let us look at the model object which will receive these parameters. We construct it as a global object at the beginning of the modelservice file in the line:

```
>>> model = ModelFactory()
```

If you examine the definition of the ModelFactory class in the modelfactory.py file supplied with the code example for this chapter, you see can see that it provides a generic interface for wrapping the training and prediction functions of different machine learning algorithms:

```
>>> class ModelFactory:

...    def __init__(self):
...       self._model = None


...   def set_model(self,modelparameters):
...       module = importlib.import_module(modelparameters.get('name'))
...       model_class = getattr(module, modelparameters.get('name'))
```

```
...     self._model = model_class(modelparameters)


...  def get_model(self,modelparameters,modelkey):

...     module = importlib.import_module(modelparameters.get('name'))

...     model_class = getattr(module, modelparameters.get('name'))

...     self._model = model_class(modelparameters)

...     self._model.get_model(modelkey)


...  def train(self,parameters,messagehandler,sc):

...     self._model.train(parameters,messagehandler,sc)


...  def predict(self,parameters,input_data):

...     return self._model.predict(parameters,input_data)


...  def predict_all(self,parameters,messagehandler,sc):

...     self._model.predict_all(parameters,messagehandler,sc)
```

As you can see, nowhere in this class do we specify the particular implementation of train or prediction tasks. Rather, we create an object with an internal member (self_ model) that we can set using set_model, by dynamically retrieving code associated with a particular algorithm using importlib. The "name" argument also comes from job.json, meaning we could load different algorithms in our application and run training tasks simply by changing the parameters of our POST request. In this example, we specify the model as LogisticRegressionWrapper, which will cause this model (and the class of the same name) to be loaded and inserted into the self_model of the ModelFactory when we call train_task. ModelFactory also has a generic method for loading an existing model, get_model, which takes as input a task ID such as the one generated in response to our train request and sets self_model to be a previously trained model object which is retrieved using this task ID as a reference. In addition, this class has methods for predict (to give the predicted response for a single row of data) or predict_all (to perform bulk scoring using Spark).

To recap, now we see that in response to our POST request, the CherryPy server hands off the information in data.json to the train function of our Flask service, which starts a background process on a Celery worker. This worker process sets the generic model object of our Flask app to a Logistic Regression, creates a Spark configuration to run the training task, and returns a task ID that we can use to monitor the progress of the model training. In the final step in the journey of this POST request, let us see how the Logistic Regression model implements the training task.

In the `LogisticRegressionWrapper.py` file, you can see the specifications of the train task:

```
>>> def train(self,parameters,messagehandler,spark_conf):
...         try:
...             sc = SparkContext(conf=spark_conf, pyFiles=['modelfactory.
py', 'modelservice.py'])
...             sqlContext = SQLContext(sc)
...             iterations = parameters.get('iterations',None)
...             weights = parameters.get('weights',None)
...           intercept = parameters.get('intercept',False)
...             regType = parameters.get('regType',None)
...           data = sqlContext.\
...               createDataFrame(\
...               sqlContext.read.format("com.mongodb.spark.sql.
DefaultSource").\
...               load().\
...               map(lambda x: DataParser(parameters).parse_line(x)))
...           lr = LogisticRegression()
...           pipeline = Pipeline(stages=[lr])
...           paramGrid = ParamGridBuilder()\
...               .addGrid(lr.regParam, [0.1]) \
...               .build()

...           crossval = CrossValidator(estimator=pipeline,\
...                 estimatorParamMaps=paramGrid,\
...                 evaluator=BinaryClassificationEvaluator(),\
...                 numFolds=2)
...           messagehandler.update("SUBMITTED","submitting training job")
...           crossvalModel = crossval.fit(data)
...           self._model = crossvalModel.bestModel.stages[-1]
...           self._model.numFeatures = len(data.take(1)[0]['features'])
...           self._model.numClasses = len(data.select('label').
distinct().collect())
...             r = redis.StrictRedis(host='localhost', port=6379, db=1)
...             r.set( messagehandler.get_id(), self.serialize(self._model)
)
```

```
...         messagehandler.update("COMPLETED","completed training job")
...         sc.stop()
...     except:
...         print(traceback.format_exc())
....        messagehandler.update("FAILED",traceback.format_exc())
```

First of all, we start a SparkContext using the parameters we defined in the SparkConfiguration we passed to this function. The parameters in our `job.json` file also include the algorithm parameters, which we parse. We then read the input data which we specified in the SparkConfiguration in a distributed fashion from mongodb into a Spark DataFrame, using a lambda function to parse the input. The parsing logic is defined in `dataparser.py`, in the `parse_line` function of the `DataParser` class:

```
>>> def parse_line(self,input,train=True):
...     try:
...         if train:
...             if self.schema_dict.get('label').get('values',None) is
not None:
...                 label = self.schema_dict.\
...                 get('label').\
...                 get('values').\
...                 get(input[self.schema_dict.\
...                 get('label').\
...                 get('key')])
...             else:
...                 label = input[self.schema_dict.\
...                 get('label').\
...                 get('key')]
...         features = []
...         for f in self.schema_dict['features']:
...             if f.get('values',None) is not None:
...                 cat_feature = [ 0 ] * len(f['values'].keys())
...                 if len(f['values'].keys()) > 1: # 1 hot encoding
...                     cat_feature[f['values'][str(input[f.
get('key')])]] = 1
...                 features += cat_feature # numerical
...             else:
...                 features += [ input[f.get('key')] ]
```

```
...            if train:
...                Record = Row("features", "label")
...                return Record(Vectors.dense(features),label)
...            else:
...                return Vectors.dense(features)

...        except:
...            print(traceback.format_exc())
...            pass
```

The `DataParser` class takes as input a parameters dictionary containing the schema of the data that—once again—we specified in our `job.json` data we included in our POST request. This information is stored in the `self._schema` property of the parser. Using this information, the parse_line function extracts the label (the response column) and encodes it as a numeric value if necessary. Similarly, the features of each record are parsed and, if necessary, one-hot encoded using information in the POST request. If the data is to be used in training (`train=True`), the parser returns the label and a vector of features. Otherwise, it just returns the features to be used in scoring new records. In either case, the features are encoded as a dense Vector from the Spark ml library (which is required for the logistic regression algorithm), and the row is returned as a Row object to be compatible with the Spark DataFrame needed for the training code. Because the fields we use as features are specified in our `job.json` data, we could train models using different columns from the same dataset without changing the underlying code.

Once the data is parsed, we construct a Spark Pipeline object to handle the stages of the model training. In our example, the only step is the model training itself, but we could potentially have transformations like the Vectorizers we examined in *Chapter 6, Words and Pixels – Working with Unstructured Data* in the context of text data as part of such as pipeline. We then create a ParamGrid to perform a grid search of the regularization parameter of our model, and pass it to a CrossValidator, which will peform n-fold validation to determine the best model. Once we have fit this model, we retrieve the optimal model from the CrossValidator results and determine the number of features and classes used in the model. Finally, we open a connection to the Redis database and store the parameters of this model after serializing it with the function:

```
>>> def serialize(self,model):
...        try:
...            model_dict = {}
...            model_dict['weights'] = model.weights.tolist()
...            model_dict['intercept'] = model.intercept
```

```
...          model_dict['numFeatures'] = model.numFeatures
...          model_dict['numClasses'] = model.numClasses
...          return json.dumps(model_dict)
...      except:
...          raise Exception("failed serializing model: {0}".
format(traceback.format_exc()))
```

Notice that we use the MessageHandler attached to this task to retrieve the task ID, which is used as the key to store the serialized model in Redis. Also, though we store the result in the same Redis instance listening on port 6379 that is used by Celery to queue tasks and update the status of background tasks, we save to db 1 instead of the default 0 to separate the information.

By tracing through the steps above, you should now be able to see how a POST request can be translated into a series of commands that parse data, perform cross-validated grid-search to train a model, and then serialize that model for later use. You should also appreciate how the parameterizations at each layer allow us to modify the behavior of this training task purely by modifying the contents of the POST request, and how the modularity of the application will make it easy to extend to other models. We also have utilized Spark, which will allow us to easily scale our calculations to larger datasets over time.

Now that we have illustrated the logical flow of data in our prediction service, let us finish by examining the prediction functions, whose output we will use in *Chapter 9, Reporting and Testing – Iterating on Analytic Systems*.

On-demand and bulk prediction

Now that we have a trained model saved in our system, how can we utilize it to score new data? Our Flask app has two endpoints for this service. In the first, we make a POST request giving a row of data as a json, along with a model ID, and ask for a score from the logistic regression model:

```
>>> @app.route("/predict/",methods=['POST'])
... def predict():
...     try:
...         parsed_parameters = request.json
...         model.get_model(parsed_parameters,parsed_parameters.
get('modelkey'))
...         score = model.predict(parsed_parameters,parsed_parameters.
get('record'))
...         return json.dumps(score)
...     except:
...         print(traceback.format_exc())
```

This time, instead of calling the `set_model` method of ModelFactory, we use `get_model` to load a previously trained model, then use it to predict the label of the input record and return the value. In the case of Logistic Regression, this will be a 0 or 1 value. While we do not provide a user interface in this example, we could imagine a simple form in which the user specifies a number of features of a record and submits them through a POST request, receiving back a prediction in realtime.

Looking at the implementation of `get_model` in LogisticRegressionWrapper, we see that we can retrieve and de-serialize the model we generated in the train task, and assign it to the `self._model` member of ModelFactory:

```
>>> def get_model(self,modelkey):
...        try:
...                r = redis.StrictRedis(host='localhost', port=6379, db=1)
...                model_dict = json.loads(r.get(modelkey))
...                self._model = LogisticRegressionModel(weights=Vectors.
dense(model_dict['weights']),\
...                        intercept=model_dict['intercept'],\
...                        numFeatures=model_dict['numFeatures'],\
...                        numClasses=model_dict['numClasses']
...                        )
...        except:
...                raise Exception("couldn't load model {0}: {1}".
format(modelkey,traceback.format_exc()))
```

Subsequently, when we score a new record, we call the `predict` function to parse this record and use the de-serialized model to generate a prediction:

```
>>> def predict(self,parameters,input_data):
...        try:
...                if self._model is not None:
...                        return self._model.predict(DataParser(parameters).parse_
line(input_data,train=False))
...                else:
...                        return "Error, no model is trained to give predictions"
...        except:
...                print(traceback.format_exc())
```

This sort of functionality will be useful for interactive applications, such as a human user submitting a few records of interest to obtain predictions, or for real time applications in which we might receive streaming input and provide predictions for immediate use. Note that thought we do not use Spark in this particular instance, we still have a nice opportunity for horizontal scaling. Once we have trained the model, we could de-serialize the resulting parameters in several copies of the modelservice, which will allow use to potentially avoid timeouts if we receive many requests. However, in cases where the volume of predictions required is large and the necessary latency is *not* realtime, it may be more effective to utilize Spark to perform bulk-scoring of records in our database. We implement this bulk-scoring capability using a Celery task in a manner similar to the train_task, specifying a predictall endpoint in the Flask app:

```
>>> @app.route("/predictall/",methods=["POST"])
... def predictall():
...     try:
...         parsed_parameters = request.json

            predictTask = predict_task.apply_async(args=[parsed_parameters])
...         return json.dumps( {"job_id": predictTask.id } )
...     except:
...         print(traceback.format_exc())
```

The associated Celery task is show below:

```
>>> @celery.task(bind=True)
... def predict_task(self,parameters):
...     try:
...         spark_conf = start_conf(parameters)
...         messagehandler = MessageHandler(self)
...         model.get_model(parameters,parameters.get('modelkey'))
...         print(model._model._model)
...         model.predict_all(parameters,messagehandler=messagehandler,sc=spark_conf)
...     except:
...         messagehandler.update('FAILURE',traceback.format_exc())
```

Again, we create a SparkConfiguration and MessageHandler, and like the predict method, we use a prior model ID specified in job.json to load a previous train model. We then call the predict_all method of this model to start a bulk scoring routine that will generate predictions for a large collection of data, and store the resulting in the mongodb collection specified by the output location parameter of the SparkConfiguration. For the LogisticRegressionWrapper, the predict_all method is shown below:

```
>>> def predict_all(self,parameters,messagehandler,spark_conf):
...         try:
...             sc = SparkContext(conf=spark_conf, pyFiles=['modelfactory.
py', 'modelservice.py'])
...             sqlContext = SQLContext(sc)
...             Record = Row("score","value")
...             scored_data = sqlContext.\
...                 createDataFrame(\
...                 sqlContext.read.format("com.mongodb.spark.sql.
DefaultSource").\
...                 load().\
...                 map(lambda x: Record(self._model.
predict(DataParser(parameters).parse_line(x,train=False)),x)))
...             messagehandler.update("SUBMITTED","submitting scoring job")
... scored_data.write.format("com.mongodb.spark.sql.DefaultSource").
mode("overwrite").save()
...             sc.stop()
...         except:
...             messagehander.update("FAILED",traceback.format_exc())
```

As with the training task, we start a SparkContext using the SparkConfiguration we defined in the Celery task, and load the input from mongodb using the Spark connector. Instead of simply parsing the data, we score the parsed records using the de-serialized model we loaded using the get_model command, and pass both it and the original record into a new Row object, which now has two columns: the score and the input. We then save this data back to mongodb.

If you open the mongo client and examine the bankResults collection, you can verify that it now contains the bulk-scored input data. We will utilize these results in *Chapter 9, Reporting and Testing – Iterating on Analytic Systems* where we will expose these scores in a reporting application to visualize the ongoing performance of our model and diagnose potential issues in model performance.

Summary

In this chapter, we described the three components of a basic prediction service: a client, the server, and the web application. We discussed how this design allows us to share the results of predictive modelling with other users or software systems, and scale our modeling horizontally and modularly to meet the demands of various use cases. Our code examples illustrate how to create a prediction service with generic model and data parsing functions that can be reused as we try different algorithms for a particular business use case. By utilizing background tasks through Celery worker threads and distributed training and scoring on Spark, we showed how to potentially scale this application to large datasets while providing intermediate feedback to the client on task status. We also showed how an on-demand prediction utility could be used to generate real-time scores for streams of data through a REST API.

Using this prediction service framework, in the next chapter we will extend this application to provide ongoing monitoring and reporting about the performance and health of our predictive models.

9
Reporting and Testing – Iterating on Analytic Systems

In previous chapters we have considered many components of an analytical application, from the input data set to the choice of algorithm and tuning parameters, and even illustrated a potential deployment strategy using a web server. In this process, we considered parameters such as scalability, interpretability, and flexibility in making our applications robust to both later refinements of an algorithm and changing requirements of scale. However, these sorts of details miss the most important element of this application: your business partners who hope to derive insight from the model and the continuing needs of the organization. What metrics should we gather on the performance of a model to make the case for its impact? How can we iterate on an initial model to optimize its use for a business application? How can these results be articulated to stakeholders? These sorts of questions are key in conveying the benefit of building analytical applications for your organization.

Just as we can use increasingly larger data sets to build predictive models, automated analysis packages and "big data" systems are making it easier to gather substantial amounts of information about the behavior of algorithms. Thus, the challenge becomes not so much if we can collect data on an algorithm or how to measure this performance, but to choose what statistics are most relevant to demonstrate value in the context of a business analysis. In order to equip you with the skills to better monitor the health of your predictive applications, improve them through iterative milestones and explain these techniques to others in this chapter, we will:

- Review common model diagnostics and performance indicators.
- Describe how A/B testing may be used to iteratively improve upon a model.
- Summarize ways in which predictive insights from predictive models can be communicated in reports.

Checking the health of models with diagnostics

Throughout the previous chapters, we have primarily focused on the initial steps of predictive modeling, from data preparation and feature extraction to optimization of parameters. However, it is unlikely that our customers or business will remain unchanging, so predictive models must typically adapt as well. We can use a number of diagnostics to check the performance of models over time, which serve as a useful benchmark to evaluate the health of our algorithms.

Evaluating changes in model performance

Let us consider a scenario in which we train a predictive model on customer data and evaluate its performance on a set of new records each day for a month afterward. If this were a classification model, such as predicting whether a customer will cancel their subscription in the next pay period, we could use a metric such as the **Area Under the Curve (AUC)** of the **Receiver-Operator-Characteristic (ROC)** curve that we saw previously in *Chapter 5, Putting Data in its Place – Classification Methods and Analysis*. Alternatively, in the case of a regression model, such as predicting average customer spend, we can use the R^2 value or average squared error:

$$\frac{(predicted - observed)^2}{n}$$

to quantify performance over time. If we observe a drop in one of these statistics, how can we analyze further what the root cause may be?

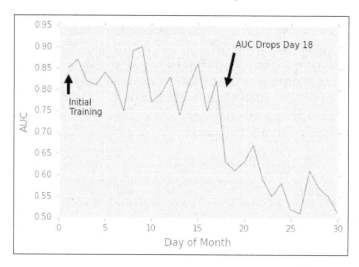

In the graph above, we show such a scenario, where we measured the AUC for a hypothetical ad-targeting algorithm for 30 days after initial training by quantifying how many of the targeted users clicked on an ad sent in an e-mail and visited the website for our company. We see AUC begin to dip on day 18, but because the AUC is an overall measure of accuracy, it is not clear whether all observations are being poorly predicted or only a subpopulation is leading to this drop in performance. Thus, in addition to measuring overall AUC, we might think of calculating the AUC for subsets of data defined by the input features. In addition to providing a way of identifying problematic new data (and suggest when the model needs to be retrained), such reports provide a way of identifying the overall business impact of our model.

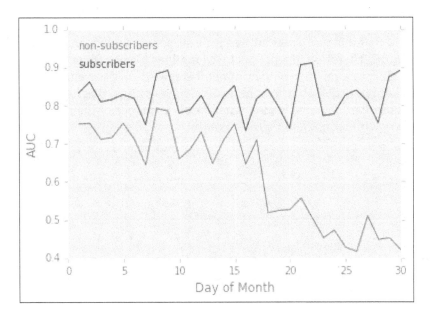

As an example, for our ad-targeting algorithm, we might look at overall performance and compare that to one of the labels in our data set: whether the user is a current subscriber or not. It may not be surprising that the performance on subscribers is usually higher, as these users were already likely to visit our site. The non-subscribers, who may never have visited our site before, represent the real opportunity in this scenario. In the preceding graph, we see that, indeed, the performance on non-subscribers dropped on day 18. However, it is also worth noting that this does not necessarily tell the whole story of why the performance dropped. We still do not know why the performance on new members is lower. We can subset the data again and look for a correlated variable. For example, if we looked along a number of ad IDs (which correspond to different images displayed to a customer in an e-mail), we might find that the performance dip is due to one particular ad (please refer to the following graph). Following up with our business stakeholders, we might find that this particular ad was for a seasonal product and is only shown every 12 months. Therefore, the product was familiar to subscribers, who may have seen this product before, but not to non-members, who thus were unfamiliar with the item and did not click on it. We might be able to confirm this hypothesis by looking at subscriber data and seeing whether performance of the model also dips for subscribers with tenure less than 12 months.

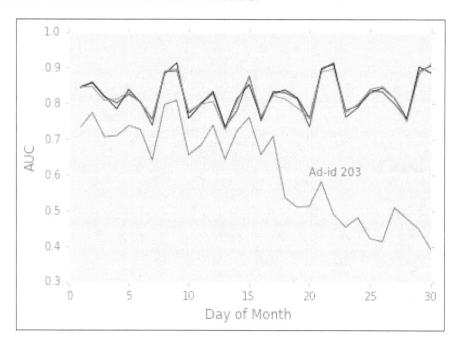

This sort of investigation can then begin to ask how to optimize this particular advertisement for new members, but can also indicate ways to improve our model training. In this scenario, it is likely that we trained the algorithm on a simple random sample of data that was biased for current subscribers, as we have more data on these customers if we took a simple random sample of event data: subscribers are more active, and thus both produce more impressions (as they may have registered for promotional e-mails) and are more likely to have clicked on ads. To improve our model, we might want to balance our training data between subscribers and non-subscribers to compensate for this bias.

In this simple example, we were able to diagnose the problem by examining performance of the model in only a small number of sub-segments of data. However, we cannot guarantee that this will always be the case, and manually searching through hundreds of variables will be inefficient. Thus, we might consider using a predictive model to help narrow down the search space. For example, consider using a **gradient boosted machine** (**GBM**) from *Chapter 5, Putting Data in its Place – Classification Methods and Analysis*, with the inputs being the same data we used to train our predictive model, and the outputs being the misclassification (either a label of 1, 0 for a categorical model, or a continuous error such as squared error or log loss in a regression model). We now have a model that predicts errors in the first model. Using a method such as a GBM allows us to examine systematically a large number of potential variables and use the resulting variable importance to pinpoint a smaller number of hypotheses.

Of course, the success of any these approaches hinges on the fact that the variable causing the drop in performance is a part of our training set, and that the issue has to do with the underlying algorithm or data. It is also certainly possible to imagine other cases where there is an additional variable we are not using to construct our data set for training which is causing the problem, such as poor connections on a given Internet service provider that are preventing users from clicking through an ad to our webpage, or a system problem such as failure in e-mail delivery.

Looking at performance by segments can also help us determine if the algorithm is functioning as intended when we make changes. For example, if we reweighted our training data to emphasize non-subscribers, we would hope that performance of AUC on these customers would improve. If we only examined overall performance, we might observe increases that are improvements on existing customers, but not the effect we actually wished to achieve.

Changes in feature importance

Besides examining the accuracy of models over time, we might also want to examine changes in the importance of different input data. In a regression model, we might examine the important coefficients as judged by magnitude and statistical significance, while in a decision-tree-based algorithm such as a Random Forest or GBM, we can look at measures of variable importance. Even if the model is performing at the same level as described by evaluation statistics discussed previously, shifts in the underlying variables may signal issues in data logging or real changes in the underlying data that are of business significance.

Let us consider a churn model, where we input a number of features for a user account (such as zip code, income level, gender, and engagement metrics such as hours spent per week on our website) and try to predict whether a given user will cancel his/her subscription at the end of each billing period. While it is useful to have a score predicting the likelihood of churn, as we would target these users with additional promotional campaigns or targeted messaging, the underlying features that contribute to this prediction may provide insight for more specific action.

In this example, we generate a report of the 10 most important features in the predictive model each week. Historically, this list has been consistent, with the customer's profession and income being the top variables. However, in one week, we find that income is no longer in this list, and that instead zip code has replaced it. When we check the data flowing into the model, we find that the income variable is no longer being logged correctly; thus, zip code, which is correlated with income, becomes a substitute for this feature in the model, and our regular analysis of variable importance helped us detect a significant data issue.

What if, instead the income variable was being logged correctly? In this case, it seems unlikely that zip code is more powerful a predictor than income if the underlying feature both are capturing is a customer's finances. Thus, we might examine whether there are particular zip codes for which churn has changed significantly over the past week. Upon doing so, we find that a competitor recently launched a site with a lower price in certain zip codes, letting us both understand the reason for the rise in zip code as a predictor (customers with the lower price option are more likely to abandon our site) and indicate market dynamics that are of larger interest.

This second scenario also suggests another variable we might monitor: the correlation between variables in our data set. While it is both computationally difficult and practically restrictive to comprehensively consider every pair of variables in large data sets, we can use dimensionality reduction techniques such as Principal Components Analysis described in *Chapter 6, Words and Pixels – Working with Unstructured Data*, to provide a high-level summary of the correlations between variables. This reduces the task of monitoring such correlations to examination of a few diagrams of the important components, which, in turn, can alert us to changes in the underlying structure of the data.

Changes in unsupervised model performance

The examples we looked at previously all concern a supervised model where we have a target to predict, and we measure performance by looking at AUC or similar metrics. In the case of the unsupervised models we examined in *Chapter 3, Finding Patterns in the Noise – Clustering and Unsupervised Learning*, our outcome is a cluster membership rather than a target. What sort of diagnostics can we look at in this scenario?

In cases where we have a gold-standard label, such as a human-annotated label of spam versus non-spam messages if we are clustering e-mail documents, we can examine whether the messages end up in distinct clusters or are mixed. In a sense, this is comparable to looking at classification accuracy. However, for unsupervised models, we might frequently not have any known label, and the clustering is purely an exploratory tool. We might still use human-annotated examples as a guide, but this becomes prohibitive for larger data sets. In other scenarios, such as sentiment in online media, remain subjective enough that human labels may not significantly enrich labels derived from automated methods such as the LDA topic model we discussed in *Chapter 6, Words and Pixels – Working with Unstructured Data*. In this case, how can we judge the quality of the clustering over time?

In cases where the number of groups is determined dynamically, such as through the Affinity Propagation Clustering algorithm described in *Chapter 3, Finding Patterns in the Noise – Clustering and Unsupervised Learning*, we examine whether the number of clusters remains fixed over time. In most cases we previously examined, though, the number of clusters remains fixed. Thus, we could envision one diagnostic in which we examine the distance between the centers of the nearest clusters between training cycles: for example, with a k-means model with 20 clusters, assign each cluster in week 1 its closest match in week 2 and compare the distribution of the 20 distances. If the clustering remains stable, then the distribution of these distances should as well. Changes could indicate that 20 is no longer a good number to fit the data or that the composition of the 20 clusters is significantly changing over time. We might also examine a value such as the sum of squares error in k-means clustering over time to see if the quality of the obtained clusters is significantly varying.

Another quality metric that is agnostic to a specific clustering algorithm is Silhouette analysis (Rousseeuw, Peter J. "Silhouettes: a graphical aid to the interpretation and validation of cluster analysis." *Journal of computational and applied mathematics 20* (1987): 53-65). For each data point **i** in the set, we ask how dissimilar (as judged by the distance metric used in the clustering algorithm) on average it is to other points in its cluster, giving a value *d(i)*. If the point **i** is appropriately assigned, then *d(i)* is near 0, as the average dissimilarity between **i** and other points in its cluster is low. We could also calculate the same average dissimilarity value for **i** for other clusters, and the second lowest value (the second best cluster assignment for **i**) is given by *d'(i)*. We then obtain a silhouette score between –1 and 1 using the formula:

$$s(i) = \frac{d'(i) - d(i)}{\max(d(i), d'(i))}$$

If a data point is well assigned to its cluster, then it is much more dissimilar on average to other clusters. Thus, `d'(i)` (the 'second best cluster for i') is larger than `d(i)`, and the ratio in the silhouette score formula is near 1. Conversely, if the point is poorly assigned to its cluster, then the value of `d'(i)` could be less than `d(i)`, giving a negative value in the numerator of the silhouette score formula. Values near zero suggest the point could be reasonably assigned in the two clusters equally well. By looking at the distribution of silhouette scores over a data set, we can get a sense of how well points are being clustered over time.

Finally, we might use a bootstrap approach, where we rerun the clustering algorithm many times and ask how often two points end up in the same cluster. The distribution of these cluster co-occurrences (between 0 and 1) can also give a sense of how stable the assignment is over time.

Like clustering models, dimensionality reduction techniques also do not lend themselves easily to a gold standard by which to judge model quality over time. However, we can take values such as the principal components vectors of a data set and examine their pairwise dissimilarity (for example, using the cosine score described in *Chapter 3, Finding Patterns in the Noise – Clustering and Unsupervised Learning*) to determine if they are changing significantly. In the case of matrix decomposition techniques, we could also look at the reconstruction error (for example, averaged squared difference over all matrix elements) between the original matrix and the product of the factored elements (such as the W and H matrices in nonnegative matrix factorization).

Iterating on models through A/B testing

In the examples above and in the previous chapters of this volume, we have primarily examined analytical systems in terms of their predictive ability. However, these measures do not necessarily ultimately quantify the kinds of outcomes that are meaningful to the business, such as revenue and user engagement. In some cases, this shortcoming is overcome by converting the performance statistics of a model into other units that are more readily understood for a business application. For example, in our preceding churn model, we might multiply our prediction of 'cancel' or 'not-cancel' to generate a predicted dollar amount lost through subscriber cancellation.

In other scenarios, we are fundamentally unable to measure a business outcome using historical data. For example, in trying to optimize a search model, we can measure whether a user clicked a recommendation and whether they ended up purchasing anything after clicking. Through such retrospective analysis, we can only optimize the order of the recommendations the user was actually presented on a web page. However, it might be that with a better search model, we would have presented the user a completely different set of recommendations, which would have also led to greater click-through rates and revenue. However, we cannot quantify this hypothetical scenario, meaning we need alternative methods to assess algorithms as we improve them.

One way to do so is through the process of experimentation, or A/B testing, which takes its name from the concept of comparing outcomes from test subjects (for example, customers) randomly assigned to treatment (for example, a search recommendation algorithm) A and B to determine which method generates the best result. In practice, there may be many more than two treatments, and the experiment can be randomized at the level of users, sessions (such as periods between login and logout on a website), products, or other units. While a truly comprehensive discussion of A/B testing is outside the scope of this chapter, we refer interested readers to more extensive references (Bailey, Rosemary A. *Design of comparative experiments*. Vol. 25. Cambridge University Press, 2008; Eisenberg, Bryan, and John Quarto-vonTivadar. *Always be testing: The complete guide to Google website optimizer*. John Wiley & Sons, 2009; Finger, Lutz, and Soumitra Dutta. *Ask, Measure, Learn: Using Social Media Analytics to Understand and Influence Customer Behavior*. " O'Reilly Media, Inc.", 2014).

Experimental allocation – assigning customers to experiments

You have an algorithm that you wish to improve—how can you compare its performance improving a metric (such as revenue, retention, engagement) in comparison to an existing model (or no predictive model at all)? In this comparison, we want to make sure to remove all potential confounding factors other than the two (or more) models themselves. This idea underlies the concept of experimental randomization: if we randomly assign customers (for example) to receive search recommendations from two different models, any variation in customer demographics such as age, income, and subscription tenure should be roughly the same between the groups. Thus, when we compare the performance of models over time between groups following this random allocation, differences in performance of the algorithms can be attributed to the models themselves, as we have already accounted for other potential sources of variation through this randomization.

How can we guarantee that users are assigned to experimental groups randomly? One possibility is to assign each member a random number between 0 and 1, and split them based on whether this number is greater than 0.5 or not. However, this method might have the downside that it will be difficult to replicate our analysis since the random number assigned to a user could change. Alternatively, we often will have user IDs, random numbers assigned to a given account. Assuming the form of this number is sufficiently randomized, we could take the modulus of this number (the remainder when divided by a fixed denominator, such as 2) and assign users to the two groups based on the modulus (for example, if 2, this would be 0 or 1 based on if the account ID is even or odd). Thus, users are randomly allocated to the two groups, but we can easily recreate this assignment in the future.

We might also consider whether we always want a simple random stratification. In the ad-targeting example discussed previously, we are actually more concerned with the performance of the algorithm on nonsubscribers, rather than the existing users who would comprise most of a random allocation in our example. Thus, depending upon our objective, we may want to consider randomly allocating stratified samples in which we oversampled some accounts to compensate for inherent skew in the data. For example, we would enforce a roughly equal number of accounts per country to offset geographical bias toward a more populous region, or equal numbers of teenage and adult users for a service with primarily younger users.

In addition to randomly assigning users to receive an experience (such as search recommendations or ads sent through e-mail) dictated by a particular algorithm, we often need a control, a baseline to which to compare the results. In some cases, the control might be the outcome expected with no predictive model used at all. In others, we are comparing the old predictive model to a new version.

Deciding a sample size

Now that we know what we are trying to test and have a way to randomly assign users, how should we determine how many to allocate to an experiment? If we have a control and several experimental conditions, how many users should we assign to each group? If our predictive model relies upon user interaction (for example, gauging the performance of a search model requires the user to visit a website) that may not be guaranteed to occur for every member of the experimental population, how many activities (for example, searches) do we need to accumulate to judge the success of our experiment? These questions all concern making estimates of effect size and experimental power.

As you may recall from statistics, in a controlled experiment we are trying to determine whether the differences in outcomes between two populations (for example, the revenue generated from groups of users in our experimental evaluation of different prediction algorithms for ad targeting) are more likely due to random change or actual differences in the performance of an algorithm. These two options are also known as the null hypothesis, often represented by *H0* (that is, there is no difference between the two groups) and the alternative represented by *H1*. To determine whether an effect (for example, the difference in revenue between the two groups) is explained by random chance, we compare this effect to a distribution (frequently the t-distribution, for reasons we will discuss below) and ask what is the likelihood of observing this effect or greater if the true effect is **0**. This value — the cumulative probability of an effect greater than or equal to the observed given an assumption of no effect — is known as the p-value, to which we often apply a threshold such as 0.05 (in the example below, this is indicated by the shaded region on the left side of the standard normal distribution).

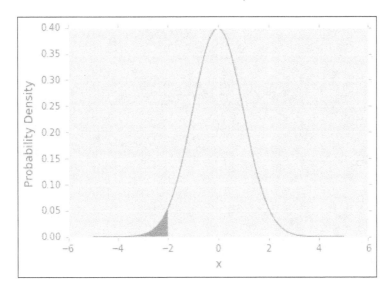

When we are assessing this statistical significance, we may encounter two kinds of errors because of the fact that any measurement of effect is subject to uncertainty. We never really know the true value of an effect, but rather measure this real, unknown effect with some error. First, we could inaccurately declare a result to be statistically significant when it is not. This is known as type I error (false positive). Secondly, we could fail to declare a result statistically significant when it actually is (also known as Type II error, or false negative).

We can ask the question how many samples we need to declare a particular effect (for example, revenue difference) significant, if there really were a difference between our two populations. While exact applications may vary, we will assume for illustration that the two groups are sufficiently large and that any difference between measured average values (such as revenue or click through rate) follows a normal distribution, which is due to the **Law of Large Numbers**. We can then evaluate this difference using the t-distribution, which approximate the standard normal distribution for large samples but does not require that we know the population mean and variance, just the mean and variance of a sample. Then, calculating the necessary number of samples requires just using the following formula (for a t-test between samples of whose variance is potentially unequal, also known as Welch's t-test):

$$T = \frac{Y_1 - Y_2}{S_{Y_1 - Y_2}}$$

$$S_{Y_1 - Y_2} = \sqrt{\frac{S_1^2}{n_1} + \frac{S_2^2}{n_2}}$$

$$1.64 \leq \frac{10}{\sqrt{\frac{S_1^2}{n_1} + \frac{S_2^2}{n_2}}}$$

$$\frac{100}{2.69} \geq \frac{S_1^2}{n_1} + \frac{S_2^2}{n_2}$$

Here, Y is the average effect (for example, revenue per customer) of each group, and S (the standard deviation) is given by the following equation:

$$S_{Y_1 - Y_2} = \sqrt{\frac{S_1^{\,2}}{n_1} + \frac{S_2^{\,2}}{n_2}}$$

Here, S_1 and S_2 are the sample variances, and n_1 and n_2 are the sample sizes of the two groups. So if we want to be able to detect a difference of 10, for example, with a p-value of 0.05, we solve for the sample size at which the t-statistic under the null yields a false positive 5% of the time (for which we use the normal approximation of 1.64, which is the value at which the cumulative distribution function of the standard normal distribution assumes the value of 0.05). We can solve:

$$1.64 \leq \frac{10}{\sqrt{\frac{S_1^{\,2}}{n_1} + \frac{S_2^{\,2}}{n_2}}}$$

$$\frac{100}{2.69} \geq \frac{S_1^{\,2}}{n_1} + \frac{S_2^{\,2}}{n_2}$$

Thus, given values for the variance of the groups in our experiment, we can plug in different values of n for the two groups and see if they are sufficient to fulfill the inequality. For this application, we might estimate the variance by looking at historical data for revenue among users of a given sample size.

If you look at the right-hand side of the preceding equation carefully, you will see that (assuming reasonably similar sample variances, which is not an unreasonable assumption in many large scale experiments such as those conducted on consumer website) this value will be determined by the smaller of n_1, n_2, since as we increase one sample size the term containing it tends toward 0. Thus, we often achieve optimal power by assigning equal sample sizes to both groups. This fact is important in considering how to decide the relative sizes of our control and experimental cells. Take an example in which we have three version of an ad-targeting algorithm, along with no algorithm at all as a control, and measure the resulting click through rate. Based on the preceding calculation, we need to decide what our main question is. If we want to know if any algorithm is better than no algorithm, we should assign users evenly between control and any of the three algorithm variants. However, if we instead want to decide which algorithm is best compared to control, we want equal numbers of users in all four cells, so that control and each treatment are of approximately equal size.

Note that the preceding calculation assumes we are interested in a fixed difference of 10 in response between the two groups. We could also just ask whether there is any difference at all (for example, the difference is not zero). The choice depends whether any lift represented by the algorithm is valuable or whether a fixed improvement is necessary to achieve the business goal at hand.

Multiple hypothesis testing

The last topic we will cover is somewhat subtle, but important due to the fact that with models with numerous tunable parameters and algorithm variations, we may often be performing a large number of hypothesis tests within a single A/B experiment. While we might evaluate each test at a significance of 0.05, if we perform 20 such evaluations, we have a probability of 20*0.05 = 1 (or almost certainty) of finding some significant result, even if it is in truth random noise. This issue, known as *Multiple Hypothesis Testing*, requires that we may need to recalibrate our significance threshold. The simplest way to do so is to divide the p-value threshold we use (for example, 0.05) by the number of tests performed (20) to obtain a new threshold for significance. This is known as Bonferonni Correction (Dunn, Olive Jean. "Estimation of the medians for dependent variables." *The Annals of Mathematical Statistics* (1959): 192-197; Dunnett, Charles W. "A multiple comparison procedure for comparing several treatments with a control." *Journal of the American Statistical Association* 50.272 (1955): 1096-1121) and, while correct, may be overly conservative in some scenarios. It assumes that we want a type I (false positive) rate of zero. However, in exploratory analyses, we often can accept some nonzero false positive rate as long as we are reasonably sure that a majority of the significant results are replicable. In this scenario, a **familywise error rate** (**FWER**) approach may be preferable. While a discussion of FWER is outside the scope of this chapter, we refer the interested reader to references on the subject (Shaffer, Juliet Popper. "Multiple hypothesis testing." *Annual review of psychology* 46 (1995): 561; Toothaker, Larry E. *Multiple comparison procedures*. No. 89. Sage, 1993).

Guidelines for communication

Now that we have covered debugging, monitoring and iterative testing of predictive models, we close with a few notes on communicating results of algorithms to a more general audience.

Translate terms to business values

In this text, we frequently discuss evaluation statistics or coefficients whose interpretations are not immediately obvious, nor the difference in numerical variation for these values. What does it mean for a coefficient to be larger or smaller? What does an AUC mean in terms of customer interactions predicted? In any of these scenarios, it is useful to translate the underlying value into a business metric in explaining their significance to non-technical colleagues: for example, coefficients in a linear model represent the unit change in an outcome (such as revenue) for a 1-unit change in particular input variable. For transformed variables, it may be useful to relate values such as the log-odds (from logistic regression) to a value such as doubling the probability of an event. Additionally, as discussed previously, we may need to translate the outcome we predict (such as a cancelation) into a financial amount to make its implication clear. This sort of conversion is useful not only in communicating the impact of a predictive algorithm, but also in clarifying priorities in planning. If the development time for an algorithm (whose cost might be approximated by the salaries of the employees involved) is not offset by the estimated benefit of its performance, then this suggests it is not a useful application from a business perspective.

Visualizing results

While not all algorithms we have discussed are amenable to visualization, many have elements that may be plotted for clarity. For example, regression coefficients can be compared using a barplot, and tree models may be represented visually by the branching decision points leading to a particular outcome. Such graphics help to turn inherently mathematical objects into more understandable results as well as provide ongoing insight into the performance of models, as detailed previously.

As a practical example of building such a service, this chapter's case study will walk through the generation of a custom dashboard as an extension of the prediction service we built in *Chapter 8, Sharing Models with Prediction Services*.

Case Study: building a reporting service

In *Chapter 8, Sharing Models with Prediction Services*, we created a prediction service that uses MongoDB as a backend database to store model data and predictions. We can use this same database as a source to create a reporting service. Like the separation of concerns between the CherryPy server and the modeling service application that we described in *Chapter 8, Sharing Models with Prediction Services*, a reporting service can be written without any knowledge of how the information in the database is generated, making it possible to generate a flexible reporting infrastructure as the modeling code may change over time. Like the prediction service, our reporting service has a few key components.

- The server that will receive requests for the output of the reporting service.
- The reporting application run by the server, which receive requests from the server and routes them to display the correct data.
- The database from which we retrieve the information required to make a plot.
- Charting systems that render the plots we are interested in for the end user.

Let us walk through an example of each component, which will illustrate how they fit together.

The report server

Our server code is very similar to the CherryPy server we used in *Chapter 8, Sharing Models with Prediction Services*.

 This example was inspired by the code available at https://github.com/adilmoujahid/DonorsChoose_Visualization.

The only difference is that instead of starting the modelservice application, we use the server to start the reportservice, as you can see in the main method:

```
>>> if __name__ == "__main__":
...     service = reportservice()
...   run_server(service)
```

We can test this server by simple running the following on the command line:

```
python report_server.py
```

You should see the server begin to log information to the console as we observed previously for the modelserver.

The report application

In the application code, which is also a Flask application like the model service we built in *Chapter 8, Sharing Models with Prediction Services*, we need a few additional pieces of information that we didn't use previously. The first is path variable to specify the location of the JavaScript and CSS files that we will need when we construct our charts, which are specified using the commands:

```
>>> static_dir = os.path.join(os.path.dirname(os.path.abspath(__file__)),
'templates/assets')
```

We also need to specify where to find the HTML pages that we render to the user containing our charts with the argument:

```
>>> tmpl_dir = os.path.join(os.path.dirname(os.path.abspath(__file__)),
'templates')
```

When we initialize our application, we will pass both of these as variables to the constructor:

```
>>> app = Flask(__name__,template_folder=tmpl_dir,static_folder=static_
dir)
```

To return this application when called by the server, we simply return app in the `reportservice` function:

```
>>> def reportservice():
...     return app
```

We now just need to specify the response of the application to requests forwarded by the server. The first is simply to render a page containing our charts:

```
>>> @app.route("/")
...     def index():
...         return render_template("layouts/hero-thirds/index.html")
```

The template in this example is taken from `https://github.com/keen/dashboards`, an open source project that provides reusable templates for generating quick dashboards.

The second route will allow us to retrieve the data we will use to populate the chart. This is not meant to be exposed to the end user (though you would see a text dump of all the JSONS in our collection if you navigated to this endpoint in your browser): rather it is used by the client-side JavaScript code to retrieve the information to populate the charts. First we need to start the mongodb application in another terminal window using:

```
> mongod
```

Next, in our code, we need to specify the MongoDB parameters to use in accessing our data. While we could have passed these as parameters in our URL, for simplicity in this example, we will just hard-code them at the top of the reportservice code to point to the results of bulk scoring the bank dataset we used to train our Spark Logistic Regression Model in *Chapter 8, Sharing Models with Prediction Services*:

```
>>> FIELDS = {'score': True, \
...           'value': True, \
...           '_id': False}
... MONGODB_HOST = 'localhost'
... MONGODB_PORT = 27017
... DBS_NAME = 'datasets'
... COLLECTION_NAME = 'bankResults'
```

Note that we could just as easily have pointed to a remote data source, rather than one running on our machine, by changing the MONGODB_HOST parameter. Recall that when we stored the results of bulk scoring, we saved records with two elements, the score and the original data row. In order to plot our results, we will need to extract the original data row and present it along with the score using the following code:

```
>>> @app.route("/report_dashboard")
...  def run_report():
...     connection = MongoClient(MONGODB_HOST, MONGODB_PORT)
...     collection = connection[DBS_NAME][COLLECTION_NAME]
...     data = collection.find(projection=FIELDS)
...     records = []
...     for record in data:
...         tmp_record = {}
...         tmp_record = record['value']
...         tmp_record['score'] = record['score']
...         records.append(tmp_record)
...     records = json.dumps(records, default=json_util.default)
...     connection.close()
```

Now that we have all of our scored records in a single array of json strings, we can plot them using a bit of JavaScript and HTML.

The visualization layer

The final piece we will need is the client-side JavaScript code used to populate the charts, and some modifications to the index.html file to make use of the charting code. Let us look at each of these in turn.

The chart generating code is a JavaScript function contained in the file `report.js` that you can find under `templates/assets/js` in the project directory for *Chapter 9, Reporting and Testing – Iterating on Analytic Systems*. We begin this function by calling for the data we need and waiting for it to be retrieved using the asynchronous function `d3.queue()`:

```
>>> d3_queue.queue()
... .defer(d3.json, "/report_dashboard")
... .await(runReport);
```

Notice that this URL is the same endpoint that we specified earlier in the report application to retrieve the data from MongoDB. The `d3_queue` function calls this endpoint and waits for the data to be returned before running the `runReport` function. While a more extensive discussion is outside the scope of this text, `d3_queue` is a member of the d3 library (`https://d3js.org/`), a popular visualization framework for the javascript language.

Once we have retrieved the data from our database, we need to specify how to plot it using the `runReport` function. First we will declare the data associated with the function:

```
>>> function runReport(error, recordsJson) {
...    var reportData = recordsJson;
...    var cf = crossfilter(reportData);
```

Though it will not be apparent until we visually examine the resulting chart, the `crossfilter` library (`http://square.github.io/crossfilter/`) allows us to highlight a subset of data in one plot and simultaneously highlight the corresponding data in another plot, even if the dimensions plotted are different. For example, imagine we had a histogram of ages for particular `account_ids` in our system, and a scatterplot of click-through-rate versus `account_id` for a particular ad campaign. The `Crossfilter` function would allow us to select a subset of the scatterplot points using our cursor and, at the same time, filter the histogram to only those ages that correspond to the points we have selected. This kind of filtering is very useful for drilling down on particular sub-segments of data. Next we will generate the dimensions we will use when plotting:

```
>>>   var ageDim = cf.dimension(function(d) { return d["age"]; });
...   var jobDim = cf.dimension(function(d) { return d["job"]; });
...   var maritalDim = cf.dimension(function(d) { return d["marital"]; });
```

Each of these functions takes the input data and returns the requested data field. The dimension contains all the data points in a column and forms the superset from which we will filter when examining subsets of data. Using these dimensions, we construct groups of unique values that we can use, for example, in plotting histograms:

```
>>>    var ageDimGroup = ageDim.group();
...    var jobDimGroup = jobDim.group();
...    var maritalDimGroup = maritalDim.group();
```

For some of our dimensions, we want to add values representing that maximum or minimum, which we use in plotting ranges of numerical data:

```
>>> var minAge = ageDim.bottom(1)[0]["age"];
... var maxAge = ageDim.top(1)[0]["age"];
... var minBalance = balanceDim.bottom(1)[0]["balance"];
... var maxBalance = balanceDim.top(1)[0]["balance"];
```

Finally, we can specify our chart objects using dc (https://dc-js.github.io/dc.js/), a charting library that uses d3 and crossfilter to create interactive visualizations. The # tag given to each chart constructor specifies the ID we will use to reference it when we insert it into the HTML template later. We construct the charts using the following code:

```
>>>    var ageChart = dc.barChart("#age-chart");
...    var jobChart = dc.rowChart("#job-chart");
...    var maritalChart = dc.rowChart("#marital-chart");
...
```

Finally, we specify the dimension and axes of these charts:

```
>>>    ageChart
...    .width(750)
...    .height(210)
...    .dimension(ageDim)
...    .group(ageDimGroup)
...    .x(d3_scale.scaleLinear()
...    .domain([minAge, maxAge]))
...    .xAxis().ticks(4);

>>>    jobChart
...    .width(375)
...    .height(210)
```

```
...    .dimension(jobDim)
...    .group(jobDimGroup)
...    .xAxis().ticks(4);
```

We just need a call to render in order to display the result:

```
>>>  dc.renderAll();
```

Finally, we need to modify our index.html file in order to display our charts. If you open this file in a text editor, you will notice several places where we have a <div> tag such as:

```
>>>  <div class="chart-stage">
...
...        </div>
```

This is where we need to place our charts using the following IDs that we specified in the preceding JavaScript code:

```
>>>  <div id="age-chart">
...        </div>
```

Finally, in order to render the charts, we need to include our javascript code in the <script> arguments at the bottom of the HTML document:

```
>>> <script type="text/javascript" … src="../../assets/js/report.js"></
script>
```

Now, you should be able to navigate to the URL to which the CherryPy server points, localhost:5000, should now display the charts like this:

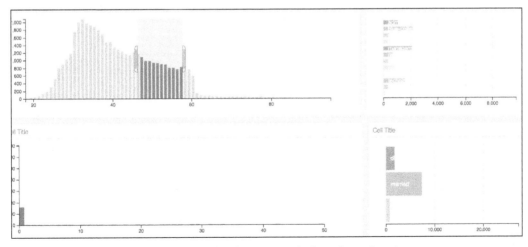

Crossfilter chart highlighting other dimensions of subset of users in a given age range.

The data is drawn from the bank default example we used to train our model service in *Chapter 8, Sharing Models with Prediction Services*. You can see that by selecting a subset of data points in the age distribution, we highlight the distribution of occupations, bank balance, and educations for these same users. This kind of visualization is very useful for drill-down diagnosis of problems points (as may be the case, for example, if a subset of data points is poorly classified by a model). Using these few basic ingredients you can now not only scale model training using the prediction service in *Chapter 8, Sharing Models with Prediction Services*, but also visualize its behavior for end users using a reporting layer.

Summary

In this chapter, we have learned several strategies for monitoring the performance of predictive models following initial design and looked at a number of scenarios where the performance or components of the model change over time. As part of the process of refining models, we examined A/B testing strategies and illustrated how to perform basic random allocation and estimate the sample sizes needed to measure improvement. We also demonstrated how to leverage the infrastructure from our prediction service to create dashboard visualizations for monitoring, which can easily be extended for other use cases.

Index

A

A/B testing
experimental allocation 298
models, iterating 297
multiple hypothesis testing 302
sample size, deciding 299-302
adjacency matrix 97
advanced analytic solution
data layer 6, 7
deployment layer 14
designing 4, 5
modeling layer 8-13
reporting layer 15, 16
affinity propagation
cluster numbers, selecting
automatically 89-92
agglomerative clustering
about 94, 95
failures 96-100
Alternating Least Squares (ALS) 222
Amazon Web Services (AWS) 55
analytic pipeline
data splitting 12
model performance 13
model persistence 13
parameter tuning 12
application layer 14
application programmer interface (API) 257
area under curve (AUC) 165, 290
auto-regressive moving average
(ARMA) 127

B

back-propagation 233

boosting 176, 177
broker 267

C

categorical data
normalizing 82
similarity metrics 78-82
Celery library
URL 273
Classification and Regression Trees (CART)
algorithm 133
classification models
evaluating 165-169
improving 169-171
click-through-rate (CTR) 2
client layer 14
client requests
DELETE request, implementing 263
GET requests, implementing 260, 261
handling 260
HEAD request, implementing 262
POST request, implementing 262
PUT request, implementing 262, 263
communication
guidelines 302
results, visualizing 303
terms, translating to business values 303
convexity 161
convolutional network
about 242
convolutional layer 242
downsampling layer 242
fully connected layer 242
input layer 242
rectifying layer 242

correlation similarity metrics 70-77
covariance 73
curl command
about 259
URL 259

D

database systems
using 266, 267
data layer 5
data mining 4
decision trees 132-137
dendrograms 94
deployment layer 14
digit recognition 249
distance metrics
about 64
blending 82
numerical distance metrics 64-69
time series 70-77
Dow Jones Industrial Average (DJIA) 70
Driver 56
Dynamic Time Warping (DTW) 75

E

e-mail campaigns, case study
about 19
data input 20
model development 21
reporting 21, 22
sanity checking 21
scoring 21
transformation 20
visualization 21, 22
Executors 56

F

false positive rate (FPR) 165
familywise error rate (FWER) 302
Flask
URL 265

G

Gaussian kernel 174

Gauss Markov Theorem 109
generalized linear models 128, 149
Generalize Estimating
Equations (GEE) 124-126
geospatial data
about 53
cloud, working in 55
loading 53-55
gradient boosted decision trees
about 177-180
versus, support vector machines
and logistic regression 180, 181
gradient boosted machine (GBM) 293
graphical user interface (GUI) 188
graphics processing unit (GPU) 249

H

H20
URL 52
Hadoop distributed file system (HDFS) 59
hierarchical clustering 94
hinge loss 173
horizontal scaling 264
HTTP Status Codes 261
hypertext transfer protocol (HTTP) 258

I

images
about 209
dimensionality reduction, for
image analysis 216-219
image data, cleaning 210-212
thresholding, for highlighting
objects 213-215
Indicator Function 191
Internet Movie Database
URL 26
IPython notebook
about 26
basic manipulations 33-38
data, inspecting 30-33
data, loading 30-33
installing 27
interface 27-29
Matplotlib, charting with 38-46

iteratively reweighted least
    squares (IRLS) 159

K

kernel function 174
K-means ++ 84
K-means clustering 83-89
k-medoids 93, 94

L

Labeled RDD 101
Latent Dirichlet Allocation (LDA) 205-208
Latent Semantic Indexing (LSI) 199
linear regression
    about 106-109
    data, preparing 109-114
    evaluation 114-118
    generalized linear models 128
    Generalize Estimating
        Equations (GEE) 124-126
    mixed effects models 126
    model, fitting 114-118
    regularization, applying to linear
        models 129-131
    statistical significance 119-124
    time series data 127
linkage metric 96
link functions
    Exponential 128
    Logit 128
    Poisson 128
logistic regression
    about 146-149
    dataset, formatting for classification
        problems 151-155
    model, fitting 162-164
    multiclass logistic classifiers 150, 151
    parameters, optimizing with
        second-order methods 158-162
    stochastic gradient descent (SGD) 155-157
    versus, support vector machines and
        gradient boosted decision trees 180, 181
logistic regression service
    as case study 267
    database, setting up 268-270

model, training 274-283
on-demand and bulk prediction,
    obtaining 283-286
web application, setting up 273, 274
web server, setting up 271, 272
Long Short Term Memory Networks
    (LSTM) 248

M

machine learning 4
Matplotlib
    charting with 38-46
message passing 90
Mixed National Institute of Standards
    and Technology (MNIST)
    database 250, 251
modeling layer 8-13
model performance
    changes, evaluating 290-293
    changes in feature importance,
        evaluating 294, 295
    checking, with diagnostic 290
    unsupervised model performance,
        changes 295, 296
models
    iterating, through A/B testing 297
multiclass logistic classifiers 150, 151
multidimensional scaling (MDS) 68
multinomial regression 150, 151

N

natural language toolkit (NLTK) library 188
neural networks
    belief networks, pretraining 238-241
    convolutional networks 242
    data compressing, with autoencoder
        networks 246
    discriminative, versus generative
        models 234, 235
    gradients, vanishing 235-238
    learning rate, optimizing 247-249
    parameter fitting, with
        back-propagation 229-233
    patterns, learning with 224
    perceptron 224, 225

perceptrons, combining 226-229
rectified units 243
regularizing, dropout used 241
single-layer neural network 226-229
neurons 226
Newton methods 158
non-relational database 266
numerical distance metrics 64-69

O

Ordinary Least Squares (OLS) 106

P

prediction service
  application, setting up 265
  architecture 258, 259
  information, persisting with database
    systems 266, 267
  sever, using 263, 264
predictive analytics 4
predictors 2
Principal Component Analysis (PCA)
  about 193-205
  dimensionality reduction, using in
    predictive modeling 209
  Latent Dirichlet Allocation (LDA) 205-208
pseudo-residuals 177
PySpark
  about 56
  classifier models, implementing 182-184
  example 141-143
  RDD, creating 58, 59
  SparkContext, creating 56-58
  Spark DataFrame, creating 59, 60
  URL 52, 56
Python requests library
  URL 260

R

RabbitMQ
  URL 273
random forest 138-140
receiver operator characteristic
    (ROC) 149, 165, 290

recommender system training, in PySpark
  case study 220-222
Rectified Linear Unit (ReLU) 242, 243
Recurrent Neural Networks (RNNs) 248
Redis
  URL 269
relational database 266
reporting layer 15, 16
reporting service
  about 304
  report application, setting up 305, 306
  report server, setting up 304
  visualization layer, using 306-310
Resilient Distributed Dataset (RDD)
  about 56, 101
  creating 58, 59

S

second-order methods
  about 155
  parameters, optimizing 158-162
server
  used, for communicating with external
    systems 263, 264
similarity metrics
  about 64
  correlation similarity metrics 70-77
  for categorical data 78-82
Singular Value Decomposition
    (SVD) 69, 197
social media feeds, case study
  about 16
  data input 17
  model development 18
  reporting 19
  sanity checking 18
  scoring 19
  transformation 17
  visualization 19
soft-margin formulation 173
Spark
  streaming clustering 100-104
SparkContext
  creating 56
Spark DataFrame
  creating 59, 60

www.ingramcontent.com/pod-product-compliance
Lightning Source LLC
LaVergne TN
LVHW060039070326
832903LV00072B/1138